LIBERALIZATION AND JOURNALISM

LIBERALIZATION AND JOURNALISM

Suraj Singh

CENTRUM PRESS
NEW DELHI-110002 (INDIA)

CENTRUM PRESS
H.O.: 4360/4, Ansari Road, Daryaganj,
New Delhi-110002 (India)
Tel: 23278000, 23261597, 23255577, 23286875
B.O.: No. 1015, Ist Main Road, BSK IIIrd Stage,
IIIrd Phase, IIIrd Block, Bangalore-560085 (INDIA)
Tel: 080-41723429
Email: centrumpress@gmail.com
Visit us at: www.centrumpress.com

Liberalization and Journalism

First Edition, 2010

ISBN 978-93-80836-14-0

PRINTED IN INDIA

Printed at Mehra Offset Press, Delhi

Contents

Preface

Today when the world is witnessing development in each and every field, there is a constant decline in values (Is the development real?)

When the world 'impossible' is somewhat losing its relevance in today's world, when nothing seems to be beyond reach, there is still despair, discontent, conflict, violence, terrorism and cultural and communal differences.

The individual urge for peace and happiness is becoming stronger and stronger with each passing day. However on a collective plan one need to reconsider our aims and activities. Steady decline in the values can largely be traced the root cause of all this unrest and unhappiness in society.

The sparkle of hope and any effort on our part that can bring happiness is like a candle of light in the space enveloped by darkness.

Peaceful world has been the main aim of mankind since time immemorial and I firmly believe that media being not only the mirror of the society but also as the leader, guide and somewhat moulder of the society can play this role.

The conflict between values is the source of many conflicts and problems. The conflict of values is not the unique phenomenon of our times but the common occurrence in both ancient and modern history.

The traditional conflict of values occurred largely in the moral realm, and its essence and focus lay in the conflict between various requirements of the same individual self. But this conflict was also moralized because personal life, either inner ideas or counteractions were put into the scope of moral valuation.

The traditional conflict of values was in fact moral conflict between good and evil, and significance and function of morality just lay in adjusting and solving all those conflicts. Complications and plurality of modern life has brought about the possibility for different value choices or pursuits, thus conflict of values occurs. The 21st century is a period of transition.

Chapter 1

Political Engagement and the Audience for News

Among the many reasons citizen had a hard time committing to being newspaper readers, one seems the most important: They found the stories did not touch on the areas of civic activity they encountered in their daily lives.

Although the newspaper retains its meaning as a symbol of adulthood, the young adults often failed to sustain the family ritual experienced in childhood. A second study on television news found that college students who turned away from newspapers did not appear to substitute another news medium to inform themselves as citizens.

Although they held television news in minimal regard, they still credited the first major news story they remembered from television with making them feel part of the larger national community. In spite of this fairly strong generation effect from watching news, many of the young adult participants considered newscasts primarily a form of entertainment, and only a few mentioned any other source far news, such as radio or the Internet.

Surveys and field work confirm that, although some older Americans may experience a strong need for news, the younger generation does not share that appetite. A growing minority of young Americans get along without what the major news organizations serve up daily, and those who do pay attention, especially to television news, do so without attaching great significance to the news as the Fourth Estate in political life. The view of the news arena as a space where the public sphere operates is declining among the young citizenry.

Because of the clear impact on the civic role for news businesses, with the potential to weaken political participation, the trends among young Americans have aroused debate about the future of democracy. Carried on without reference to other countries, the debate raised questions requiring comparative research abroad. Are the increasingly negative experiences with news among young citizens peculiar to the United States? Or do the changes pertain as well to young adults in other contemporary societies? To search for answers, this monograph presents the results of two qualitative studies abroad that closely replicate the U.S. research, examining newspaper and then television news experiences that college students recount in life history narratives.

Spain was selected as a comparative case for several reasons. The most compelling comes from data on the young audience for news: Among Western democracies, only in Spain is news viewership reaching an almost universal national audience and newspaper circulation growing among young citizens. Spain provides a setting within another advanced country that differs from the United States in most particulars: Spain's development came recently, as did its return to democracy. Besides their differing language and parliamentary monarchy, young Spaniards grew up in close-knit extended families and attended highly structured schools that emphasized rote learning. More important, the Spanish media arena diverges greatly from that typical in the United States. Where local newspapers and commercial broadcasting dominate the U.S. press, national newspapers and public television predominate in Spain. In such a contrasting political and media settings, young citizens will likely report distinct ways of informing themselves as citizens.

The decisions of young adults in another country present opportunities to build grounded theory. By looking at groups that contrast strongly with those previously studied, field work can seek cases that break the rule, clarifying the contours of the new relationship to news emerging among the young. The process may also generate concepts useful to understanding subjective experiences of the news arena. Comparing groups reared under a greatly differing news arena permits a search for common patterns. Any strong similarities found to cross cultural or national boundaries would contribute to the general understanding of subjective experience. The comparison could yield insights into the structure of generations as the news media globalize. Expected differences might indicate alternative policy choices for news organizations and their role in informing citizens.

THEORY AND METHOD

The idea of comparing nations has long been employed to build theories of politics and society. Since Durkheim and Weber, "the father of crossnational research", tried to understand modern society by holding it up against historical and primitive groups, scholars have used examples from different nations as a way to illustrate their ideas, from the social Darwinism of Spencer and the functionalism of Radcliffe-Brown, to the structuralism of Levi-Strauss. Herbert Blumer criticized these comparisons to remote societies as an exercise in nostalgia.

Comparative studies of contemporary nations, on the other hand, give observers a vantage point closer to home, reducing the danger of romanticizing a traditional or historical society. Interest in comparative research was surging, principally at the intersection between sociology and political science, when Seymour Martin Lipset wrote his classic studies. The new field, political sociology, took on several topics that cross the borders of the two fields, such as the fate of democracy, the role of the media, and the participation of individual citizens as part of different generations.

Defining and measuring "the political culture of democracy" and "the social structures and processes that sustain it" inspired the pioneer study of comparative political attitudes in the United States, United Kingdom, Germany, Italy, and Mexico. The news media clearly took part in these structures and processes. To illustrate the patterns found in survey questions about media use and political interest, the authors also conducted life history interviews.

During the early 1960s Americans facing the cold war, fearing a domino effect if small nations fell to Communism, wanted to know how to encourage the broadest democracy without causing instability. "How can the apathetic peripheral man become the aspiring participant man without a deep seachange in the psychic weather?" asked Daniel Lerner.

The answer was found in Lipset's three requirements for political democracy; a regular means to change officials, a loyal opposition, and (important for this study) a mechanism for the largest possible share of society to participate. Communication seemed to provide one of the most likely mechanisms. "In the world today - whether you like it or not, whether it is advisable or not, whether it is good policy planning or not - tremendous developments in communication," Lerner went on, "are occurring in every country".

These changes at mid-century began to shrink the global community, and several contemporary studies identify communications (including newspaper consumption) as a strong indicator of political development.

Subsequent studies have paid most attention to voting, but the news media also provide a key to citizens' involvement in democratic governments. As mass communication grows, clusters of older social, economic, and psychological commitments end, and citizens become more open to new patterns of action.

The commitment to participate in politics can clash with the roles the media play in generating economic profits, and this contradiction may limit their legitimacy and effectiveness in the political system. News media can block as well as encourage change, because "the construction of political reality is essentially a 'mediated' process". Young adulthood, when political reality takes firm shape in personal commitments, is rarely studied.

Socialization research emphasizes childhood and

adolescence and pays little attention to the media, although media research shows that television often provides the earliest encounters with politics in the United States. Cross-national research on media and politics usually focuses on media content, not audiences, and mass media researchers have called for more comparative study of public communication.

This chapter on young citizens and the media has two theoretical aims. One is to describe and delineate elements in the structure of subjective experience. In his suggestions for studying the media, Blumer proposed that they do not operate within clearly demarcated and distinct outlets and forms, such as newspapers and television, but instead act within a larger zone that he called an arena. Viewed from the perspective of citizens' symbolic interactions, subjective experiences with the news arena have been little studied.

To extend understanding of the political sociology of news, this monograph employs a descriptive strategy to discover grounded theory. After identifying other groups for comparison, a principal task is to describe subjective experience in detail, thus adding to the store of empirical observations of responses to the media arena. To build theory, groups are chosen as negative cases, selected to delimit the news arena and clarify its role in young citizens' experience.

That Americans increasingly reject news invites the search for cases where a different news arena holds sway. Cross-national research looks for similarities between nations because "if the same factor produces the same effects in two very different situations, its influence tends to be confirmed". National distinctiveness makes finding the same processes less likely in more than one country, and so similarities are not only unexpected but also valuable to add to the general understanding of the media arena. Differences contribute as well, and the most important source of contrast, of course, is national history.

As they confront problems, the citizens of various countries find alternatives and reach different decisions. Their contrasting responses can be used to suggest policy options.

Another theoretical aim is to examine generational change. Generations are produced only in modern societies, where rapid changes produce longterm shifts in ideology. Events give each new group of children a different set of experiences that tie them strongly to others their age. What people know about politics is influenced by their position in a generation, and studies of generations suggest that their collective memories emerge not only from massive traumatic events such as wars and large scale demographic shifts but also from mass exposure to events shown in the media. Karl Mannheim noted that an actual generation, whose coming of age coincides with a set of common experiences, does not necessarily interpret those shared events uniformly.

The conflicting meanings they assign events divide them into what Mannheim called generational units. Maurice Halbwachs agreed that collective memories play a central role in distinguishing different social groups and classes. Mannheim further suggested that, although their life spans may overlap, different age groups experience the same moments of history differently, each generation living in its own subjective era, as he called it.

This has been borne out in subsequent research. Finally, Mannheim proposed that national differences effectively separate people of the same chronological age; citizens in Germany and China in 1800 could not form part of the same actual generation because they could share no formative experiences.

The growth of news organizations that extend beyond national borders, the consolidation of media ownership globally, and the resulting international spread of political reporting styles raise the question whether citizens of nations separated by geography and language had begun to share sufficient media experience by the end of the 20th century to form a generation in effect.

These theoretical considerations guide the study: the search for commonalities that indicate new social and political meanings for news crossing national boundaries, the observation of differences with an eye to discover alternate policies for American news organizations as they inform citizens, and the testing of boundaries of subjective experience between a political generation and its units in the United States and Spain.

As a practical matter, choosing countries is the first task in any crossnational comparison. For the greatest detail and depth, a binary analysis comparing only one country to another -works best. Because it "leaves out neither the specific nor the general," binary study can contribute "to an understanding of general phenomena". The choice of countries requires a balance.

The two should share enough to make reasonable comparisons but also have enough differences to make for robust results. The United States shares with Europe many cultural, political, and economic traditions, including the modern phenomenon of youth culture. Within Europe, Spain differs from the United States perhaps more than any other nation. The United States and Spain stood as complete opposites in the early 1960s. Among developed American and European nations, Spain had the lowest newspaper circulation (70 per thousand population) and the penultimate rate for televisions (13.1 per thousand population) - only the Portuguese owned fewer sets.

During the Franco era, Spain also had no meaningful gauge of voting. By contrast, the United States had newspaper circulation in the middle of the range (326 per thousand population, compared to the United Kingdom, 506 per thousand population) and the highest number of television sets (306.4 per thousand population).

The percentage of U.S. citizens who actually voted, while not high (64.4 per cent in 1960), ranked with those nations lacking mandatory voting laws. The United States also had the highest level of college enrollment (1,983 per hundred thousand population) and Spain (258 per hundred thousand population) the lowest (Britain had 460 per hundred thousand population, but a larger share of enrollees graduated).

Perhaps because of these differences, most Americans know little of Spain beyond the tourist cliches of bullfights and flamenco, necessitating a brief overview of recent political, media, and generational history.

POLITICS

Unlike the United States, Spain experienced an extended pause from democracy during the Franco regime, which had a profound impact on the country. The "executions, the imprisonments, the torture, the lives destroyed by political exile and forced economic migration point to the exorbitant price paid by Spain for Franco's `triumphs' ". Despite these depredations, Spanish citizens remained committed to the ideal of civic culture. Under Franco, citizens in the different regions of Spain preferred democratic rule by "all of us" rather than by one caudillo, even in the most conservative strongholds. The commitment to democracy was based on the culture of Spain, rather than springing from economic factors or social structure.

In Franco's later years, Spain underwent a "Prussian-type economic development . . . beginning in the mid-1950s and promoted by national ruling classes". Preston characterized the 1960s as a period of robust economic growth resulting in broad social changes. Business and professional people became independent-minded in increasing numbers, and unrest from the worker movements applied growing pressure for change.

The Franco regime did institute some liberalizing policies, such as the Press Law enacted in 1966. Liberalization took firm root in such places as the universities, where Marxist publications became widely available and prominent intellectuals criticized the regime, calling for reform, and where "tolerance at the ideological level was unquestionable". Spain also experienced greater contact with the outside world, through flows of migration from Europe and increases in tourism primarily from the western hemisphere.

The assassination in 1973 of Carrero Blanco, the ultraconservative head of Franco's government, "was a factor of overwhelming importance". He was replaced by Carlos Arias Navarro, who, although not progressive, did support limited reforms. In his most important act, televised on February 12, 1974, he announced that "the national consensus in support of the regime must in the future be expressed in the form of participation". Arias Navarro's speech opened the door for Francoist institutions to reflect more political pluralism, although that aim faced repeated setbacks. The regime then enacted a Statute of Associations, which allowed groups to register, although few did (and opposition political parties remained prohibited).

The hopes for reform in the early 1970s clashed with economic frustration over Franco's "paternalistic regulation of the labour market", as well as his policy of keeping Spain out of the European Economic Community.

The energy crisis put a break on increases in the standard of living for the working class, which lacked political rights and became increasingly militant. By 1975, "it had become clear that socioeconomic and institutional change as well as modifications in political beliefs at both the mass and elite level of Spanish society had eroded away the underpinnings of the authoritarian regime". Franco himself became ill, and the media kept a vigil outside the palace. The extreme measures to postpone his death, the machinations to extend the regime, and the hope of installing a new head of the Cortes (Parliament) who would resist change - these things came to light only later. At the time, Spaniards witnessed only the head of government in tears, announcing Franco's death on TVE1, the state channel.

TRANSITION

Franco left behind a constitution that envisioned Prince Juan Carlos becoming king. This went as planned. The king would have ruled only as the successor to Franco, without full dynastic legitimacy, but then his father Don Juan de Borbon renounced his right to the throne. Arias Navarro continued as head of the government from November 1975 until the king replaced him in July 1976 with Adolfo Suarez, who followed a strategy of seeking pacts with the right and the left.

He got the approval of the military and Cortes for a Law on Political Reform, ratified in 1976. The process secured the right to form political parties, granted political amnesty, dissolved the state labour unions and the single Francoist Movimiento party, and then set free elections for the Constituent Assembly.

The consensus completely rejected Franco's plan: "trade unions were legalized, political parties, including the hated Partido Comunista de Espana [PCE], were permitted". Extremists of the right wing began a violent backlash, which reached a nadir in Madrid, January 23 to 28, 1977, during the semana negra or "black week" that left student activists and lawyers, as well as policemen, murdered. The fate of Spanish democracy seemed uncertain.

In May 1977, during preparations leading up to the first general, multiparty elections, the Union Centro Democratico (UCD) formed a centre-right coalition of political forces. The communists (PCE) "played a major role in the transition and . . . gained 20 per cent of the vote in the 1977 election", and the socialists (PSOE) won more than a quarter of the vote (28 per cent and 118 seats). The centre coalition (UCD) received one-third of the votes (165 seats) and began a period leading a minority government that lasted until 1982 (in the 1979 general election, the UCD won 34 per cent and 168 seats, and the PSOE won 30 per cent and 121 seats).

The country put its economy on abetter footing with the Moncloa Pacts in October 1977. The accords imposed austerity, with budgetary control, tax reform, limits on wage increases, and a devalued peseta. As a result, inflation decreased (from 29 per cent) and exports went up, but unemployment also increased. The accords caused discontent when many of the promised reforms failed to materialize.

"Inevitably," Preston wrote, "the most dramatic difficulties encountered by Spain's newborn democracy were the direct legacy of Franco's rule". One of these, the Basque separatist movement (ETA), enjoyed some popular support through the 1970s. The rigid centralist policies of the Franco regime had left such regional movements stronger, especially those in the Basque country and Catalunya. Although the new constitution adopted in 1978 recognized regional autonomy, the separatist movements still presented a violent threat. A military trained to distrust democracy presented another difficulty.

This bore fruit when Lieutenant Colonel Antonio Tejero led a group of senior military officers in an attempted coup d'etat on February 23, 1981. The king went on state television to denounce the failed attempt, and the public responded with mass demonstrations. From 1977 to 1982, the socialists remained the principal opposition party. Then the socialist era arrived: "Felipe Gonzalez became prime minister in 1982, after his party's crushing victory in the elections that year. His second administration saw Spain enjoy dramatic levels of economic growth. His third administration was marked by internal party strife, exacerbated by growing evidence of corruption".

Following an unexpected victory in 1993, the government became increasingly mired in charges of corruption and was defeated in 1996 by the Partido Popular (PP), which formed a minority government with Catalan support. The 1996 elections marked the end of the transition from the Franco era. Since the transition, Spain appears to have entered a period of stability, similar to the quiescence characteristic of the mature U.S. democracy.

At a time when the left-leaning socialist party controlled Spanish government, the United States by contrast had a series of conservative administrations. A decline of trust in the U.S. government and its institutions marked the period. Surveys of opinions and attitudes since the transition to democracy indicate a Spanish citizenry consistently moderate in ideology and supportive of democratic principles.

They also have low levels of political interest and information. From the late 1970s through the late 1980s, a consistent share (about three-quarters) said they knew little or nothing about politics. When asked their general response to politics, a majority expressed boredom or indifference, while one-third expressed interest and enthusiasm and one-fifth expressed annoyance and disgust. These survey results lead researchers to identify an "outstanding feature in the political attitudes of Spanish people, namely, their political passivity".

MEDIA

In a study in the 1960s, the United States and United Kingdom plotted high and near the regression line correlating communications (an index computed from newspaper consumption, newsprint used, telephones installed, and mail volumes) and political development. Spain stood near the middle in communications development and the low-middle in political development, well below the average. This combination suggested a country poised, because of its communications development, to experience a spurt in political development - an accurate prediction, as it turned out.

Under the Franco regime, changes in the laws governing the press took a first step toward liberalization. The 1966 reform changed the process (but not the fact) of censorship, ending it before publication but imposing "post hoc suspension or closure", so that editors had to guess what might get censored. "Franco, the Falange, the Army and the principles of the regime could not be criticized, but for all the limitations, the law constituted a real change, and the most reactionary elements in the regime were furious at the implications".

The policy change "gave rise to hopes of more substantial political change". Under the new law, periodicals such as the newspapers Informaciones, Ya, and Madrid and the magazine Diario 16 published criticism of the government and called for reform, working within the constraints of the regime. Publications also sprang up in regional languages such as Catalan.

Spanish television was founded as a state monopoly in the 1950s. "Under the Franco regime, television held the key to reading the eyes and ears of the Spanish population" because, unlike newspapers in the country, "television commands massive audiences". After Franco's death, government control continued over what were by then two state channels, TVE1 (also called La Primera) and TVE2 (La Dos). Newspapers gained much more freedom, and the transition saw several newspapers start up. The most important national paper to emerge, EI Pais, established a left-leaning socialist editorial line, in contrast to the right-leaning monarchist position of the newspaper ABC. The strong political agendas of Spanish newspapers did not come as a novelty. Much earlier, for example, "Franco spoke of the monarchist daily ABC as an `enemy'".

During the period of socialist rule, two important shifts occurred in the Spanish news media, bringing them closer to their U.S. counterparts. On one hand, the government revised (by some accounts timidly) the broadcasting laws. "In the 1980s, Spanish television evolved from a public monopoly, with only two state channels, into a competitive multi-channel system".

Two new channels began free broadcasting, Antena 3 and TeleS, and a third emerged based on subscription, Canal Plus. On the other hand, Pedro J. Ramirez founded in the late 1980s a national newspaper, EI Mundo. Ramirez, who worked as a young intern in the Washington Post newsroom the day Nixon resigned, introduced investigative journalism at EI Mundo. The paper took a strongly anti-socialist line against Felipe Gonzalez and his government. Ramirez made himself a household name in Spain by pushing the stories of corruption in government to the forefront of the political agenda.

The national newspapers in Spain circulate throughout the country, alongside (and in competition with) the local and regional press, and both continue growing in circulation. By the 1990s, all the older Spanish newspapers had reformatted themselves as smaller tabloids. The press has adopted an aggressive pattern of redesigns and received a number of awards, particularly El Mundo for reporting and EI Pais for design. U.S.-based journalism associations have named both of these among the best newspapers in the world. The changes in newspapers accompanied an erosion of press partisanship, with an increase in claims to professionalism among reporters and in market orientation among publishers.

Television news also has a history of partisanship in Spain, although less overt than the printed press. A study of the 1993 election, for example, shows that the state-controlled TVE1's favorable coverage of Gonzalez and the socialist government became especially pronounced in the pre-campaign period. In that election the private channels, Antena 3, Tele5, and Canal Plus, first covered the campaign in full. The entry of commercial broadcasters "has created a new audience map, and all the networks and stations are increasingly guided by ratings". As a result, public broadcasting, although still dominant, has seen a continual erosion of its audience and income.

Despite some growth, newspapers still do not receive wide readership in Spain, and total circulation reaches only one in ten of the population. The press has been expanding, however, with the number of newspapers published increasing since the 1980s. At the same time, the trends have been toward greater concentration of ownership, including the growth of newspaper chains and cross-ownership of television and radio stations and magazines. These trends have parallels in the United States.

Electioneering in the news media of various countries has begun to follow a pattern as elections become Americanized. That trend makes a clear picture of U.S. news essential for understanding the Spanish media. Historically, the U.S. news media have operated under market competition with only limited government regulation. Public broadcasting arrived late and has played a very small role. The press remains predominantly local, with competition at that level declining as newspapers have closed or consolidated.

Coverage of politics has changed substantially since the 1960s, when newspaper reporters and television correspondents gave a largely descriptive chronicle of the candidates' words and movements during election campaigns. Studies show that U.S. journalists have increasingly described presidential campaigns using the metaphors of conflict or the horse race, positioning themselves as political interpreters for the public. As a result, media organizations may have largely supplanted political parties as the principal power brokers in the selection of U.S. leaders.

Competition for readers and viewers has imposed entertainment values on U.S. news. Since the 1960s, television journalists have greatly shortened politicians' sound bites and increased the relative share of time and emphasis given to their own judgments about campaigns. Newscasts became dramatically more visual in the 1970s, at the time when they reached a pinnacle of audience share and advertising revenues. Seeing themselves in competition with television, newspapers followed suit, updating their designs at a rate that accelerated in the early 1980s.

Both television and newspapers began to face audience declines in the mid-1980s, as cable expanded the alternatives for news (including CNN and C-SPAN). Newspaper executives identified and attempted to slow the erosion of readership among young adults. By the early 1990s, news executives viewed computer networks as a potential competitor. Unlike the ideological competition among Spanish newspapers, the U.S. press sees itself as part of a news market, where television broadcast news competes with cable and radio and where newspapers - most of them local monopolies - compete with broadcasters. Driven by market considerations, the U.S. news media aim for the greatest visual and emotional impact within the constraints of the widest possible audience appeal.

YOUNG ADULTS

A persistent puzzle of Spain since Franco has been the political culture that survey researchers characterize as passive, with low rates of participation, weak party allegiance, and limited social capital, as measured by memberships in civic associations and neighborliness. Despite low participation, the levels of cynicism and efficacy in Spain during the transition were no worse than those in the United

Kingdom and the United States, and in general the "political culture in Spain did not differ too greatly from the political cultures of stable democracies".

The period of rapid change in Spain did, however, produce clear differences between generations. Those in young adulthood during the late 1970s belong to what has been called the transition generation, born after 1951 and reaching adulthood after Franco. In 1980, 21to 25-year-olds had the highest feelings of political efficacy and lowest cynicism of any group.

On the whole, the young voiced more support for democracy, had more interest and confidence in politics, participated more, and had greater party allegiance, while they indicated less trust in the actions of authorities and in their country as a whole than did older Spaniards. General levels of participation ranked lower, but the young were among the most likely to participate in politics. The idea "of a generalized lack of interest in politics among the youngest age group is not borne out" at that time. They culminated a trend in which each succeeding generation, in response to the dictatorship, identified more strongly with the left in Spain.

Young adults of the post-transition generation are even less the product of their country's period under Franco than were their parents. Born near the time he died, they are reaching adulthood with Spain fully integrated into the European Community. They appear to be moving away from the left. Recent surveys show that they have levels of political interest similar to those found in 1980. The highest level of interest appears among those recently of voting age, and the level and growth of their interest corresponds to the availability and access to information such as news about politics. Their most common modes of political participation include voting, informing themselves, joining associations, and discussing politics. They report being most influenced by the media and by friends, followed by their families and by schools. They overwhelmingly support democracy as a political system, although they tend to judge their own country's system harshly in comparison to others in Europe.

The survey data tend to contradict popular wisdom among the transition generation that their heirs in the posttransition era are less interested in and knowledgeable about politics, and more disengaged from and cynical about public life. No previous field work has examined this contradiction.

In the young generation's media experience, the newspaper landscape has had regular growth in circulation and in the number of newspapers published. Unlike their parents, they see EI Pais as a fixture and, of course, the anti-socialist, crusading EI Mundo as a novelty. Despite growth, newspapers form a small part of the media environment, but they offer a range of competing ideologies (contrary to the rule in the United States or in Spain under Franco).

Newspapers during the young adults' lives have been constantly changing - not only growing but redesigning and altering formats requiring regular adaptation and adjustment by the audience. Television, however, remained under state control through most of their formative years. Public broadcasting provided the only news on television through the 1989 campaign, when the post-transition generation entered its teenage years. The addition of private channels occurred in the political calendar during the next two elections, just as the young generation reached voting age.

In other ways, the new generation of Spanish citizens presents a particularly interesting case. The country saw a baby boom immediately after Franco's death. Upon reaching an all-time high, the birthrate then dropped in subsequent years to reach the lowest level in the world. As a result, the group reaching young adulthood in the mid-1990s is the largest in Spain's history.

Their demographics create a case study in contrasts. On the up side, they have experienced the expansion of education and stabilization of democracy. The number of Spaniards completing college doubled between 1973 and 1992, and successive elections since the transition to democracy have produced rising levels of voting and other participation among the young. On the down side, the large size of the generation has caused problems. With general unemployment high (22 per cent at the time of the 1996 election), discontent among young voters became a factor cited in the defeat of the socialist party. The counterpart cohort of young Americans is also part of a bulge generation, the children of America's earlier baby boom, and they have suffered similar economic consequences, with the attendant levels of discouragement.

INDICATORS TODAY

By the 1990s, the political and social gap between the United States and Spain had closed substantially. The share of Spanish workers employed in white collar jobs had grown dramatically (from 30 to 44 per cent, 1960 to 1981). Television had reached close to saturation in 1994 (99.3 per cent of households), and half had more than one set (49.9 per cent) and a VCR (57.6 per cent). However, the average electoral turnout remains much higher in Spain (73.9 per cent of eligible voters, since the death of Franco, 1977-1993) than in the United States.

On average, Spaniards use the media in very different patterns (according to 1996 data from ASEP). They view only three and one-half hours of television a day (210 minutes). The state channels still receive a third of the audience share (TVE1 at 28 per cent, TVE2 at 10 per cent), with private channels dividing up most of the rest (led by Antena 3 at 26 per cent, Tele5 at 19 per cent). Satellite channels from abroad play a much smaller role. Large differences appear especially in the printed press (according to 1996 data from FIEJ). The number of newspapers continues to grow (up 13.6 per cent from 1990 to 1994), as does daily circulation (up 36.6 per cent). Over the same period, the number of dailies in the United States declined (by 4.5 per cent), and weekday circulation was also down (by 5.3 per cent).

METHODS OF STUDY

Although political sociology since its founding has relied on data from statistical samples of various nations to use as indicators of political and social life, qualitative methods have also played a role. Personal essays written by citizens were considered a standard technique. In recent guides to crossnational study, half of the recommended methods require field work, and qualitative tools seem especially useful to examine subjective beliefs. Because survey data "necessarily abstracts institutions events, and processes from their unique social and cultural context", field studies become all the more important.

Autobiographical techniques have a long history in studies of the media and citizens, beginning with the groundbreaking examination of Polish peasants and immigrants to the United States. The full length autobiography has generally been used in the social sciences to study foreign or marginalized others. Bv simplifying and focusing autobiography more narrowly, researchers found a way to apply the technique to the mainstream. Blumer asked young people from many walks of life to write shorter narratives about one aspect of their experience, their memories of and reactions to movies. This technique, the limited life history, has found wide application in recent years among scholars in the social sciences and cultural studies.

The limited life history technique is especially effective for spanning time - the longitudinal section - as political culture is transmitted across generations. Life histories also impose an expanded view of political participation, not only including such elements as party affiliation and political interest included in questionnaires but also leaving open a full range of other activities, whatever participants choose to address in their narrative essays.

To find out about young Spaniards' subjective experiences with news, colleagues helped me collect life history narratives from young adults in Spain. During 1996, sixty-two undergraduates at three Spanish universities contributed their news experiences. The universities are located in three very different regions in Spain: the capital, Madrid, the industrial Navarra region, and the depressed autonomous community of Canarias. Because each of the universities draws from a wide area, the mix of participants included many other regions of Spain. The participants form what is called a "saturation sample", the qualitative standard for gathering sufficient examples. Saturation, the point at which any additional examples would add only particulars without increasing the general understanding about the group, is reached in most studies somewhere between twenty-five and thirty.

The study group is appropriate for two purposes. It first allows a close replication of the studies of U.S. college students. Second and more important, it represents the small but significant sector in Spain of the affluent and educated young. They form not only the core of up-scale audience members that news executives seek to attract and sustain but also the source for the next generation of political leaders, activists, and attentive citizens essential to democratic government.

The participants were asked to write a short life history essay, beginning with their earliest memories and continuing to their current activities. They received the same instructions as did the U.S. groups in earlier studies, translated into Spanish, one set for television news and another for newspapers. About a third of the participants agreed to write two essays, one on each medium, to allow a comparison of their ways of writing and thinking about the two. All participants also completed a questionnaire with standard demographic, media use, and political items, the same completed by the U.S. groups but translated into Spanish.

The group is not intended, of course, to be a representative sample at the morphological level. The questionnaire was collected to allow a clear comparison to the previous studies as well as to national measurements of young Spaniards. In the survey responses, the volunteers did resemble the U.S. groups from previous studies: mostly communication majors, predominantly white, and roughly two-thirds women. Unlike the U.S. participants, a slightly larger share of Spanish volunteers haled from cities and large towns (80 per cent), with most of the remainder from smaller towns and rural areas (16 per cent). Their parents also differ, the largest share of whom attended only some high school

(72 per cent of mothers, 50 per cent of fathers) and work mostly in labour and in the home.

The Spanish students reported higher levels of media use than did the Americans (the mean for each measure is shown). They read newspapers more often (5.4 days "last week") and watched newscasts more (6.1 days). More of the Spaniards said they read a national newspaper (36 per cent), local paper (40 per cent) or both (20 per cent), and none reported reading a student paper. There were no non-readers. For television news, more Spaniards reported watching local news (52 per cent) and national news (54 per cent and some watch both), but satellite and cable received no mention. There were no non-viewers. Besides their higher attention to news, they paid slightly more attention to audio-visual media. They said they watched a bit more television on average (84 minutes "yesterday") and listened to radio somewhat more (58 minutes). In contrast, they spent substantially more time with the newspaper (31 minutes). They read more books (2.1 "last month") but fewer magazines (3.6). They also watched many more movies (8.4 viewed, plus 1.0 rented).

The participants' media use roughly matched audience statistics for urban Spaniards their age. In national surveys (all figures from 1996 ASEP data), young adults generally used print media and radio more heavily than did older adults. Young adults read newspapers more (50 per cent "yesterday") than did all adults (37 per cent), although the gap appears to be narrowing.

The same share of young and older adults watched television (89 per cent), but slightly more of those under 30 watched news (76 per cent compared to 73 per cent "yesterday" for all adults). The study group, although smaller in number than the U.S. volunteers, was much more geographically diverse than either of the U.S. groups. However, the saturation sample did not yield sub-populations large enough to break out for comparison. The differing minority populations in the two countries did not permit comparison in any case.

I also gathered fifteen essays from Spanish adults older

than 29, ten about newspapers and five about newscasts. These get mentioned parenthetically in the following sections. The older group, all white, split evenly by gender. They ranged from 30 to 52 years old, with the mode at 36. Their parents hold roughly the same types of jobs and attained about the same educational level as in the younger group. However, the older adults came predominantly from small towns and rural areas (53.3 per cent). They paid much more attention to newspapers, reading more days (6.3 "last week") and for longer intervals (37 minutes "yesterday"). They watched television news less often (5.3 days "last week") and spent less time with television (66 minutes "yesterday"). In fact, all their uses of media fell substantially lower (except movies rented, 4.5 "last month").

To help compare these life histories, I studied the newspaper essays separately from the television essays. For each group, I first read a small number (about a fifth) to look for the recurring themes found in the previous studies and revised the list as needed (this amounted to adding a few items). A Spanish assistant then used the translated and annotated list to code the essays for the presence or absence of each theme. To check reliability, I recoded some of the essays (20 per cent). The reliability coefficients between coders are quite good on average.

In reporting the results, I have stayed as closely as possible to the form and structure of the two earlier studies. Although lengthy, this strategy produced a wealth of description and allowed the maximum direct comparison to the studies being replicated.

The analysis in the next two sections, then, weaves together three strands: qualitative readings and quotations from each group of essays, the quantitative results of coding, and related questionnaire responses. To these dimensions I have added the following types of comparisons: with the counterpart group from the United States, with Spanish national statistics when available, and with records of important news stories since the mid-1970s, drawn from two chronicles the leading national newspapers published.

Quotations from the essays given in the following two sections identify the writer's gender, hometown size, and frequency of attending to the news medium (occasional 3 or fewer days "last week," regular 4 or 5, and habitual 6 or 7). Age is shown because I followed the Spanish norm of including adults under 30 (the U. S. statistics on young adults usually, but not always, include only 18- to 24-year-olds). Unless indicated, the writer came from a town. Partisan Newspapers and Ritual

In broad strokes, the Spanish essays on newspapers reaffirmed the centrality of daily rituals for acquiring the reading habit. Although they did not present their newspaper experiences as uniformly by periods as did the Americans, the Spaniards did provide detailed accounts of the newspaper ritual for each stage in the U.S. chronology: in early childhood at home, middle childhood in school, and transition to adulthood, with various influences and political consequences in the present.

Unlike the Americans, the Spaniards became newspaper readers (and in quotations from these essays, the writer read the newspaper habitually, unless otherwise noted). Many aspects that make the Spanish press more attractive and accessible to young adults flow from the partisan ideologies newspapers overtly espouse. The partisan distinctiveness was echoed in the Spanish essays themselves, which on the whole seem much more varied and individualistic than the U.S. essays.

CHILDHOOD

At first the newspaper simply existed in the jumble of early childhood memories. Spaniards and Americans alike said they had a hard time remembering their first glimpse of one. An urban male occasional reader, 21, wrote, "It's like trying to remember seeing abed the first time or the bathroom of your house. They've always been there and there just wasn't a first time." A few did report a memorable first encounter:

When I was five, snooping in the old family bureau, I discovered a pile of yellowed papers, gnawed by mice. I unfolded it and found before my eyes a kind of revelation: one of those newspapers from before, on sheets so large you could roll me up in them. That was the first time I saw a newspaper. -a male regular reader, 25

Many of the essays, like the U.S. group, said they experienced newspapers as a constant presence (70 per cent) throughout their upbringing. Once the newspaper emerged from the tog of early childhood, however, the initial uniformity in Spanish and U. S. experiences dissolved.' The strength of habit and family training came through strongly among the Spaniards. A majority of their essays described newspapers as a part of family routine (56.7 per cent), a share exceeding that found in the U.S. essays. None of the Spanish writers concluded from the repetitive nature of their early experience that newspapers therefore had little importance or played no role in their lives.

The Spaniards described many ways the news routine unified them with parents. Two-thirds of the essays said that their first encounters with newspapers occurred in the presence of parents (66.7 per cent), and many of those who did not cite parents instead mentioned grandparents. The essays talked of morning rituals for purchasing bread and newspapers that made them feel part of the adult world. An urban female, 21, wrote, "When he took me to school, we used to stop at some kiosk and he gave me money so I could buy the paper. Since I was very small, it gave me the illusion of going alone to buy it, and I felt grown up."

Spaniards reported more parental encouragement than did the Americans. Quite a few essays said parents urged them to read the paper (40 per cent), and on the questionnaire a majority (66.7 per cent) said parents encouraged them either "strongly" or "somewhat" (compared to very few essay mentions and much lower ratings by the U.S. group). The Spanish parents also encouraged their children to read books (83.3 per cent, only slightly below the U.S. group), suggesting that the difference springs from their beliefs about newspapers, not about reading in general.

Some Spanish parents went beyond urging and read

aloud or discussed the newspaper. Unlike the Americans, more Spaniards said their parents read to them from the newspaper (20 per cent). They also described the family having conversations based on the newspaper.

I remember my father in the kitchen reading the paper while my mother served lunch. He also, after reading something interesting, commented about it to my mother, and they both began a conversation, filled with constant exclamations. -an urban female, 20

With all the urging they received as children, the Spaniards expressed impatience with parents (6.7 per cent) only about as often as the U.S. group, but they less often defined the paper as exclusively for adults (33.3 per cent, compared to almost half of the U.S. essays).

The gap between the child and the newspaper as an adult activity seems smaller in Spain. Responses to the format of the paper, for example, created less of an issue among the Spanish participants. Children from both countries encountered broadsheet pages as youngsters, but the Spaniards then watched the changeover to tabloid size. About a third of the essays mentioned the change (30 per cent), and none talked about continuing frustration with the large pages, as the Americans did. Instead, they remembered large broadsheets fondly as objects from childhood. An urban female, 20, recalls, "With that enormous paper I could make the biggest paper hats you've ever seen." Although some young Spaniards mentioned the ink rubbing off, none expressed the sort of irony on the subject found in the U.S. essays. An urban female, 21, said she liked newspapers because "it didn't matter if I tore them up or spilled on them because the next morning a new one appeared in my father's hands."

The Spanish essays did not reveal the climate of conflict apparent in the U.S. stories, although the gender and power order for reading the paper worked about the same in both countries. The Spaniards mentioned fathers being first (30 per cent) a bit more often than Americans did, but the Spaniards also mentioned mothers reading first (10 per cent), or "parents" (6.7 per cent), or others, especially grandparents (13.3 per cent). (This represents a change from the previous generation, according to the older Spaniards, who said twice as often that their fathers used the newspaper first.) Only one essay reported sibling rivalry over newspaper access. A female regular reader, 21, said "there were even fights in my house because both of us wanted to be the first to read it. In the end, what always ruled was the strong arm." Although some of the gender issues Americans discussed surely exist in Spanish home life, most of the essays did not seem troubled by the disparity between gender roles.

The Americans expressed much more conflict with the newspaper as a form and object, with its role in defining the power relationships within the family, and, most important, with the adult world it represents. Americans defined their situation by the yawning rift in their social world, between themselves as small children and the distant, sometimes incomprehensible world of grownups.

SCHOOL YEARS

When describing the newspaper during their middle childhood years, the Americans reported resenting the pressure from parents and teachers, who nagged and cajoled at home and assigned difficult homework to make them read. The Spaniards told a strikingly different story. Parents and teachers made their expectations known through gentle persuasion, acting as models by reading and discussing news, and through in-class activities, not homework. At home, the Spaniards said their parents would repeat a proverb - a touchstone of the transition generation - to the effect that one cannot change the world unless one knows something about it. Several essays cited the phrase. There seems to have existed a general expectation that young people would eventually read newspapers, and that was that.

The schools the participants attended appeared to have integrated newspapers into the curriculum much more than did those of the U.S. group, not only as an art medium or tool but also as content. An urban male, 23, described a reading circle, where "someone had to read a small book or story and then retell it aloud to the other children, but I remember the time when instead of books they gave us the task of looking in a newspaper for 'good news.'" Two-thirds of the Spaniards (66.7 per cent) reported schoolwork involving newspapers (more than three times the share of U.S. essays).

Where most assignments for Americans involved homework, many of those who mentioned assignments in Spain said they took place during class (80 per cent, others did not specify and only one mentioned homework). Half of those who said they used newspapers in school (55 per cent) described role-playing, games, or a publishing activity built around newspapers. In many cases, the training described appears to have sprung from something akin to a media literacy approach, in which children are armed with intellectual tools to see through or pull apart media messages. After repeating the proverb about changing the world by knowing it, an urban female, 21, said, "Little by little, from the doubts that she raised in class, I began to realise the importance, not so much of the newspapers, but of what gets reported in them."

Spanish teachers often modeled their own newspaper interest, the essays said, by mentioning what they read to students (19 per cent of those reporting school activities) and by bringing the paper to class.

The strangest thing was that my religion professor, during exams and tests, hid behind the newspaper as if absent from what was going on in the room, but when somebody opened their mouth or turned around to copy, he would call on them and threaten them with suspension. -an urban male.

Of course, the incidents where teachers simply read during exams (not included in the above percentages) added to the uses of the newspaper in school. The essayists rightfully did not consider such occasions part of their schoolwork, but they pointed to teachers' demonstrated interest in newspapers, sanctioning them as acceptable activity during certain moments of the workday.

Outside of school, only a minority of the essays described

using newspapers (36.6 per cent). Paper routes - and home delivery - hardly exist in Spain, and recycling did not begin until recently. These activities received no mention. Nor did any essays mention newspapers used in churches or in scouting, an absence that reflects traditionally lower involvement in clubs and associations among Spaniards. (A third of the older Spaniards made a point of saying they never used the paper in other settings.) The few outside uses of newspapers varied extremely, with no example repeated by more than one participant.

Many participants nevertheless described newspapers as a constant presence in their school years (70 per cent). Those who did not experience newspapers as a constant typically grew up in a small town, and in fact, the smaller the city or town, the less constant a role the newspaper played (ranging from 85.7 per cent among urbanites to 60 per cent among townsfolk). (Just under half of the older participants called newspapers a constant, following the same hometown pattern.

A rural female, 33, wrote that seeing her father occasionally read the newspaper influenced her own attitude: "The fact that a person who hardly knew how to read would take the trouble to buy a paper and then spend hours reading it meant it was something important." The difference between father and daughter reflects the generational experience as people moved to urban areas and education became compulsory after 1971.) Some of the young adults did describe their parents modeling newspaper use and, for instance, mentioned that adults often conversed about what they had read in the paper (23.3 per cent).

Regarding their middle childhood, the Americans described lower institutional support for newspapers in school (but not elsewhere), expressed resentment over homework, and reported cheating to evade the assignments. The Americans presented a scene of conflict and economic activity surrounding newspapers, in contrast to the Spanish emphasis on persuasive modeling and critical training. These tendencies might have been even stronger had political circumstances not constrained them. As an urban male regular reader, 26, recalled, "My school years coincided with our transition to democracy, which meant that my teachers used the newspaper with real caution."

TRANSITION TO ADULTHOOD

The Spaniards described moving smoothly into newspaper reading, where the group in the United States followed a rocky and often unsuccessful path. The few Americans who conquered what most considered a dull and ungainly product told dramatic conversion stories. Only a quarter of the Spanish participants described the newspaper as boring (26.7 per cent), and a few said they always found it interesting (6.7 per cent). They seemed satisfied that adults read newspapers and accepted reading as the mature thing to do. Several aspects of the content and format contributed to their successful transition into adult reading.

The Spaniards conceived of newspapers primarily as an information source (93.3 per cent); the Americans largely did not (5.5 per cent). (All the essays by older Spaniards defined the paper that way.) A few Spanish essays mentioned the difficulty of reading the newspapers, but lacking a store of factual knowledge did not produce the series of attempts and failures the U. S, essays described. The Spaniards usually expended not so great an effort:

Little by little I adopted my family's tradition of reading the newspaper over breakfast, until I got to the point where now if I don't read the paper at breakfast, it's like having coffee without sugar. By 15 1 remember being caught up completely in the tradition. -an urban female, 19

Although their progress toward more demanding content developed in parallel with Americans - from softer, more familiar stories gradually to national and international events - the Spaniards focused more on news and less on the entertainment. The comics, for instance, entered only occasionally into the Spanish narratives (which referred to a generic pastimes page containing games and puzzles). What attracted and held the Spaniards' interest was hard news. Not all the essays addressed the subject (63.3 per cent), but of those that did a majority called news the primary draw (68.4 per cent). A smaller percentage keyed their interest to sports (21 per cent), and the remainder said they preferred other subjects, such as arts and leisure.

The tabloid format helped the Spaniards move from softer content (in the back of the single section) to serious news (in front). U.S. broadsheets actually create a barrier to that progress by separating different kinds of news physically into sections. The Spaniards often described the habit, what a male regular reader, 24, called his mania "for reading the pages backwards, that is, starting from the back."

News of local places and people attracted young people in both countries. An urban female, 21, said, "My mother always kept them on the dining room table, and I leafed through them because I liked seeing the pages with places and people I knew." Among the minority who described memories of a first story (13.3 per cent), a few recollect seeing their family or friends in the paper, just as the Americans did. I don't remember the first paper I read entirely but can recall one of the first I bought, looking for a picture of my school ping-pong team, so I started buying papers out of sheer vanity. -an urban male regular reader, 26

That closeness to home, what journalists call proximity, provided a universal hook - for some a school paper, for others a local paper - but living in Spain provides an expanded sense of the local. The Spaniards included not only such events as a plane crash in a nearby airport but occurrences throughout their country (which is no larger than a state or region of the United States), such as the Pope's visit, and even international news, such as malnutrition of children in Africa, happens fairly close by.

A sense of the newspaper as informative, an amenable format, and proximity to other countries all build on the Spaniards' newspaper experiences in childhood. In the end, they simply became readers, often as preteens (unlike the U.S. group). "When I began to acquire a `certain taste' for the harmless vice of reading the press," said an urban male, 23, "I was about 11 years old." As young adults, a majority of the

Spaniards said they read the paper habitually (53.3 per cent), and another quarter regularly (26.7 per cent). The remainder said they read occasionally, and none reported being nonreaders. (Almost all the older participants said they read the paper habitually [6.2 days "last week"].) Only one essay by a young adult contained any of the shame or embarrassment for sometimes failing to read the paper (an emotion found more often in U.S. essays).

The Spanish participants said they read the paper regularly 15.4 days), uniformly across gender, age, and parental education, with one exception: hometown size. On average, the city-dwellers said they read the paper habitually (5.7 days). The lower rate of readership among town-dwellers (4.9 days), although not extreme, revealed the status of newspapers. Several of those from small towns or rural areas described the newspaper as a accouterment of "the upper class," as a 25-year-old male puts it, "that is, those who read newspapers were cultured, intellectuals, and people with money." Participants from the provinces described their interest in newspapers as part of a process of self-improvement, to lift themselves out of a marginal world into the mainstream. (An essay by an older provincial male, 49, said that "newspapers had an immense attraction, they were the door opening onto a new and unknown world.")

The smooth and direct move into readership among the Spanish provides an extreme contrast to U. S. examples of bumps and failures. Both cases, however, shared a key attraction: the importance of softer, local news. Coverage touching on young people's lives in Spain, as in the United States, gave the participants the surest entrance into the newspaper reading habit.

INFLUENCES

The participants adopted a sophisticated stance toward newspapers, calm and accepting but not uncritical. They actively compared various news sources and read newspapers with a bemused skepticism and tolerance. The frequent changes in design and reduced format, as well as the ideological differences among newspapers, invited greater awareness of how journalists construct news. The Americans, by contrast, adopted a stance fraught with internal conflict before journalism they see as monolithic. The U.S. essays protested too much - how unimportant the newspaper was, how little it influenced them, and how indifferent they felt toward it - and then contradicted themselves, citing specific examples of its influence on their actions.

The Spaniards considered the press important but not as a guide to conduct. Many more of them denied the influence of newspapers on their actions (66.7 per cent) than did the Americans. The Spaniards less often called newspapers unimportant in their current lives and rarely reported an attitude of indifference. Their essays were also much more consistent. Fewer described any actions the newspaper influenced (10 per cent), and none of these went on to deny the influence (a contradiction common to the U.S. essays). The Spaniards offered a balance, one-sixth expressed positive attitudes toward newspapers and another sixth provided specific critiques. (The essays by the older generation took this even further, most offering praise while many offered criticism, often along with praise.) Almost half the young adults replied on the questionnaire that they considered news accurate only "some of the time" (46.7 per cent), and they rated the overall job of the news media just below the midpoint (2.4 on a four-point scale) between "excellent" and "poor." Their attitudes came out in the essays:

At home we always buy one paper, not because it seems the best, since there isn't one that we like everything about. You could say that it's the one we dislike the least. Many times they publish stories in a way we disagree with, such as getting the facts wrong about a demonstration when they estimate the number of people. But each paper has its own morality, and I understand that, so I enjoy comparing newspapers. It's the easiest way to get close to the truth. -an urban female, 21

An important component of the young adults' sophistication came to light when they entered into comparisons of the various news outlets. A third of the essays did so. They compared national to local newspapers, newspapers to radio coverage of the same events, and television news to the printed press. A 20-year-old female wrote, "I figured out that simply the order that stories appear in two papers revealed a discrepancy in their editorial principles." A male regular reader, 24, said "television has made it so these days people take a different attitude toward the press, that of critical reflection about the events carried out before our eyes." With the newsstand as the primary distribution point, the Spaniards confronted a wider array of choice and comparison each day.

They declared their skepticism much more often (46.7 per cent) than did the Americans (13.4 per cent), and a qualitative difference emerged as well. Where the Americans expressed an almost cynical doubt about newspapers, the Spaniards seemed matter of fact. Of course newspapers give a limited view of the world, the Spaniards implied, and of course they cannot be relied on completely-one cannot be gullible. "Newspapers aren't infallible Bibles whose arguments we must believe and follow in lockstep. You have to be critical of the critics and benefit from their arguments when adopting one position or another," wrote an urban male regular reader, 26, who also thanked "the press for stimulating in me the ideal of tolerance, of listening to different opinions without prejudice, and for sharpening my critical sense, including toward the news itself." Tolerance emerged as another theme in the Spanish essays. An urban female occasional reader, 21, said, "It has helped me broaden my view of the world and see that there are a lot of people, all very different. This wider view has made me more tolerant of those around me." Such expressions, quite common in the Spanish essays, hardly entered the U.S. ones.

The Spaniards' sense of the constructedness of newspapers might result from the process of change that ended broadsheets in Spain. More than half of the essays noted changes in the visible farm of papers (56.7 per cent), and they most often cited the change in format (52.9 per cent). They said they felt surprised when papers reduced their size.

One suburban female, 21, said her first impression was "that they didn't have as many things to report," but then she found "reading much more manageable." A large share also recalled the shift from black and white to colour printing (41.2 per cent). The U.S. essays hardly noted any design or format change.

The Spaniards, in response to the flow of changes in their newspapers, built an expectation for more. A female regular reader, 24, noted the "modern formats, new styles, and very different looks" add value, "so that newspapers don't get monotonous." An urban male occasional reader, 21, said, "The newspaper I read even now continues changing and searching constantly for a more agile form that allows it to reach the public in the most direct way." Such young readers conveyed a sense of riding the wave of change.

The sophisticated attitude also emerged when participants described the ways newspapers affected their moods. About half reported some type of emotional influence (56.7 per cent),5 and of these almost two-thirds said they experienced anger or disgust (64.7 per cent). In most cases, the feeling amounted to an annoyance at the depravity of humanity, but sometimes the participants said the manner of reporting, rather than the content, annoyed them. For example, several of the essays written by those living in the Basque Country pointed out how their experience differed greatly from the impression newspapers gave of constant violence by ETA, the Basque separatist group. A few of the Spaniards said they felt fear or happiness (10 per cent), but twice as many reported sadness, usually over the state of the world. Here again, news of ETA played a role. An urban male, 23, said, "I felt terrible anguish" after reading the newspaper account of an ETA car bomb that killed two people.

Finally, a common mood among the Spaniards, absent among the Americans, described the tranquillity a newspaper encourages, for which they used the English term "relax." (This mood also turned up in essays by older adults. For example, an urban female, 36, who read regularly, described it as "a moment of leisure and introversion. It gives me a secret pleasure to read the paper abstractedly in a green space, a cafe, or a public bench in the sun.") Although the U.S. essays lacked any specific reference to relaxation, they did give a much more serene impression than did the counterpart essays on newscasts. The newspaper experiences for both countries have that tranquillity in common. Despite the presence of political violence within Spain, for instance, the Spanish newspaper essays did not mention fear as often as did the U.S. essays.

In contrast to the U.S. approach, press practices in Spain encouraged a sophisticated stance. The ideological clarity of Spanish newspapers positioned readers at the nexus of political choices, a freedom echoed in the farm of newsstand distribution, and the format and design changes clarified the inventedness of the newspaper form. The participants responded to news as mediator, not as the neutral conduit the Americans saw in the U.S. press.

POLITICS

The political experiences in the essays often sprang from the more strongly partisan stance in the Spanish than in the U. S. press. The Spaniards described a three-step recipe for handling the outpouring of partisan news. First, some of them used several news sources:

Luckily my own political opinion doesn't derive from reading just one daily because, as I said, I usually go through several throughout the day, and ... I squeeze out what I consider the most ... closely adjusted to reality. -an urban male, 28

Second, they employed their knowledge about the political leanings of each paper. "Knowing more or less the ideologies of the newspapers in my country, I try to read critically," wrote an urban female, 20, who concluded that "not all politicians are as good or as bad as they appear." Some essays listed their newspaper preference as a shorthand way of describing their own political position, rather than the other way around. Saying one always reads El Pais, far example, reveals a preference for the left-wing liberal interpretation of events, whereas a dedication to ABC suggests a disposition to conservative and monarchist interpretations.

With a clear sense of the differences, the Spaniards said that, third, they then contrasted what they learned from the news, especially about political matters. "What I do is read and compare so that I can act in the most balanced manner, according to my personal convictions," said a suburban female, 21.

That personal compass helped them retain a discriminating distance. As a rural female, 22, put it, "Reading the newspaper has . . . helped me get a more critical view. . . . I've arrived at the conclusion that many times it's best to read without getting too caught up." Especially during elections, wrote a female regular reader, 21, "I think . . . the facts and opinions are the least trustworthy, due to the number of interests that hide behind that information."

Sometimes participants said the news discouraged them, especially considering what a male regular reader, 25, called "the role certain papers played in our country during recent years by denouncing cases of corruption."

Disappointment with politics came more often from women. "In my political views, reading the daily paper has filled me with irony," wrote an urban female occasional reader, 21. "I think it's better to take it with humor." On the whole, the essays by women seemed slightly less politically oriented than did those by men. The difference also turned up on the questionnaire item for political interest (men 1.2 and women 1.5, on a three-point scale of "very," "somewhat," and "not at all" interested).

In the end, the competing political ideologies in a variety of newspapers, along with some citizens' skills at parsing the messages they read, built a stronger connection to politics. In fact, the young adults seemed to connect with politics more through newspapers than they did through political parties, for which they said they had little sympathy. Only a minority expressed an affinity with any of the three main political parties, socialist PSOE, leftist IU (both 10 per cent), or conservative PP (13.7 per cent), and fully half left the item blank or wrote "none." Yet almost all rated themselves "very" (80 per cent) or "somewhat" (36.7 per cent) interested in politics.

It comes as no surprise that the Spanish participants became newspaper readers while the Americans did not. The Spaniards gave the impression of participating from their earliest years in a family project to bring them into the newspaper-reading habit at home, placing them, of course, within the minority in a country without widespread newspaper reading. The young adults remembered their parents as not pushy or nagging but encouraging, a result that confirms Mannheim's observation of how rarely didactic approaches work in transmitting values between generations. The process comes clear in this extended example:

I remember that my parents used to read me the strange and odd events that happened, from briefs on the last page, and they also explained any important news they'd read. They also urged me to read the paper. They would say, "Oh, did you read this or that happened?" as if for me to have read it were an ordinary thing. That way they encouraged me to take the time, because it was really interesting. They still do that, but now I almost always say yes, I've already read it. What was certain was that I didn't especially like reading the paper. I could read one or two articles but I got tired right away. - an urban male, 24

The essays also said that newspapers enjoyed substantial support from teachers. Unlike the U,S. model of homework, Spanish schools made daily newspaper reading appear painless, through in-class activities and the reinforcement of teachers' behaviour. The media literacy approach, teaching children a critical distance from the press while emphasizing the importance of things reported there, appears to have produced more assiduous reading, rather than the opposite.

The teacher's idea for the class was for us to read a lot of papers of different ideological stripes, to analyse events from different points of view. I refer to this because it was when I changed my attitude toward newspapers. From then on, they interested me much more and I read them differently. I focused on the editorials, as well as on the political stories and their different interpretations. -a female, 27

The material side of the press encourages reading in Spain. Newspapers all have a manageable format, and almost all have reduced the problem of ink rubbing off on the hands. Regular redesigns, whatever their meaning to older readers, appealed to these young adults, who expressed impatience with papers that failed to ride the wave of change. Clear competition at the newsstand also helped build their interest. From a wide selection - national, regional, and local dailies augmented by sports and business papers - some young adults purchased several newspapers just to see how a story was covered (this despite the high cover price, usually equivalent to more than a dollar a copy).

The competition seems not to have degenerated into pandering, although a few of the essays mentioned a recent shift toward more graphic and disturbing coverage. The local paper "has tended to become more aggressive," said an urban female, 19: "All you have to do is compare the same news story in different newspapers." An urban male, 24, wrote that as newspapers try to sell serious news by running it "between curiosities and lighter news, . . . entertainment slowly takes over."

These differences teach some important lessons for newspapers in the United States, despite the contrast in social settings and the Spaniards' exceptional access to news, education, and other advantages. Local newspaper monopolies typical in the United States probably do not encourage readership among the young, but neither do competing papers unless they have ideological differences obvious enough for readers to perceive a difference and sustain the variety.

A clear ideological line, which some U.S. editors might fear would drive readers away, apparently has had the opposite effect in Spain. Support from parents and from teachers seems to have sprung from or responded to the sobriety of the Spanish press as well as its commitment to a political point of view regardless of economic consequences.

At school, the U.S. curricula that emphasize doing the hard work of reading at home probably backfire and create resentment.

On the other hand, U.S. resistance to media literacy curricula, because of fears that they will produce troublesome, critical readers, did just that in Spain, with the effect of increasing their interest in newspapers. The empowered readers read more. Finally, although they liked the smaller format and regular design change, the young Spaniards responded with suspicion to efforts to sell the news by packaging it for entertainment value. Their sophistication as readers produces just the sort of tolerance that political theorists expect from a free press in democratic societies a hopeful outcome of ideological competi tion, media literacy, and design innovation.

The similarities between the U.S. and Spanish groups, although far fewer, have more to teach. In both countries, the fate of newspapers paralleled their respective abilities to make news reading a daily ritual at home. Including newspapers as a constant presence in the schools also seems uniformly crucial. The routines of publication and the schedules of production and delivery - the temporal bases of newspapers in modern societies - are just what new electronic versions of newspapers conspicuously lack. Information without a physical form that must get manufactured on regular deadlines may float unattached to temporal processes until readers or electronic publishers invent some other ritual as a replacement.

The same content of the newspaper-another commonality-appealed to the young adults in both countries. News in the paper had to touch close to their lives in each case. Both groups found themselves drawn into the newspaper specifically (as opposed to other news sources) through stories involving people and places they knew. Newspapers have other strengths.

Americans as well as Spaniards mentioned the power of news to recognize events as important and make people seem worthy. At the same time, the content encouraged a placid response: newspapers did not in either country produce the fear incited by U.S. newscasts. In general, when the newspaper's strengths as a setter of daily ritual, as a giver of status, and as a facilitator of calm rationality combined with truly local news content that overlapped the social worlds they inhabited, young adults became readers.

The similarities in the two groups could provide a list of goals for the U.S. press: altering the regulatory environment, the structure of the industry within local and national markets, as well as the content of news and the format for presenting it. Newspapers in the United States would have to make a host of changes at every level to replicate the Spanish experience.

Such a wholesale revision of the U.S. press seems well beyond reasonable expectations for printed newspapers, but perhaps not for electronic forms. The comparison of narratives from Spain and the United States does help account for the failures and successes of newsprint among young citizens, pointing to ways publishers can convey the political information needed to sustain democratic participation.

NEWSCASTS AND POLITICAL GENERATIONS

The young Americans in previous research seemed to resist the idea of writing a life history with newscasts, but the stories they related reveal various conflicts with what they considered a powerful political actor.

They saw themselves as weak compared to television news, which they then attacked with all sorts of criticisms of bias, sensationalism, and triviality. The Spaniards took a greatly different view that led them to feel empowered themselves. That central story emerges from the details reported in this section.

One general observation deserves mention as preface: The forms of news they encountered seem implicated in the ways the young adults in both countries thought and talked about their experiences. Depending on which medium they described, the participants had different ways of writing. About a third of the Spaniards (twelve in all) volunteered to write two life histories, one about newspapers and the other about newscasts.

The two essays by a single writer had a consistency of skill, language, and complexity, and those who wrote at length tended to do so for both topics. However, most of the television vignettes they retold were slightly shorter (and within shorter paragraphs). The ease of simply referring to images, as well as the abrupt shifts in topics, resulted in essays that did not run quite as long, regardless of which essay came first or whether the writer made small economies by referring in one essay to things already related in the other.

On the whole, the television essays seemed less detailed, tended to mention more images, and told less elaborate stories with thinner descriptions - a pattern similar to that found in the U.S. essays. The contrasts require more formal study because language differences make comparing essays from the two countries difficult. At least within each national setting the structures of the medium, or perhaps the habits of thought each encourages, were reflected in the ways the young adults wrote about their experiences. In short, the forms of news may delimit how people understand their political worlds.

THE NEWS RITUAL

The participants described a much stronger ritual for watching television news in Spain than in the United States. The differing historical development of television, as well as the cultural heritage in Spain, made watching newscasts a universal practice, reinforcing the importance of family routines for the success of televised news.

Compared to the history of the U.S. medium, television entered Spain later and the industry converted to colour more recently, producing among the participants a greater awareness of the television as a material objects Some of the Spaniards (12.5 per cent) used that sense of the television set to begin and frame their essays (none of the U.S. essays did):

It's easier to remember when you got your first television set or when you changed from black and white to colour (I was nine), just as it's not easy to remember when you saw a car for the first time, although you can always remember the first one you owned. -an urban male, 21

Such material memories extended to the appearance of the newscast. "I remember that they began with a clock that covered the whole screen," said another urban male, 21, "which we used to check our own to see if it was exactly on the time shown." An urban female, 21, recalled that "the broadcast had only one person and was presented about like the radio news used to be, reading from a sheet of paper." Another said the news "seemed made by hand."

In national custom, watching television news became deeply entrenched in Spain.' The midday break from work for many Spaniards traditionally runs from one and four o'clock, and the afternoon news at three consistently has therefore ranked among the highest rated television programs. "It seemed incredible that my grandparents ate lunch and dinner as fast as possible so they could watch the news," said an urban female regular viewer, 25. "At home it wasn't such an obsession, but we did always eat lunch with the national news in the background." An urban female, 19, said, "At home the television news has always been sacred, at midday as well as in the evening. Whenever the symphonic theme music came on at home, the living room fell silent."

The television ritual dated from the childhood of the young adult generation. (A majority of essays by older adults said they specifically did not watch at a routine time and place. In the Franco era, not everyone owned a television set. "The only television in my village was owned by the parish church," said a rural female occasional viewer, 41, "and we would go there to watch, paying in advance." The older adults also noted the greater appeal of news during the transition. "My interest in TV news," wrote a male regular viewer, 43, "surged as soon as the Franco dictatorship ended. Since that moment I've watched newscasts with real interest as often as possible.")

Although just about everyone adopted the news-viewing habit after Franco's death, attention to broadcast news has even older roots. An earlier generation became attracted through radio in the 1930s. Their grandchildren, the young adults in the study, described the grandparents' current habit of watching el pane and commented on the name, derived from the Spanish Civil War, when people called radio bulletins from the front el pane militar.

The strength of the family news practice produced some conflict, the essays said. Describing the news anchor, an urban female, 21, said, "How could a lady that my parents didn't even know personally get more of their attention than I, their own daughter?" Almost a third (31.3 per cent) mentioned feeling resentful of parents for their news-watching habit, a rate greatly surpassing the very few such expressions in the U.S. television essays. History here intervened with the process of adding more television sets to the home giving Americans the option to choose other programs. Multiple television sets came later to Spain and hardly get mentioned.

The participants said that in small urban apartments they had few alternatives. "For the smallest ones this began the most painful thirty minutes of the entire day " said an urban female, 21. "It was a torture to not be allowed to talk or squeal for such a long time."

The Americans faced frustrations not only with both parents, who dictated which programme to choose, but also with their fathers, who relaxed with the news while mothers cleaned up. When such differences appeared in their essays, the Spaniards either did not remark on or did not make much of them. The Spanish state monopoly until the 1990s had no commercial competition, making the news on Television Espanola (TVE1 or La Primera) the news.e A further U.S. frustration, with the racism of newscasts, received no mention at all among the Spaniards.

A combination of some gender equality and fewer contested role norms tended to mute the feminist reaction to news watching in Spain. In many cases participants described home routines that included women and men equally. Newscasts themselves also included women. The state channel had female anchors from the participants' earliest memories. Since the addition of a second state channel and three private channels, women continue in anchor positions, although usually in secondary posts (presenting the sports segment, for example, or the weather, both of which appear in national newscasts). The Spanish women also accepted male prerogatives with tolerance. A suburban female regular viewer, 25, said that "it was one of the few things my father always wanted to watch, because the rest of the programs on television didn't interest him much."

Even when the essays mentioned being told to be silent during the news (21.9 per cent), the demand reiterated the communal quality of the activity. An urban male, 24, said, "I remember that when it didn't interest me and I'd start to talk, my grandparents and parents would all go `Shhh!' and I had to be quiet." No essays mentioned parents getting angry in the authoritative way found in the U.S. cases. The Spanish group also recalled that conversation reinforced the news-watching ritual (9.4 per cent), which hardly received notice in the U.S. group.

During the midday meal, someone in the family would bring up a topic of conversation and refer to what they would see on television. That way I kept getting more interested in the news and in what happened in the world, because if not, I would never understand the conversations at home. -an urban female, 20 Frustrations the Americans felt led them to a feel indifference toward newscasts. Even with the relatively high level of childhood frustration, only some of the Spaniards expressed indifference (9.4 per cent). The ritual in Spain had largely the opposite effect. An urban male, 24, wrote, "A lot of times I could stand watching the newscast because, if all the grown-ups were full of interest and anticipation, they must have been expecting something."

OUTSIDE THE HOME

The Americans described a variety of ways institutions reinforced news watching. Many remembered watching newscasts in school, usually aimed at having fun and entertainment. The Spanish essays revealed much less institutional activity supporting television news. A majority said newscasts never had any role at all during school (71.9 per cent). (An even larger share of older Spaniards agreed.) "It's true that in some courses like language arts they covered some things about news," wrote an urban male, 21, "but they were almost always related to newspapers rather than to televised stories."

When they mentioned in-school experiences, only a minority said they ever watched news at school (9.4 per cent). A few mentioned role-playing (6.3 per cent). One participant, 24, said her class had an assignment to "act out the work of television journalists, although without knowing anything about the technical process." Such tasks took a fairly serious tone, not meant to entertain. The activity the Spaniards most often cited, class discussion (9.4 per cent), trained them to think critically and present articulate arguments about the news. Teachers, often in language arts classes, explained the ways newscasters "employed the language," said a 24-year-old participant. The approach went without mention in the U.S. essays, where the only discussion they noted happened in the school yard.

For homework, fewer of the Spaniards reported assignments involving television news (9.4 per cent, and 56.3 per cent denied receiving such assignments). (Even more of the older Spaniards concurred.) A few young adults who did have homework described how their families worked with them. One participant asked to watch a news story on an assigned subject said I sat with my father, and with great patience he started to translate the news into a more understandable language.... But he not only told me what they said but also tried to reconstruct the history, so I could contextualize the news story. -an urban female, 21

Although not in schools, watching the news did occur in other public places, the essays emphasized. An urban female, 19, said, "I discovered that the newscast was sacred not only at my house, but anywhere else you went - everybody was paying attention, at my grandmother's, my friends' houses. or any restaurant or cafeteria."

The newscast ritual emerged primarily outside of school life in Spain. The television essays mentioned class discussions, role-play, and homework assignments much less often than the newspaper essays did. The symbolic environment of Spain in that respect matched what the U.S. groups described. While reaching a much wider audience, Spanish newscasts received a much lower level of support that did newspapers in the cultural values the essays described.

GENERATIONAL MEMORY

Television news emerged in the previous study as a force that-through an initial major news story - helped young adults identify with their generation. The U.S. essays focused on the explosion of the space shuttle Challenger as the event to catch attention. Coming from a wider span of ages (eleven years instead of six), the Spanish essays did not agree on a single first event. In those recalling a first story (43.8 per cent), three major events stand out. The story most often cited (12.5 per cent), the death of Generalisimo Franco, lasted more than a month in 1975, prolonged as doctors went to extraordinary measures under pressure from those wishing to extend the Falange regime. The final announcement left a strong impression:

I do remember one image . . . that had an impact. It was of Carlos Arias Navarro [the head of government] crying before the camera as he announced the death of Franco. I've seen that image many other times, but I believe that the reiteration has served to reinforce in memory that first time it appeared. -an urban male, 24

The young adults also said they (like the U.S. group) shared a universal response with family and friends. A 24-year-old female remarked that after the announcement, "I recall my parents' faces marked with fear for what would happen next."

The event occurred very early in the lives of many participants, some of whom instead referred to one of two subsequent incidents (each 9.4 per cent). Regarding one, the attempted coup d'etat in 1981, a rural female, 22, said, "I remember having seen the news about the golpe de estado of February 23." The essays cited the image of Lieutenant Colonel Antonio Tejero firing shots in the chambers of parliament, with the TVE1 cameras broadcasting live. Others cited, without elaboration, the election of Felipe Gonzalez and the socialist party (PSOE) in 1982.

The important moments in Spain's transition to democracy contain the qualities also found in the U. S. first-story accounts. The essays did not for the most part describe the event, but instead merely pointed to its name or date or principal protagonist. In most cases, the Spaniards said they experienced the event as communal, not in the schools, where the U.S. students watched the shuttle explode, but at home with the family. Both groups remembered the event primarily as visual - in Spain an image of Franco, the king, the colonel, or Felipe Gonzalez, with another telling detail such as tears or senators diving for cover.

Finally, the element of surprise came through in both groups. Even for Franco's death the actual moment, although not unexpected, caught some families with one member away, adding fear to the surprise.

Among the other first news events they recalled, a few mentioned the space shuttle explosion that played so prominently in the U.S. group. Whatever the event, the participants all assigned similar meanings to their first news story. Besides defining the event as universally shared and understood, they centered the retelling on the operation and importance of the news media.

Repetition also played an important role. "I no longer remember if I saw it the year it happened." said a 19-year-old female. "They repeat it almost every year." Finally, the essays follow a pattern of mentioning discussion, which reinforced the event, its significance, its universal interpretation and emotional charge. The shared understanding of a key moment (and in some cases the same moment) in their interaction makes television news central to forming a generation's identity.

BECOMING A VIEWER

A majority of the U.S. television group reported regular or occasional news viewing, and the group's essays generally did not describe any rites of passage leading to a commitment as a viewer. None of the U.S. television essays told a story of trying to join the audience and failing, unlike their counterpart newspaper essays. Although less tortured than the accounts of the U.S. newspaper group, the television essays by Americans reported a variety of tensions and conflicts. Many recalled their parents urging them on, and some complained about the nagging.

Others said they faced social pressure from overachieving relatives or friends. Those who acquired the habit wrote with derogatory language - far from the self-righteous attitude among the U.S. newspaper readers - identifying their high level of news viewing as an addiction, with binges or other extreme swings from time to time. Little wonder they developed an inconsistent and desultory habit of attending to newscasts.

The Spaniards acquired a much higher commitment to watching the news, without much anxiety or complaint. According to the questionnaire, they watched daily for the most part.ll Many identified themselves as habitual viewers (78.1 per cent], and of these, most said they watched every day (84 per cent of habitual viewers). Regular viewers made up the next largest group (18.8 per cent), only one reported viewing only occasionally, and none reported not watching at all. The only difficulty they cited, newscasters' use of complex language, turns up infrequently. "It was a challenge to connect with what they tried to say, and keeping up to date was a difficult task," said an urban female, 20. "I think only now am I really understanding the news."

The Spaniards said they reached high levels of viewership without much parental urging. Only a minority of the essays said their parents gave any overt encouragement (18.8 per cent), and nearly as many said their parents did not encourage them at all (12.5 per cent). They rated the level of parental encouragement at the midpoint (3 per cent) on the questionnaire, indicating their parents neither encouraged nor discouraged them. The neutral rating makes sense. With the custom of news watching a given, parents had little reason to urge it on the young. A majority called the news a constant, repetitive presence during their middle and late childhood (78.1 per cent).

The content of news programming more often provided the impulse. Several essays mentioned one particular programme: "I remember from a very young age my parents watching `Informe Semanal.' I didn't know what it was, but there were some reports I liked," said an urban female, 21. "At home 'Informe Semanal' is something of an institution." The Saturday evening programme appears to have had the same traditional position among Spanish television news magazines as held in the United States by "60 Minutes" (which no U.S. essay mentioned). The Spanish programme runs more to documentary without a hard news treatment:

One Saturday, during those cold, boring winters of my adolescence, I found myself wide-eyed, watching a story from "Informe Semanal" and without realizing it I got caught up in those reports. I still didn't like the regular newscasts, but on Saturdays I had a regular date to get to know the world. - a female regular viewer, Most participants did not mention the age at which they began watching news for their own interest, rather than as part of the family ritual. Those who did, specified an age ranging from 9 to 16, of course, a strong family tradition made the issue moot in most cases. The essays more often said when the news they watched daily simply began to interest them. Some called their own progression normal. "I've always chosen freely the programs that were broadcast," wrote a suburban female regular viewer, 25. "At first I liked the children's shows, later I preferred movies, and finally news programs began to interest me."

In sum, the Spaniards wrote without the disparaging comments of the U.S. newscast viewers and without the self-righteous tones of the U.S. newspaper readers. None of the Spaniards expressed regrets, apologies, or hostility for failing to view (of course, all but two watched news at least regularly). From a young age, the participants considered news viewing an activity for adults (37.5 per cent of the essays mentioned this explicitly), and the general tenor of the writing seems to accept the news as the natural avenue toward adulthood. The routine at home grew uneventfully into an adult habit.

FORM AND CONTENT

The young Americans previously studied did not recall many changes in the look of news. They considered newscasts information, especially appreciated for its visual form, and they had regrets for missing the show. Their preference for news and weather (in that order) reinforced the sense of the centrality of news.

In contrast, the Spaniards considered newscasts with somewhat more reserve. They less often equated television news with information (78.1 per cent) or remarked on missing the broadcasts (perhaps because they simply missed it infrequently). Several essays did highlight the value of the visual content of news, just as the Americans did. An urban female, 21, cited the example of getting a sense of other countries. "With the visuals, it's much easier to remember," she said.

The Spaniards, however, had more awareness of its constructed look, commenting more often on the changes in the newscast (40 per cent). The end of the dictatorship brought a general thaw in the style of newscasting. "Back then," said one urban female, 21, "the news was cold and distant from the viewer." (The older Spaniards remembered the old broadcasts vividly.

"The news, back in the time of Franco, was censored and very filtered, and seemed gray and terribly discouraging to me," wrote a 40-year-old male. "They presented a Spain in positive stories that seemed dull and ingenuous, and an exterior world in negative ones, as somewhat dangerous . . . .")

The entry of commercial channels opened the state television stations to competitive pressures, with a resulting increase in sensationalism. A few of the young adults noted specific visual and technological changes in the previous five years, but mostly they commented on the accompanying shift in the tenor of news content, from the values of serious knowledge to the values of entertainment, a transformation that mimics U.S. newscasts.

Everything now seems more like a variety show, like something serious in content but perfectly planned to keep viewers watching the station. The package shines brighter all the time. The coif of the anchor and the smile of the co-anchor contrast with the quantity of negative images and stories. It's quite depressing to watch the news these days. -an urban male, 24

Just over half the Spanish essays expressed a preference for a particular content (56.3 per cent), and weather (the Americans' second favourite segment) figured hardly at all (6.3 per cent). In both countries, news topped the list. For some Spaniards, the interest started early, as it did for a 22-year-old female, who wrote, "I found it enjoyable to know what happened in places with odd names, although at first I didn't understand a thing."

News shared first preference with sports (both 28.1 per cent) among all participants, but by gender the males (like their U.S. counterparts) mentioned sports most often (37.5 per cent, and not one called news a top preference). The women, on the other hand, listed news most often (37.5 per cent) followed by sports (25 per cent), a notable attraction not shared by U.S. women. In some cases, the writers credited interest in sports with leading to their commitment to watch all the newscast, just as in the U.S. examples. "Little by little I began to pick what interested me, at first sports more than anything else," wrote a rural female, 22. "Later I began watching the entire newscast."

The Spaniards acquired the habit of viewing with relative ease, primarily through the news and sports, but they also acquired a critical distance. Besides a sense of how journalists construct news (a result of recent Spanish media history), their response to sports stands in contrast to the Americans' second choice: weather. Sports covers invented games, where weather supposedly reports reality.

INFLUENCES

The Spanish essays were reticent to talk about their moods in detail, and fewer of them said that television news changed their emotional states (53.1 per cent) than did the Americans. Spanish television, at least before the 1990s when commercial stations appeared, did not emphasize danger and violence, and the essays did not refer to many cases of fear during childhood. The Spaniards, even more often than the Americans, listed the various emotions they felt without elaborating. When they did specify, the essays gave examples of human suffering, just as the Americans did. For example, an urban female, 21, wrote, "The images of the charred bodies affected me so much I didn't watch the programme again for several years."

The emotion the Spaniards most often cited, anger (25 per cent), appeared more frequently for women (29.2 per cent) than for men (12.5 per cent), just as in the U.S. group. An urban female, 21, wrote, "The images of terrorist attacks and resulting activities always affect me, but instead of fear, they make me feel anger and helplessness, and that sensation stays with me all day. " The participants sometimes directed their anger toward government policies and politicians. "The story that made me mad, not that long ago and I believe it angered not only me but all of Spain - was the coverage of corruption," said a rural female occasional viewer, 23. (The story she cited enters in the next section.) Anger also focused on the newscasts themselves. An urban male, 21, said the news "provokes my indignation because of the way the stories are treated, usually from the most macabre angle."

Next often the Spaniards cited fear (21.9 per cent), but at less than half the rate of the Americans. In contrast to the U.S. group (in which women, especially from the cities, expressed fear strongly), the Spaniards had no major gap between the numbers of men and women reporting fear or its qualitative expressions. In a typical example, a 26-year-old female regular viewer said, "When the news reports come out about anorexia or depression, the statistics on the incidence of these illnesses are frightening." Such statements cited fear without expressing much emotion.

Sadness, the Americans' most frequent emotion, the Spaniards mentioned least frequently (6.3 per cent), citing happiness twice as often (12.5 per cent). Every instance of these two feelings came from an essay by a woman (in the U.S. group, only women said they ever felt sad, but men expressed happiness more often than did women).

In their emotions, the U.S. group tended to passivity, with men understated in their responses, and women experiencing more volatility. The Spaniards, male as well as female, took a somewhat more active stance, reacting most frequently with anger and newscasts and their content (while understating the passive emotions such as fear and sadness). That pattern extended as well into the actions they took in response to newscasts.

A substantial minority of the Spaniards said television news did have an influence on their actions (34.4 per cent), but none mentioned any changes in dress, hairstyle, or tone of voice - the authoritative airs that some U.S. women said they imitated. Nor did the Spaniards mention news affecting any decisions about their present or future jobs or family. They reported only one action that newscasts influenced: using information in conversations.

If there is something that stands out from watching news on television, it's the comments we make afterward, whether in the family, with friends or around other people. We have the custom of commenting on a news story and exchanging opinions about it. -an urban male, 23

Another important difference in how the news activated the Spaniards but left the Americans reactive appeared in the precautions they said they took. The tenor of fear did not come through among the Spaniards, who mentioned no precautions and did not appear to share the U.S. fear that one wrong move might spoil their lives. As a result, a majority of the Spaniards (53.2 per cent) maintained that television news did not influence their actions. Like the Americans, they seemed dismissive of the idea that news might affect them. Unlike the Americans, they did not then contradict themselves by listing specific ways the news affected their appearance and actions, including major life decisions.

POLITICS AND MEDIA

The young Americans writing about television news reported a limited interest in politics to match their moderate viewing habits. Unlike their elders, they told no stories of using the news to take political actions. The young adults tended to define themselves as ineffectual and relatively powerless, seeing television news (often mentioned with the generic phrase "news media") as a potent political actor. Some essays mentioned observing cynicism in themselves or in peers as a response to media power and their own political impotence. Although they gave a positive overall rating to the job news outlets do, they saw entertainment values corrupting the news. Somehow the media, they believed, supplanted political parties and weakened political discourse, limiting their own options. Some of the Americans saw their only option as a choice between television news and newspapers.

The essays from Spain revealed a stronger interest in politics, which also turned up in the questionnaire. The group gave itself a mean rating between "very" and "somewhat" interested in politics (1.5 on a three-point scale). Although higher than the national average, the rating reflects the group's median age (21), when Spanish youth have the highest political interest (Institute de la Juventud, 1991). The participants also linked their political interest with media use. In the questionnaire, those "very" interested in politics watched news habitually (6 days "last week"), and those "somewhat" interested said they watched slightly less (5.5 days "last week"). None reported being "not at all" interested in politics.

The Spaniards most often mentioned a type of action they call a political decision, which they usually defined as making a choice between political alternatives. Some essays also mentioned voting, and several specified other actions. "These days the news still has an impact on me," said a female regular viewer, 26, "and perhaps those are what in a given moment made me try working in a non-governmental organization or making a donation or whatever else to help out." Such levels of participation match survey results (Institute de la Juventud, 1991), in which a majority of 18- to 29-year-olds said they voted in elections (69.2 per cent) and about half said they usually followed political stories in the media (51.9 per cent). Consonant with other statistics, only a small share of participants reported joining associations (13.8 per cent).

When they wrote about politics, the participants considered the use of power central, and they saw themselves, not television news, as capable of exercising power. The exception, a 20-year-old female, remarked, "Everyone knows perfectly well how important a politician's image is when televised. It's the only medium that they can count on to reach the entire population and share their ideas." Even this passage places the politicians, not the journalists, at centre stage and lacks the sort of cynicism found among some Americans. Instead, the Spaniards appear to play down the importance of the news media generally and television news particularly in their political world. They rated the overall job the news media do in Spain (2.4) lower as a result. An urban male, 21, said, "More than a few times the newscasts give too much importance to an exchange of insults between politicians." The Spaniards saw the shift toward spectacle in television news as confirmation of their judgment that television news can play only a partial role in their political thinking.

Such a critical stance toward television news appears to go hand in hand with their own sense of potency and independence. The Spaniards emphasized their own position as decision-makers. "I think the stories get too little coverage to be used as the only base for information," said an urban female, 21. More than a quarter of the essays described comparing the various news media (28.1 per cent). A rural female, 22, said that newscasts led her "to take a more critical view, since the different ways of presenting stories on the different television networks give you contradictory images. Only after thinking about them can you then form your own opinion."

The essays also brought newspapers into the discussion. "I always like to watch several newscasts to see the different ways journalists have of narrating the stories," said a suburban female regular viewer, 25. "I also like to contrast this with the press." The Spaniards did not treat newscasts and newspapers as competitors, between which to choose. Instead each news outlet had a use. As did their compatriots who wrote about newspapers, the television group also took a sophisticated attitude, judging television news harshly but also acknowledging its usefulness. I've always thought that assimilating information from newscasts is relatively complex.

The bombardment of information is so rapid it's difficult to absorb what they say. Now I also believe it's much more powerful seeing images on television than reading them in the paper. Television touches my emotional fibre as a spectator. a suburban female regular viewer, 25

The essays most often cited one political topic: the corruption scandals surrounding the former socialist (PSOE) government (a current issue in the news just after the 1996 election). Revelations by news outlets illustrated the importance of a free press in Spanish democracy, the essays said. More than half of the essays talked about the value of television news (56.3 per cent) since the transition to democracy. The scandal coverage, followed by a substantial young adult vote against the socialists, appeared to have especially enhanced the participants' sense of power to make political decisions, independent from the older generation that repeatedly elected socialist governments.

Instead of concluding that the media have somehow supplanted political parties and weakened political discourse, the Spaniards discounted the role of newscasts as only one source among many. They emphasized their own thinking, as well as their ongoing political discussions with family and friends.

MEDIA CRITICISM

Complaints about bias in media coverage played prominently among the Americans. Women and members of minority groups such as African Americans included examples of discrimination in their essays and vented their harsh judgments of newscasts as a result. Similar complaints of bias did not play so prominent a role among the Spanish group. Several participants from the Basque region, however, did decry the false impression television reports gave of life in their communities.

A person from Jain, for example, who sees the news, must think that in the Basque country and Navarra we all go around armed and that it's almost like Bosnia. But if you live here, you realise that's not reality. -a suburban female regular viewer, 22

In general, however, the essays did not censure newscasts for discrimination. The only example parallel to the U.S. criticisms involved images of women. A suburban female regular viewer, 25, wrote: "I remember seeing a room full of men. One of them brought in a girl of seven or eight. They tied her with esparto rope ... and proceeded to cut off her clitoris." The essay described this "montage of images," intended to expose discrimination, as an example of the cruelty to women "they show on television every day." Several women complained of the recent turn of television toward shocking or violent news. The essays dated the shift to the arrival of competition. They denounced the new commercial channels for trying to attract viewers without considering the repercussions:

What I like least about TV news is how very morbid they are, how, when something happens, they thoughtlessly show it all without thinking of the consequences. They only care about being as dramatic as possible, and sometimes the scenes they show ... can harm the people involved. -an urban female, 19.

Although not as prominent as in the U.S. essays, such complaints mark a shift in the meaning of television news to the Spaniards. Both groups appear to share a sense that news has become degraded under commercial pressures. The transformation that the Americans noted, however, has just begun entering the situation the Spaniards describe.

The experience of television news among the Spaniards presents myriad contrasts to the U.S. group. Many of the differences result from the distinct historical contexts in the two countries.

The recent change from dictatorship helped produce a more widespread custom of news watching, which some attendant resentment hardly weakens. More of the young Spaniards became viewers without much overt parental encouragement and with little support from the schools. Instead the reinforcement of daily practice built a deep commitment.

The Spaniards, despite their constant attention to television news, tended to discount its importance. Changes in news form gave them a greater awareness of the constructedness of the newscast. The Americans, by contrast, saw their preferred content (news and weather) as information about a factual reality and responded with sadness and fear. The Spanish group reacted to news with anger, a relatively active emotion, and the women expressed less fear.

In general, the Spaniards presented themselves as more independent of television news. It influenced their actions less often, although they reported more conversations about it than the Americans did.

The most intriguing differences occurred in the political realm. The young Spaniards, at least in the particular moment after an election, took more interest in politics. They not only engaged in discussion but saw political decisions as theirs to make.

They followed politics and watched television news more than the Americans did, but at the same time they had a lower opinion of the news media. Where some in the U.S. group felt powerless, the Spaniards did not. They described themselves as free to make choices and saw an array of options for informing themselves. The Americans instead tended to see the necessity of choosing between television and newspapers, and some of them saw the media as powerful. By rejecting this view, the Spaniards avoided falling into the cynicism found among the Americans.

The U.S. television news industry cannot, of course, replicate the national historical experience of Spain, but the different experiences the Spaniards reported can recommend practices for U.S. newscasters interested in creating a high level of commitment to and critical independence from news. The Spanish example suggests a reasonable alternative to the U.S. definition of a news market, in which television must compete with newspapers in a winnertake-all contest. Such a view probably does not contribute to young adults' sense of their own options.

In Spain the media cooperate as a way of competing in the news arena. Newscasts commonly highlight newspaper stories, show images of the pages, and then go on to illustrate alternative points of view. The practice teaches viewers to read newspapers, watch the newscast, and listen to radio with the intent to learn more by comparing and drawing their own conclusions.

It is tempting to attribute the cross-fertilization among news media to the growing consolidation of media outlets in Spain. However, the television news segments highlight the main stories of all the principal newspapers. In the United States, as a result of cross-ownership such as the Chicago Tribune and the WGN super-station (Channel 9), newscasts plug only the company's own newspaper and Web version.

The case clearly differs in Spain, where anchors present news as a cooperative endeavor in which each medium has its use. Newspapers provide flexibility in time - they await the opportune moment - but their efficiency and convenience define newspapers as private reading. Television news has a programme schedule, and that inflexibility in time helps build a family ritual, although it also makes newscasts ephemeral.

By emphasizing and promoting alternative sources, the U. S. news media could provide a sense of abundance and variety similar to what the young Spaniards note. The sacrifice each medium in Spain makes in its own position as an authoritative source is small. The cooperative spirit does not dispense with competition but highlights it, producing a rising tide of news coverage that lifts all ships, for the young as well as for newspapers, electronic news, and newscasts. The young gain a sense of independence freedom to explore and make decisions. In the bargain, the news outlets get what they need most, viewers (and readers) who stay attentive and critically aware.

SIMILARITIES

The experiences of the U.S. and Spanish groups do have some important parallels. In both settings, a ritual at home supplied the most powerful and universal meanings of newscasts. Viewers acquired the practice through the rhythms of childhood experience. The temporal quality, then, came not just from the news as something new, but in the daily-ness of the process, especially in Spain. The ritual also involved the presence of parents, who shared in witnessing both the news and the family watching the news. In this sense, news watching depends on generational experience. The older generation, in Spain as in the United States, appears to have transmitted the practice through daily example more than through preachment, as predicted. Schools probably cannot reproduce the experience.

The young generation also brought its common experience to the news, and, in turn, the news of both countries contributed to the memories of the new political generation. The experience of being caught up in a national event occurred in both countries, which tends to confirm the generationbuilding effect of television news. In some cases, young adults in both countries shared the same initial news event.

The international reach of some major stories appears to tie young people in what may be an emerging trend toward actual generations, to use Mannheim's term, that cross national boundaries. That first news story does more than initiate the young generation's memory. At the same time, the common experience of the two generations, in the presence of news, ties them together in the national political identity, although as Mannheim predicted, their qualitative experiences of the event differ.

At the centre of television news stands the image. The young viewers valued the images of people and places they would not otherwise know. Such images helped them define what belongs within the nation as well as without, to the familiar us and the foreign them. The everyday procedures of news work do not often manufacture the kinds of images vital for linking young people to news. The events that tie the young generation to the old and fuse them all into national consciousness usually happen unexpectedly and overtake the newscasters at the same time. The element of surprise makes a difference. The news that marks a generation's memory transcends the daily routine of news and leaps outside the boundaries of the newscast as a temporal ritual.

One final commonality, the shift away from serious content and toward the rhythms and style of entertainment in the newscast, plagued both countries. The transformation, quite advanced in America, appears implicated in the dispirited and cynical attitudes among young citizens. The changes young adults observed in Spain presage a similar reaction among the generation to come. The stronger ritual in Spain, as well as the custom of comparing news outlets, has built sturdy links between generations, at least for the young adults studied here. However, the move toward sensational coverage and ratings competition seems most likely, in the long run, to harm Spanish broadcasters - their own reputation and position in the constellation of news options.

When developing the life history technique in the early twentieth century, Herbert Blumer attempted to create a lens for looking at the facts of his participants' childhood encounters with movies. The idea was simple: just ask them. The critique of empiricism in the intervening years suggests that life narratives, rather than simply reflecting the past, instead operate as a primary tool in the construction of identity in the present. The stories young adults wrote for this study do reveal the occasional event from history, such as the military coup in Spain, but their importance lies elsewhere. The stories give insight into subjective responses, the meanings and values young citizens assign to events in past.

Their narratives are public documents, not revelations of private goings on. The method of collecting written stories, despite the consistent offer of anonymity, generates an official version of events as the participants would like them seen. The picture they offer of themselves as audience members represents their ideal, along with a frank admission in many cases of how they fall short of that model.

In their experiences as citizens and members of media audiences, the young adults depict themselves as public persons. That image comes as close as possible to citizenship, making life histories an appropriate tool for understanding how the young adults explain their identities as citizens. In short, life narratives reveal not historical facts (although they allude to them) but symbolic interpretations, which in turn influence how the young act out their citizenship.

The success of the news industry in the United States and elsewhere depends on a range of decisions, from editorial content to corporate strategy, which rarely take into account the symbolic worth of the enterprise. As young Americans abandoned news over the past twenty years, the loss, although financial in the short run, has symbolic weight in the long run. Yet research has not usually examined that elusive quality, the subjective value of news. A cross-national comparison of how young citizens understand the news helps fill the gap.

The contrasts between subjective experiences in Spain and the United States shed light on the consequences of a news arena organized for market competition. Some things that U.S. journalists avoid most assiduously may in fact provide antidotes to the declining role of newspapers in the political life of young Americans and to their disregard for newscasts as an alternative. An explicit ideological position seems foremost among them. Reporting that consistently covers events from two opposing sides puts journalists in the role of neutral arbiter and leaves citizens out of the decision-making loop, as mere spectators. In the United States, the ideology of balance makes for powerful journalists but weakened young citizens, who respond by disengaging and in some cases turning cynical. Taking a political position and speaking consistently from it has had the opposite effect in Spain.

Another activity that U.S. journalists avoid may suggest a second remedy: a willingness to talk directly about the competition, its news decisions and ideological aims. When news organizations compete mainly in the market, mentioning the competition becomes a taboo, an unseemly intrusion of money matters into the high-minded business of public information. Fairly uniform coverage, which accompanies the silence about competitors, enhances the authority of journalists as professional news-handlers and leaves citizens with branded versions of what amounts to the same news product. In the United States, the limited choices reduce young citizens to mere consumers, who respond with boredom and indifference. Talking about the many points of view available in competing news outlets creates a vibrant news arena with the opposite effect among elite young adults in Spain.

The similarities in subjective experience between Spain and the United States suggest further remedies. In both countries the key that opens newspaper reading and news watching to more young citizens is daily ritual, observed in the example of parents and teachers. Didactic methods such as those employed in recent Newspaper Association of America campaigns seem ill-advised. The results reported here imply that the campaigns would have better success if built from in-school activities rather than homework, and in any case, getting parents to engage with news daily seems essential, and school work ancillary.

As news has become more professional in the United States, journalists have moved away from reporting the local and the particular, preferring to cover more significant and impressive events. In all the groups studied so far, however, young citizens report that local events most sparked their interest. The trends in U.S. journalism go against the subjective preference for news that stays close to young citizens' social worlds, reporting on familiar people and nearby places. Re-focusing on the local community, as the recent public journalism movement proposes, may help slow the decline in interest among young citizens.

In the context of remedies, it bears repeating that in the groups from both countries, models of entertainment and commercialism for news produce a similar negative response. The young adults' interpretations bring to mind the logic of the traffic jam. When passing an accident, drivers may prefer not to look but cannot resist. Despite their mounting frustration over so-called "gaper's delay," each car slows down at the scene of mayhem (which always reveals less than it promises).

Young adults react to shocking and entertaining news in much the same way, looking against their better will, but resenting their brief union with the crowd. For the purveyors of news, any short term gain in ratings or circulation from such coverage only feeds a longterm malady: the weakening subjective sense of the value first of news to citizens and then of citizenship itself.

All these recommendations interrelate. In the end, the U.S, news industry would be wise to target older adults primarily, organizing all efforts around building a daily habit. Whatever the cost in the near term, seriousness will build a more lasting commitment.

Techniques that draw from entertainment and advance commercialism may attract momentary attention from a young audience while doing damage to parents' willingness to incorporate news into daily living, thus sacrificing the next generation of viewers and readers. U.S. news businesses likewise would benefit by making their usually unspoken ideological stands overt, contrasting themselves clearly and openly to other news outlets. Whether motivated by politeness or professional brotherhood, journalists who fail to highlight honest disagreements about news in effect devalue not only political ideology but also the news itself. News deserves better. Variety and conflict between news organizations create, paradoxically, a cooperative news arena, increasing interest among the public rather than limiting the audience for news.

BUILDING THEORY

Besides the policy implications of the research, the Spanish case study and the comparison with the U.S. studies also contribute to theory. Three principal insights deserve elaboration, two that advance existing theories generations and political participation - and one that builds grounded concepts from subjective experience.

Similarities between the Spaniards and Americans help clarify the role of news in the formation and structure of generations. First, the young adults in each country share memories of particular moments in their national history covered in the news, especially, in the case of Spain, the events in the transition to democracy. That groups from both countries also share memories spanning national borders - such as the explosion of the space shuttle - suggests the emergence of cross-national generations, which were a conceptual impossibility at the time Mannheim wrote. Although probably not sufficient to form an actual generation, their common experience does point to an emerging global news arena and a potential internationalization of citizenship.

Second, the college students in each country might form a distinct unit within their own national generation. A next step should investigate groups of young adults from other socioeconomic levels. In the United States those who enter college form a large unit, but further study could profitably compare them with others who do not. Additional study seems especially appropriate in Spain, where fewer young citizens attend universities and read newspapers. That need does not, however, reduce the importance of an initial comparison of elites in the two countries.

The present study sheds light, for instance, on the persistent puzzle of participation in Spain. How could a citizenry deemed passive on many survey measures accomplish and sustain so successful a transition from dictatorship to democracy?

The evidence presented here contradicts the statistics for the population as a whole and expands the understanding of surveys focusing on youth (Instituto de la Juventud, 1991). Instead of the picture of a post-transition generation hopelessly disengaged from politics, the participants (unlike their U.S. counterparts) knowledgeably and willingly tackle political issues, foreign and domestic, while disparaging political parties and even their own government. Clearly the general indicators of knowledge, involvement, and efficacy fail to measure the dimensions of a subjective environment where, to paraphrase the classic statement by V S. Pritchett, nothing mediates - no association, party, medium, state, or church - between Spaniards and whatever power directs their world.

Capturing the particular moment of transition in Spanish history, contrary to expectation, does not diminish the importance of such results. Besides the obvious ways that the transition heightened citizens' sense of the importance of politics and their own decisions, the evidence suggests that the transition generation acted with circumspection, constraining their tendency to criticism when modeling media literacy. Nevertheless, further study should compare young adults in other countries where transitions have occurred, such as Brazil.

Finally, the study suggests a concept grounded in the contrast between young Spanish citizens and their counterparts in the United States. The comparison reveals a pattern in which several aspects of the participants' responses tend to cluster together in what can be termed a subjective posture.

On one hand stand many of the Americans, whom the earlier studies describe as responding with indifference to politics and activism, with resentment toward the media, and with a sense of fear and powerlessness. Another posture turns up in the essays by Spaniards, who have considerable interest in politics leading to activism, view the media with a detached but critical eye, and respond to news by comparing and making choices among political options. The two postures, or clusters of subjective responses, seem to mark endpoints on a continuum.

Certain kinds of enrichment or impoverishment define that range, which, for lack of a better term, might be called subjective affluence. The term affluence, of course, refers here to something other than material poverty. Both countries are relatively well off, and the groups studied enjoy substantial economic advantages. Their differing postures, where the observed personal responses cluster, have striking parallels, however, within the surrounding media environment.

The Americans experienced an arena for news driven by commercial competition. The news media avoid taking overt ideological stands, in favour of a uniform standard of coverage. A market mentality furthermore drives news outlets to employ the techniques of entertainment, along with an emphasis on private tragedy and public violence, to make the news more captivating (that is, to win higher ratings or circulation). The Spaniards experienced a very different news arena. The driving force of partisan ideology aims to present an politically coherent depiction of public affairs, and, moreover, holds up examples of other news media and their differing news judgments.

Of all the evidence presented, recent changes in Spain support most strongly the interpretation that these two arenas mark (in lived experienced) the endpoints on a continuum. Participants described a shift within the Spanish arena toward the U. S. version of things.

They bore witness not only to external events, as media outlets Americanize, but also to subjective events, as the young Spaniards themselves responded to that changing media environment. The subjective postures in the two countries link, not to their material prospects in this case, but with their responses to the symbolic arena. The subjective postures and the news arenas interact and together define the relative wealth of the subjective environment.

In short, subjective affluence describes a symbolic

continuum independent to some degree from economic affluence. Despite material abundance, the Americans experience a symbolic poverty, brought on by trends that now have begun spreading to Spain. Further study of subjective affluence could clarify the complex relationships emerging between news and citizens, while examining the long-term consequences for trust and interest in the press and in politics.

Chapter 2

Pressure and Performance During a Political Crisis

The Nigerian press faced its most turbulent years to date between 1993 and 1998, a span that has been described as the "darkest period of its 140-year history." This was the period between a national election that was to lead to democratic rule but was annulled by the military and the sudden death of General Sani Abacha, which revived the transition to democracy.

Though most of the repressive measures against the press were not new, their scope was unprecedented. Between 1994 and 1995, for instance, three publishing houses, which by an editor's estimate accounted for 50 per cent of Nigeria's newspaper market, were simultaneously shut down for about 18 months. Moreover, there were unprecedented incidents of murder and attempted murder of journalists and pro-democracy activists.

The atmosphere of fear was therefore unprecedented, except, perhaps, during Nigeria's civil war. Yet, the press remained considerably robust and outspoken during what Nigerians have come to call the June 12 crisis, in reference to the date of the annulled election in 1993. The election of a civilian government in 1999 formally ended the crisis; yet, it remains a strong undercurrent of Nigerian politics.

The Nigerian playwright and Nobel laureate Wole Soyinka wrote of the Nigerian press milieu during the 6-year crisis that it provided "one of the most fascinating fields of research in the plethora of mainstream, underground, fake underground, pseudo-mainstream, and so forth publications.... " Indeed, the June 12 crisis provides significant insight into the dynamics of government-press relations in a transitional-democratizing press system. This study examines the dynamics and suggests the implications. It is an analysis of the Nigerian press's fate and performance during the June 12 crisis.

The events of the crisis will be theoretically situated in media systems analysis. The paper will examine especially the interface of the emergence of an independently oriented news media and a government's exercise of power in the context of a legitimation crisis. Ultimately, the paper will suggest the relative advantage/disadvantage of journalism professionalization and orientations in the context of a national crisis.

The focus of the study is the independent press, especially the leading news magazines Tell, TheNews, and Newswatch. As will be discussed later, despite the diversity of ownership of the Nigerian press, the independent press has come to determine its tenor.

Data for the analysis were gathered by examining issues of Tell, TheNews, Newswatch, and other independent magazines and newspapers published during the crisis, especially 1993 through 1995. Data were also drawn from periodic reports on the Nigerian press by the U.S.-based Committee to Protect Journalists. These sources were supplemented with interviews of Nigerian journalists, among them the editors of Tell and TheNews, and personnel at the Committee to Protect Journalists.

SOCIETAL CONTEXT OF JOURNALISM

To fully understand the pressures on and performance of the press in any country, one has to consider the economic, political, and socio-cultural contexts of that press, along with the resulting professional orientation of the journalists. Such a holistic approach reflects the complex reality of all human undertakings and has been suggested by a host of theorists and applied to various aspects of communication research.

In their seminal volume on media systems, for instance, Siebert, Peterson, and Schramm developed their "four theories of the press"- authoritarian, libertarian, social responsibility, and communist - by analyzing the political, economic, cultural, and philosophical orientations of different groups of countries.

Though their thesis has been shown to reflect the cold-war ideology of the time and some specifics of their exposition faulted for undue generalization, the general orientation of their work has endured, with modifications.

Employing similar factors of analysis, Hachten, for instance, modified the Siebert-Peterson-Schramm classification and came up with five categories: authoritarian, Western, communist, revolutionary, and developmental. Even this more realistic classification is flawed, however, as many countries still straddle the categories. An understanding of a given press system requires the analysis of the factors of that press system rather than its slotting into a category.

Downing has suggested the expansion of such factors to include, among other things, insights from anthropology, geography, history, linguistics, and psychology. And Mowlana has referred to aspects of these factors as the ecology of communication, a term he uses "in a broad sense to include all the symbolic environments in which human and technological communication takes place." For purposes of analytical parsimony, three factors - the political, the socio-cultural, and the economic - are specifically discussed here. However, as should be evident, the three factors are discussed to subsume several others.

Regarding the political factor, the system of government is a determining factor in press practices. Pluralist democracies are inherently more accommodating of press freedom, and dictatorships are less tolerant. However, even among dictatorships, the imperatives of power and legitimation cause governments to negotiate explicitly or implicitly depending on their circumstances.

As several social theorists have noted, power is a relational attribute rather than a boom that is lowered at will.

It is at its most effective when exercised without coercion, and each instance of coercion entails some risk of diminution or even loss of power.

As Flathman, among others, has noted, there is a distinction between power and authority: the latter subsumes legitimation and the former does not. Thus, the extent to which power may be exercised non-coercively is partly a function of authority.

Accordingly, even autocratic rulers who have all the instruments of coercion at their disposal often seek legitimation and approval to enhance their authority. Leaders such as Gamal Nassar of Egypt, Kwame Nkrumah of Ghana, and Josip Tito of Yugoslavia, for instance, all relied considerably on populism and charisma to co-opt acquiescence. They employed coercion when their authority and co-opting failed to bring about conformance.

The form of government aside, a country's politics reflects basic facets of the society, including ethnic and religious pluralism and class structures. The distribution of political power varies depending on whether a country is ethnically homogenous or heterogeneous, whether there is a significant middle class, and the extent of the development of civil society.

Countries with diverse ethnic and religious groups - especially those like Nigeria where there is a rough parity in the population of the major groups - require a greater balancing act in matters of governance. Accordingly, they invariably have a built-in opposition, formal or informal, and an inherent capacity for resisting despotism. Similarly, a large middle class and the attendant civil society play a role in shaping the exercise of political power, irrespective of the form of government.

The resulting dynamics of power bears strongly on the function of the press, especially in its relations to the state. Countries such as India and Nigeria that are pluralist in ethnicity and religion also have dynamic press systems that often reflect the fractious nature of their politics. The press in such countries is also more capable of resisting repression.

Even in countries with a monolithic political order there is increasing pressure from global trends toward more open press systems. Such pressures come from new technologies of communication, increasing synchronization in global economic and political values, and diplomatic relations. In some instances, international press attention to a domestic situation has led to reform, as in the case of violence against Brazil's street children, for instance.

Regarding the socio-cultural factor, a press system reflects the general character and values of the society in which it is based, as well as the educational background of the people who staff the newsrooms. Studies of the Chinese media system, for instance, note the conforming impact of Confucian values. Similarly, analyses of Nigeria's civic and political culture suggest the impact of the absence of such values in public life.

For instance, in his book We Are All Guilty, Orewa argues that Nigeria's political instability reflects a general indiscipline in institutional and civic culture. Indeed, political culture - a society's values regarding the appropriate form of government - is an important consideration. One has to note, for instance, that the success of dictators often depends on the inclination of people to accept dictatorships. In many developing countries, including Nigeria, where the military have taken over power, the coups have often been preceded by public opinion in their favour. The implicit values bear on the ensuing government's behaviour toward the press.

Studies of the African press have also pointed to the effect of traditional reverence for leaders, polemical tendencies toward opponents, and the dictates of oral communication on mass media content. Doob has written, for instance, that, "In traditional African societies the prestige of established leaders is carefully maintained so that in their normal roles as communicators their communications are likely to evoke approval." Such tendencies have been cited to explain the often adulatory and partisan content of the Nigerian press.

Education also plays a role in the development of a press system. To begin with, literacy is a prerequisite for the use of the print media. Accordingly, newspaper and magazine circulation tends to reflect the literacy rate in the given country. Moreover, the performance of the news media is a reflection of the education and training of the personnel, including their professional socialization.

Regarding the economic factor, the press requires funding and sustenance, and the source of funds has a direct bearing on press content and control. In general, the news media are funded in one of three ways: by governments, by political parties or their supporters, and via the market-place. Of course, these forms of sponsorship are usually not exclusive. Rather a press system may be characterized by its dominant form of sponsorship, which usually determines its orientation.

The press in communist countries, for instance, is funded directly by the government, and its content reflects its role as an agent of the government. Similarly, early in the history of press systems in many non-communist countries, political parties were major owners of newspapers and magazines or were closely aligned with them. Such ownership and alignment typically marry politics and the press, and so determine the content and tenor of the latter.

In contrast, the press in contemporary capitalist democracies tends to be funded through the marketplace, making them more independent of the government. In such systems, however, advertisers exercise more clout than the government, and their interests may "have a higher priority than the desires of readers." A critical orientation toward the government is more likely, in part because of the independence from government and in part because such criticism often has popular appeal.

In countries in crisis or those undergoing transition in their political and/or economic system, the inherent tension also manifests in press practices. Such has been the case in Russia, other former Soviet republics, eastern Europe, and African countries. In these countries, stresses in the social system or sudden adjustment to new economic realities cause certain irregularities in press practices, including undisciplined exercise of press freedom and "cash journalism"

- the acceptance of money in return for writing favorable stories or covering them up. The practice of cash journalism is also common in China, where there is tension between communist control and officially sanctioned free enterprise. In sum, economic imperatives in any press system produce stresses or pressures that have an impact on journalistic practices.

It should be emphasized that despite the general tendencies just summarized, the relationship between press systems and any given factor described above is not inevitable. Rather, the actual impact of a given factor is a function of other elements of the social system of which the press is a subsystem.

As Vasquez has noted, for instance, government funding of the media in Sweden has much less impact on press freedom there than does similar funding of the press in communist and developing countries. The overall effect of the factors has to be seen in context and in totality.

JOURNALISM PROFESSIONALIZATION AND ORIENTATION

As suggested by the review above, journalism professionalization reflects the political, social, and economic system of which a given press system is a part. Indeed, the elements of professionalization, in general, are related to the factors of press systems just summarized. These elements are specialized education, a public service rather than commercial orientation, autonomy, and a high level of related ethical standards in practice.

It has been argued that journalists acquire these attributes through three levels of socialization: the societal, the professional, and the organizational. Societal socialization refers to the overall impact of the social system on individuals and their values, and it accounts for differences among countries even given comparable politics and economies. The professional level refers to processes such as education, training, the development of particular orientations, and the articulation of values and standards through journalism associations. As will be further explained soon, there is an increasing global harmonization in this respect, though differences remain.

The third level of socialization, the organizational, is the process by which individual news media inculcate their particular values and preferences in their journalists. This level of socialization distinguishes, say, one newspaper from another within the same press system in their professional orientation. Beam has suggested that professionalism is best studied at this level. Such an approach does, indeed, have empirical advantages, but it is limited in its representation of professionalization. Analyses that reflect all three levels of socialization better reflect the reality.

Various categories have been developed for classifying journalists' orientations. In a psycho-social taxonomy that reconciled the contradictory claims that journalists are autonomous rebels and that they are motivated by altruistic service to society, Schwartz demonstrated that they fall in either category, what he labeled "inner-directed" or "other-directed."

Janowitz identified two orientations as the gatekeeper and the advocate, the gatekeeper being committed to scientific detachment and objectivity and the advocate being oriented toward interpretation and criticism. A similar taxonomy developed by Johnstone, Slawski, and Bowman classifies journalists as neutral and participant.

In a more recent study of American journalists, Weaver and Wilhoit rejected the neutral-participant typology as a misnomer and developed a four-type classification as adversarialist, interpreter, disseminator, and populist mobilizer. They found that the dominant orientation was the interpretive, which entails a blend of investigative reporting and analysis.

This is followed closely by the disseminator orientation, which emphasizes rapid transmission of information to the widest number of people. The adversarialist orientation, with its emphasis on skepticism toward government and business, was found to be a minority orientation. Only a small percentage of journalists were classified as populist mobilizers, those who stressed giving voice to the public and setting public agenda. The various orientations were found to co-exist in various degrees, creating what Lahav has described as "the inherent contradiction between the press as a political organ and the press as an objective medium."

Press systems and the nature of professionalization may be said to be characterized by the dominant orientation at a given time. Historically, press systems have started out in the partisan-advocacy orientation and, to various degrees, moved toward more detached reporting. Janowitz concluded in his analysis that the gatekeeper approach to journalism enhances professionalization and that professionalization, in turn, makes the advocacy orientation more viable.

In the United States, the drive toward professionalization has been traced to the Civil War, when partisanship became so extreme and crude that embarrassed practitioners began to seek reform. The impetus re-emerged after World War I following the resurgence of sensationalistic propaganda. Some early trade publications, undertook the articulation of values and standards and were embraced by journalists. Ultimately, the need to mass-market news accelerated the drive toward objective and non-partisan news.

In the 1920s, Walter Lippmann articulated what became "a central principle in the professionalization of journalism": careful gathering and accurate, balanced, and objective reporting of facts.

Lippmann proposed a scientific orientation to news, which requires "the habits of ascribing no more credibility to a statement than it warrants, a nice sense of the probabilities, and a keen understanding of the quantitative importance of particular facts." Though it cannot be said that Lippmann's high standards have been attained anywhere, journalism professionalization has advanced along the lines of his recommendation. Various professional organizations have long emerged in part for this purpose.

Their canons typically reflect the need to maintain credibility with the public, a goal that is broadly defined to encompass the press's independence, social responsibility, and adherence to the standards of facticity, accuracy, objectivity, fairness, and balance.

With varying degrees of emphasis, these standards are subscribed to by journalists in various regions of the world. Studies have shown that even in systems where the press is not independent, some journalists aspire to these values or at least subscribe to them in principle.

For instance, while acknowledging that its founding charter imposed "certain political responsibilities," the Pan African News Agency nonetheless stipulates as follows in its stylebook:

A news agency exists to provide news to newspapers, radio and television stations and it lives on credibility. Those who subscribe to its service have the confidence that its news and features will always be factual, objective and balanced and that it can always be relied upon to provide good quality service promptly. Indeed, as Head and Ibelema have noted, professionalization in various press systems has to be judged in terms of journalists' exemplification of these ideals to the extent possible within their systemic constraints.

Studies have shown that professionalization provides some protection from outside interference and attacks. Dimmick's study shows that various media industries moved toward or intensified efforts at professionalization during periods of intense scrutiny or threats from the outside. Some scholars have gone as far as to characterize the practice of objectivity as a mask for journalists' agenda or as a "strategic ritual" and professionalization as an "agent of legitimation."

The rise of journalism professionalization has, however, raised concerns that the watchdog role of the press might be blunted. Merrill contends, for instance, that the American press was becoming so socially responsible that it was "in danger of becoming one vast, gray, bland, monotonous, conformist spokesman for some collectivity of society." Some studies have indicated, however, that professionalization has no such effect. This study provides some insight on this debate.

JOURNALISM PROFESSIONALIZATION AND ORIENTATION

Journalism professionalization in Nigeria has been affected particularly by the political factor, especially the press's ownership by or affiliation with political parties and governments early in its history. As will be elaborated on in the section that follows, that historical pattern, which changed significantly only in recent years, has determined the nature and extent of Nigerian press professionalization.

Suffice to note here that the ownership pattern limited journalists' autonomy, an important element of professionalization. Though political ownership limited crass commercialism, it did not give rise to a true public service orientation, another important element of professionalization. Rather - at least until recently - journalists were propagandists for specific groups and organizations.

The propaganda orientation of the press also bears on its ethical standards. As operatives of particular parties and governments, journalists often did what they had to in order to thrive. The limited formal education of many Nigerian journalists was also a factor in this regard. It not only affected the development of skills, but also limited the opportunity for pre-employment socialization, an important part of professionalization.

The education factor has changed substantially in recent years, however, with the influx into the profession of university graduates in journalism. Still, press practices have generally reflected the elements of professionalization just summarized. Even when journalists subscribe to high ethical standards, they violate them when necessary to safeguard their employment.

Tony Momoh, who has variously been the editor of Nigeria's Daily Times and the Federal Minister of Information, once said of the Nigerian press that it was the freest in the world because it was not constrained by any norms. Momoh refers here to the feisty nature of the Nigerian press, which reflects the country's fractious politics. Momoh's characterization of the Nigerian press contrasts starkly with

Merrill's claim that the U.S. press was becoming so socially responsible that it risked being bland. Though Merrill's and Momoh's claims may not fully represent the respective press systems they describe, they may be said to suggest a continuum on professional tendencies.

The Nigerian press has historically exhibited two complementary tendencies: partisan, often polemical advocacy and adulatory journalism. These tendencies do not fit neatly into any of the journalist-role typologies summarized earlier, as is often the case when models developed in the West are applied to other countries. However, Weaver and Wilhoit's typology seems most relevant. The Nigerian press's partisan orientation is consistent with the adversarialist and interpreter categories, especially the first. As will be explained later, the tenor of the partisan-advocacy orientation changed significantly by the 1990s; however, the tendencies still underlie journalistic practices.

Bourgault has attributed the Nigerian press's partisan advocacy and adulatory tendencies to Africa's oral tradition. Bourgault notes the similarity between the functions of the praise-singer in many African cultures and that of the sycophant-journalist. And Obafemi Awolowo, one of Nigeria's nationalist leaders and pioneering politician-journalists, writes that early Nigerian journalists "were accorded recognition at social functions" only as a "'socio-journalistic contract'" in return for flattering coverage.

Though oral tradition is a plausible reason for the sycophantic aspects of Nigerian journalism, it is not as cogent in explaining the contentious and abusive aspects. As Wilcox writes in an analysis of African journalism, "Most traditional African cultures have a high respect for authority and it is considered disrespectful to challenge or gossip about ethnic and now national leadership."

The combative and polemical tendencies of the Nigerian press are rooted rather in the press's colonial history and sustained by Nigeria's contentious politics. Emmanuel Dagogo Jaja, one of Nigeria's independence-era editors, writes, for instance, that: "In the days just prior to independence, the only Africans active in journalism were politicians, and no one thought of newspapering as a profession.... Journalism was then regarded as a field for misfits and agitators."

Ainslie writes of the Nigerian press of the 1960s that its political loyalties, in a system characterized by regional/ethnic-based politics, tended to produce polemical journalism of personalized abuse rather than debate on issues. Also, a report on press freedom by the human rights organization Article 19 states that the "period of multi-party civilian rule was not a high point in Nigeria press history" because all "but a very few newspapers aligned themselves with fiercely competing and often corrupt political parties." Press partisanship is also evident during military rules, though not always as overt or polemical, the exceptions being the years just before Nigeria's civil war and just before and during the June 12 crisis.

Professional press associations, including the Nigerian Guild of Editors (NGE), the Nigerian Union of Journalists (NUJ), the Newspapers Proprietors Association of Nigeria (NPAN), and the umbrella group the Nigerian Press Organization (NPO), have aspired to standardize professional norms. In 1979, the NPO established a code of ethics, which espoused much the same values as U.S. codes and those of the International Press Institute and the International Federation of Journalists. However, as Nwosu has asserted, the codes are routinely ignored.

A study of the ethics of Nigerian journalists found that those who worked for privately owned newspapers tended more to subscribe to an adversarial ethics than do those who worked for government-owned newspapers. However, the latter group expressed greater awareness of professional codes, though they refrained from practicing those that would cause conflict with their employers.

This finding bears on recent transformations of the Nigerian press, especially the rise and dominance of newspapers and news magazines that are independent of governments and political parties and are in many cases founded and run by journalists.

ORIGINS OF PARTISAN-ADVOCATORIAL ORIENTATION

As already noted, the Nigerian press's partisanship has origins in its history, and that history bears on its fate and performance during the June 12 crisis. The history may be broken up into four periods: the nationalist, regionalist, state-oriented, and independent press eras.

This classification reflects major ownership and editorial orientations dating from the early years of the press to the present day. The Nigerian press became politically aligned quite early in its history. Though the first newspapers, dating back to 1859, were published for educational and entertainment purposes, political advocacy soon became a major thrust.

The first noted case of political journalism in Nigeria was in 1863, when R. Campbell, a West Indian of African descent who has been described as a "brilliant and courageous" writer, "practiced journalism to fight the then existing slave trade." In 1891, John Payne, a Liberian trader in Nigeria, began publishing the Lagos Weekly Record, in which he attacked the policies of the colonial government.

The thrust of the Nigerian press became decidedly political from the 1920s, with the formation of political parties and their establishment of newspapers as organs of agitation. Though most of the papers had obvious regional interests, they aligned in their crusade for independence or some form of self-determination or political rights for Nigerians and other Africans.

The pre-independence press was thus largely nationalist in ideology and orientation. A major exception was the Daily Times, which was established as a commercial enterprise rather than a political instrument and was funded largely by foreign investors. The rest of the Nigerian press began making the transition from nationalism to regionalism as political independence became increasingly a reality and internal political rivalry emerged as a preoccupation.

However, the birth of the regionalist press was not complete until the late 1950s and the years just after independence. This period witnessed the flourishing of newspapers sponsored by the regional and federal governments.

After the Eastern Nigerian government established the Eastern Outlook (later renamed the Nigerian Outlook), other regions and the federal government followed suit. The federal government established the Morning Post in 1961, the Western Regional government established the Daily Sketch in 1964, and the Northern government established the New Nigerian in 1966 (to replace the Nigerian Citizen). The Midwestern Region, which was excised from the West in 1963, established its own newspaper, The Observer, in 1968. The rise of the regionalist press presaged the demise of the nationalist newspapers, most of which were defunct by 1975.

The regionalist newspapers maintained Nigeria's advocatorial press tradition through the early years of independence and democracy. The vibrancy of the press reflected a political structure in which four powerful ethnic-oriented regional governments competed among themselves for resources, while vying for control of or influence at the federal government. As noted earlier, such inherent political pluralism is usually accompanied by a contentious press.

Just before Nigeria's civil war between 1967 and 1970, the country was broken up into 12 states to replace the four regions as political divisions. The state-oriented press emerged during and after the war, as each state sought to establish its own news media. Among the state-owned newspapers established at this time were the Chronicle (South-Eastern State), Daily Sketch (Western), Nigerian Herald (Kwara), Nigerian Standard (Benue Plateau), Renaissance (East Central), and Nigerian Tide (Rivers).

It was during this period, in 1976, that the federal military government bought 100 per cent interest in the New Nigerian, the North's dominant newspaper, and 60 per cent interest in the Daily Times Company, which till then was Nigeria's largest and most successful publishing house. Significantly, the acquisitions were made the same year that the federal government-owned daily Morning Post and Sunday Post ceased publication after years of falling circulation and revenue losses.

The acquisitions, coupled with the limited geographic appeal of the state-owned newspapers, created a vacuum for national non-governmental newspapers and so gave rise to the birth of the independent press - the fourth (and current) press era - beginning in the early 1980s.

This era is marked by the rise and dominance of newspapers and magazines established by wealthy entrepreneurs and groups of journalists. The first major publications in this era were the National Concord and The Guardian.

The papers soon became major rivals of the government-owned newspapers, including especially the Daily Times and the New Nigerian, both of which had begun to decline in circulation as well as influence. The Concord, The Guardian and their respective founders - Moshood Abiola and Alex Ibru, respectively - also were to feature prominently in the June 12 crisis.

Though independent, the National Concord became identified with the National Party of Nigeria, the country's ruling party during the four years of what Nigerians call the Second Republic. Dissenting senior staff members subsequently left the Concord group and founded Newswatch in 1984/85, and the magazine gained instant popularity.

This development established a trend that would soon characterize the independent press era, namely the founding of publications by journalists intent on pursuing editorial orientations which though often still partisan were less circumscribed by political affiliation.

Among other publications established this way were the dailies Vanguard and This Day and the weekly magazines Tell and TheNews. The decline of the federal and state government-owned newspapers intensified at this point, and most were reduced to publishing less frequently and in skeletal forms.

Thus, the independent press era is characterized by the dominance of national publications that were not owned by governments or political parties, though their political sympathies or even agendas were transparent in most cases. This era is also marked by the influx into journalism of "a well-educated and politically committed crop of reporters." Olurunyomi writes that "Not only were these young men and women prowling their beats with the confidence of brilliant college graduates, they had also undergone an activist baptism of fire from the anti-apartheid and student movements." This explanation is similar to Flacks's analysis of the ideological ferment within American professions resulting from the influx of graduates radicalized by the campus activism of the 1960s.

The founding of Tell magazine in 1991 and TheNews magazine in 1993 and their subsequent role in the June 12 crisis are particularly illustrative of the ownership trend that characterize the independent press era and the impact of that trend on press performance. The departure of some senior staff members of the Concord group to found Newswatch in 1984 was replicated in 1991 when editors at Newswatch who felt the magazine was becoming too staid and conservative left to found the more radical Tell.

Tell's philosophy was to be more advocatorial in the tradition of the nationalist press. Nosa Igiebor, Tell's executive editor and one of the founding publishers, cited the activist journalism of Nnamdi Azikiwe, Obafemi Awolowo, and other nationalists of the colonial era as his inspiration. That philosophy characterized Tell's performance during the June 12 crisis and kept it in the forefront of defiant opposition throughout the crisis.

Like Tell, TheNews was established by a group of senior journalists who left the Guardian group after it was briefly shut down by the military government in 1992. The journalists left the Guardian group rather than agree to an apology for a story as demanded by the government as a condition for ending the shutdown. Like Tell, TheNews was established with an activist journalistic philosophy. The founders believed that "the military had hijacked the [Nigerian] polity," resulting in "a loss of federalism." They saw the magazine then as an "instrument of social engineering" "to catalyze debate and [its] direction," to fight against corruption, and to resist any attempt to muzzle their effort. As will be shown later, the consonant philosophy of the two magazines, along with their relative youth and non-establishment status, informed their reportage and enabled their resilience in the face of concerted effort by the government to muzzle them.

Indeed, it is useful at this point to summarize the factors whose confluence determined the course of the events described below. In politics, there was a legitimation crisis involving military leaders who usurped power at a time the populace was weary of military rule and the economic hardship it helped engender. Along with the ensuing civilian-military divide, there was inter-ethnic tension resulting, in part, from the military's domination by an ethnic/regional segment of the population. Despite the economic difficulties, the press - especially the independent press - also grew at this time, spurred in part by the general resentment of the military government and in part by the growing availability of new technologies that facilitated newspaper and magazine production.

The government also began to license commercial broadcasting at this time. This rapid growth of the news media put a strain on the availability of trained and experienced personnel (despite the influx of graduates noted earlier) and the weak economy strained their viability.

The June 12 crisis therefore featured an illegitimate and insecure government that sought to perpetuate itself through co-opting and coercion, an expanding press that was developing true independence for the first time and was still searching for its professional compass in the midst of an inhospitable economic climate, and a weary populace that included significant numbers of radicalized people. As will become evident below, the tenor of the repression and the press performance reflected all of these factors.

In their systems analysis of the mass media and politics, Gurevitch and Blumler propose an approach that emphasizes the "complementarity of roles." They posit that any given political system would tend to produce a corresponding role for journalists and a matching audience expectation. Conversely, any given journalism orientation would tend to produce a certain audience orientation which would put pressure on people in politics to perform in the appropriate direction. As with most structural/functional analyses, Gurevitch and Blumler's tends toward harmony. However, one could envision a situation in which the circumstances and roles in a system become conflictual rather than complementary. That was the situation in the June 12 crisis.

THE CRISIS

The June 12 crisis may be said to have its intermediate origin in the military overthrow of the just re-elected civilian government of Shehu Shagari on the eve of January 1, 1984. General Muhammadu Buhari, who headed the ensuing military government, was himself overthrown in August 1985 and succeeded by General Ibrahim B. Babangida. After numerous transition programs that stopped short of actualization, the Babangida regime finally conducted presidential elections in June 1993.

Unofficial results of the election showed that Moshood Abiola, a wealthy businessman from Western Nigeria, won the election decisively, but the Babangida government withheld the results and subsequently annulled the election on June 23. In response to the ensuing outcry, Babangida stepped down and picked a civilian, Ernest Shonekan, to head a transition government that would conduct another election. Though Shonekan is also from the West, the gesture did not mollify the opposition.

Given that his appointment was brokered and signed on to by top members of the two parties that contested the election, including Abiola's party, the press might have embraced the agreement if it was still tethered to political parties as it used to be. But the era of the independent press ensured that it maintained its own course.

Subsequent strikes and other forms of resistance made the interim government virtually ineffective. In a few months,

General Sani Abacha, the defence minister who was left over from the Babangida administration, forced Shonekan to resign and hand over power to him. What, in effect, was another coup essentially marked an end of the transition to an elected government. Opposition to military rule intensified, as did concerted advocacy for reinstatement of the June 12 election. When Abiola sought to declare himself president in 1994, on the anniversary of the election, he was arrested and imprisoned until his mysterious death in 1998.

The annulment rubbed hard on three sensitivities: the political, the ethnic, and the economic. Politically, there was a strong yearning for electoral democracy, resulting from a near-consensus that the military had overstayed and had, in any case, failed to fulfill its rationalization for seizing power. Nigeria's worsening economy, perhaps more than anything else, intensified disillusionment with military government. And then there was the ethnic factor, the increasingly vociferous complaint of Southerners that Northerners had presided over the federal government since independence. Nullification by a Northern-dominated military of a national election that was won by a Southerner for the first time in Nigeria's history was seen as confirmation of a Northern conspiracy to dominate.

Therefore, reaction against the nullification was immediate and determined, propelled especially by the ethnic and political factors. There were street demonstrations, especially in the West, Abiola's home base, along with national labour union strikes, which were pronounced across the South. Strikes by workers in the crude oil production industry, Nigeria's economic mainstay, all but crippled the economy.

The Nigerian press weighed in heavily on the June 12 crisis mostly along partisan lines. As Patterson and Donsbach have shown, even journalists in non-partisan press systems are influenced by personal feelings in their news judgment. With the issues so weighty and emotions so high, the traditionally partisan Nigerian press became wholly advocatorial. The concentration of the news media in the West determined the thrust of the advocacy. An essayist for the

Vanguard newspaper noted this reality in a scathing column written after Nigeria's return to democracy in 1999:

By sheer numbers, most of Nigeria's print and electronic media are headquartered in Nigeria's South-West zone. From there, ensconced smugly in a cocoon of sorts, they exert an awesome influence. And even though some of them are not owned by the Yorubas who populate this zone, the media in the South-West zone nonetheless capture the atmospherics of this zone.

Thus, the thrust of press advocacy was a campaign against nullification of the June 12 election, which took on the dual hue of ethnic agitation and pro-democracy activism. Whereas the broadcast press, most of which was government owned, downplayed the crisis and generally covered the issues so as not arouse the government's ire, the major newspapers and magazines took on a crusading role, publishing anti-government/military investigative pieces and searing editorials.

GOVERNMENT REPRESSION

The military government reacted harshly. However, despite the massive security apparatus at its disposal and its grim determination to perpetuate itself, its repression was made ultimately ineffectual, at least in part, by its simultaneous and confused quest for authority and legitimacy. The government combined harsh measures with attempts to gain approval from the Nigerian public and world opinion, as studies of dictatorships would predict. The contradictions inherent in such an orientation resulted in harsh but haphazard actions against the press.

In 1994 alone, the Committee to Protect Journalists (CPJ) listed about 40 incidents of assault on the press in Nigeria, not including intimidating phone calls and interrogations by members of the State Security Service. Among the incidents were 22 instances of detention or jail, 9 instances of occupation and/or closure of news media, and several cases of physical assaults and confiscation of publications, including up to 300,000 copies of various issues of Tell magazine.

The Babangida and Abacha regimes legalized the repressive actions through numerous decrees, some of which were promulgated and applied retroactively. This is an instance of searching for authority to legitimize a coercive exercise of power, a practice the military government continued throughout the crisis.

Though Babangida abrogated his predecessor's Decree No. 4 of 1984, he promulgated the Treasonable Offenses Decree in May 1993, about a month before the election that he annulled. The Treasonable Offenses Decree went beyond Decree 4 to impose the death penalty against anyone whose speech or writing is determined to be disruptive of "the general fabric of the country or any part of it."

Following denunciations from within and outside Nigeria, the decree was suspended a few weeks after its announcement. The next month, the government announced the promulgation of another law, the Offensive Publications Decree No. 35, under which law enforcement could confiscate publications deemed disruptive of the transition programme. Under this decree, several journalists were jailed and thousands of copies of publications seized.

When Babangida nullified the June 12 election, attacks against his government became even more vociferous. On August 16, the regime announced two additional significant decrees to rein in the press. Newspapers Decree No. 43 of 1993 required annual registration of newspapers with costs to each paper totaling about $10,000, a considerable amount in the context of a developing country. Newspapers Decree No. 48 of 1993, which was retroactive to July 22, proscribed the Concord group, Punch Newspapers, Sketch Press, and the Bendel Newspaper Corporation, all in the West and Mid-West. These publishing houses had been raided and occupied since July 22, 1993.

When Abacha ousted Shonekan in December 1993, he released the jailed journalists and re-opened the closed media houses in a gesture to pro-democracy activists. But he also issued the ominous warning that he would close the media houses again if offended. It did not take long before the threat was effected. On June 11, 1994, security officials again shut down the offices of the Concord and Punch groups, and on August 15 did the same to the Guardian group. The publications' offense was probably their insistence on de-annulment of the June 12 election and, in the case of the Guardian, a report of conflict within the administration.

To nullify federal courts' damage awards against the government and orders that the publications be allowed to reopen, the Abacha regime, on September 5, announced decrees No. 6, 7, and 8 of 1994, which retroactively proscribed each media house for six months from the dates of their closure. Here again, the government sought, on the one hand, to appear to be law abiding in not ignoring the court's order and, on the other hand, to keep its harsh measures in place. In December, the proscription of all the three publishing houses was extended for six months. Then in June 1995, the government announced a second six-month extension, after the three media houses refused the government's conditions for their deproscription.

The conditions included a pledge to not publish embarrassing information about the government and to not press legal actions over the proscriptions. That a military government included such a requirement is clearly indicative of its strong concern for its image and its quest for approval. And that the press turned it down is also indicative of the extent of its defiance and resilience. Thus, for about 18 months during the height of the crisis, the government effectively silenced three of Nigeria's four largest media houses, which among them published 15 newspapers and magazines and accounted for half of the newspaper market.

The comparable though somewhat different fate of Tell and TheNews, two of the most defiant publications during the June 12 crisis, further illustrates the determined, though uneven, nature of the government's repressive measures. TheNews was proscribed by the Babangida government in July 1993, barely five months after the magazine's debut. However, rather than negotiate with the government on the terms of its deproscription, as was the norm when the press was largely an instrument of political parties, the editors founded another magazine, Tempo, which published underground and, in the words of the editor, "was extremely pungent and uncompromising." Such adaptability would have been improbable without new technologies or had TheNews been a part of the political or even corporate establishment. The government hunted unsuccessfully for the publication's site and for the editor, Dapo Olorunyomi.

After Abacha took over power in 1993, he deproscribed TheNews, which, along with Tempo, resumed searing reportage and commentaries on the government. When the Abacha regime sought to muzzle both publications, they again went underground, in what the editor described as "guerilla journalism."

The Abacha regime could have formally proscribed TheNews and Tempo, even without locating their premises, but it did not. Rather, after trying unsuccessfully to arrest the editor, security officers in exasperation arrested and briefly detained his wife, a freelance journalist.

Unlike TheNews, Tell was never proscribed though it carried equally searing commentaries and damning reportage. However, Tell's staff was readily the most harassed during the crisis.

Several were jailed and assaulted by security officers. To minimize the risk, they too began to practice guerilla journalism. For periods of time the senior journalists avoided their newsrooms, homes, the airports, and other places where they could easily be identified. So frequent was the visit of plain-clothed security officers that even food vendors near Tell's premises began to recognize the security agents and to alert Tell's staff. Any editors present would escape through back doors.

But frustrated agents soon began to assault whomever they found. "They took anybody they see, for as long as you worked with Tell. It didn't matter whether you were big or small, it didn't matter whether you were an accountant or a reporter."

Once, the newsroom librarian was so severely beaten he

spent several days in the hospital. Members of the State Security Service soon took to keeping a regular surveillance on the magazine's premises and the editors' homes, sometimes openly, sometimes disguised as visitors. The editors sometimes got caught and imprisoned, and copies of the magazine were routinely confiscated by security personnel.

The harassment took its toll on Tell's operating expenses. For a period in 1996, the magazine shed its glossy-colour cover to cut expenses and minimize losses in event of confiscation. Still, along with TheNews and a number of other publications, it maintained a defiant editorial stance against the government until the end of the crisis.

For the most part, the government was reactive and did not seem to have any coherent policy, other than the desire to rein in the press. Therefore, though the government did not seem to deem any measures too harsh, the application was haphazard and inconsistent.

Often journalists were jailed and publications shut down for the same material that others carried without sanction. It seems, however, that on the whole, the government seemed less concerned with excoriating press attacks, which were routine, than with reports that raised doubts about its legitimacy or viability, cast aspersions on its intent, or revealed inner scheming or maneuverings - whether or not the reports were true. This is consistent with the concerns and actions of dictatorships in other parts of the world, including Brazil and Indonesia.

In addition to the contradictions of power inherent in the Abacha regime, several other factors seem to account for its inconsistency and the harsh measures themselves. To begin with, the Abacha administration did not seem to have a coherent philosophy of governance.

Abacha seemed insecure and distrustful of his immediate formal subordinates. Accordingly, he surrounded himself with personal aides to whom he delegated responsibilities that would ordinarily go to portfolioed members of the cabinet. Such authority was haphazardly delegated as deemed necessary to manage particular situations. Decision-making was, in effect, ad hoc. Inevitably, there was a degree of disorder in the military and disarray in the administration.

Second, there was Nigeria's traditional politics of pluralism and the inherent robustness in public discourse, which made totalitarian censorship difficult to implement. This structural impediment to repression, coupled with the courage of journalists and fueled by anger and resentment, facilitated defiance and proved difficult to manage.

Third, the introduction of mobile modern communication technologies such as laptop computers, online technology, and fax machines also facilitated "guerilla journalism," which seems to have confounded the military regime. Thus, technology facilitated resistance in much the same way that it helped thwart the military coup against Mikail Gorbachev in 1991.

But, again, the most important factor in the Abacha administration's dealing with the press is the contradictions inherent in the government's determination to retain power by all means and its need to legitimate itself through public approval, both internal and external.

The contradictions were comparable to that faced by Anwar Sadat of Egypt when, possibly to please American policy makers, he sought to liberalize Egyptian politics while also stifling criticism. Similar contradictions have also been identified in the media policies of Zimbabwe's Robert Mugabe, who crafted a media system which though independent in principle is controlled through an intricate ownership and governing structure.

Given that such contradictions reflect on all but one of the above factors and explains both the government's gestures toward and repressive measures against the press, they will be more extensively discussed. Despite Abacha's image as unresponsive to public opinion and political pressures, he seemed concerned about internal and external acceptance, even as he employed harsh measures to retain power. Accordingly, he undertook repressive measures as he thought necessary to ensure his viability even as he extended gestures intended to facilitate acceptance.

As already noted, when Abacha assumed power in 1993, he revoked several repressive decrees and released journalists who were detained by Babangida's government, of which he was a powerful member as the minister of defence. Among the journalists he released was Nosa Igiebor, the editorin-chief of Tell.

He also deproscribed TheNews. When the gestures did not mollify the opposition press, Abacha re-imposed harsh decrees and began massive arrests, including again of Igiebor in December 1995. Also, in 1994 Abacha appointed Alex Ibru, the owner of the Guardian, one of his fiercest critics, as the interior minister.

The gesture was consistent with authoritarian governments' tendency to find legitimation through inclusiveness. When the Guardian remained adversarial in its coverage and commentary, Abacha's government, of which Ibru was still a member, shut it down. Ibru resigned soon after. Then in February 1996, about two years after the Guardian was proscribed, Ibru barely survived an assassination attempt.

The contradictions may also explain why publications were no longer proscribed after the Concord, Guardian, and Punch groups were deproscribed in 1995. The Abacha government seemed thereafter to have abandoned that approach to repression, possibly because proscriptions, unlike the arrest of individuals, affected the larger public and was patently draconian. Accordingly, arrests and detentions continued, and there was an increased incidence of attacks on news houses, including bombings, assassinations, and attempted assassinations, which could not be directly linked to the government.

The contradictions may be most manifest in the resort of the government or its agents to counterfeit journalism as another counter measure to the opposition press. During the height of the crisis, counterfeit editions of Tell, TheNews, and other publications were occasionally distributed in major cities in Nigeria, carrying news stories that lauded the military government. By 1996, a number of pro-Abacha publications had also come into existence, headed by people with no known journalistic background. The publications were believed to be funded by Abacha's operatives. They, however, never gained the stature of the opposition press. Thus, the contradictions in the government's goals engendered drastic, sometimes desperate, measures but also helped ensure their ultimate failure.

PRESS DEFIANCE

Despite the risks and the economic pressures brought about by a severely weakened economy, the opposition press, on the whole, continued through much of the crisis to report on various facets of public life and offer critical opinion.

Their resilience reflected various factors: individual courage often sustained by resentment and anger, ethnic loyalty, which provided considerable structural obstacle to authoritarianism and the rise of stealthy and portable media technology.

Thus, the opposition press not only survived the repressive measures but remained relatively robust venues of information, public debates, and criticism. Even advocacy for the reinstatement of the June 12 election, which the government seemed to find criminal, remained strong. And government malfeasance and suspicious intent were investigated and reported on, especially by the leading opposition papers.

The publications were often skeptical of the government's pronouncements regarding transition to democracy. During the period leading up to the June 12 election in 1993, for instance, the press frequently noted indications that Babangida had no intention of actually handing over power to an elected government.

For instance, in an extensive cover story before the election in 1993, Tell detailed an interview in which Nigeria's former military head-of-state, Olusegun Obasanjo, among other things, questioned the sincerity of the transition programme.

When about two weeks after the election Babangida

announced the annulment, Tell and other publications which raised the same fears were vindicated.

After the annulment and the subsequent institution of a representative constitutional conference, the press again carried news stories and analyses that indicated that the conference was Abacha's diversionary tactic to mollify the opposition.

There were reports about Abacha's manipulations to have favorable representations in the conference. When the conference eventually came up with a draft of a constitution, the press reported that Abacha was pressuring for an amendment. The draft was subsequently amended.

When the constitution was eventually released and another transition programme set in progress, the press again warned of Abacha's schemes to stay in power. The press's alarms were again confirmed when each of the five approved political parties successively endorsed Abacha as its presidential candidate. The momentum toward the realization of this scheme ended with Abacha's death in 1998.

Following the annulment, the government was particularly sensitive about calls for the installation of the presumed winner of the June 12 election. Yet, opposition publications were unrelenting in pressing the case through scathing commentaries and excerpts of interviewees. Among the defiant cover stories carried during the height of the crisis were:

"Why IBB is on the run."
"Abacha's secret deal with IBB. How he schemed for power. Tension in the barracks."
"Abacha and the Kaduna Mafia."
"Forces That Will Chase Out Abacha."
"Abacha's days are numbered."
"The North rises for June 12."
"Fresh Alarm Over Coup Suspects."
"Abacha's New Offensive."
"Despotism Let Loose. Why Abacha is adamant. Hangs on to power."
"Abacha Must Be Probed."

"Aso Rock's N.8 billion bribe for soldiers... To secure 8-year presidency for Abacha."

"Nigeria held hostage. Abacha's years of terror."

"Confrontation. Politicians take on the military."

An examination of individual articles in the publications further shows the extent of the defiance. In a speech a few months after the annulment - a speech that was published as a column in Tell - Obasanjo warned the new government not to "make itself a laughing stock" with actions that went against global trends. Obasanjo's reference to global trends was evidently intended to play on the military's concern with acceptance.

When, on seizing power, Abacha announced that he would appoint civilian administrators to run the states and almost immediately reversed himself, Tell derided the explanation that the reversal was to reflect public opinion. In a column titled "Abacha and his magicians," Tell's editor-in-chief, Nosa Igiebor, wrote: "Clearly and simply Abacha's somersault was a settlement of the increasingly and dangerously restive sections of the military. After all the Babangida junta of which Abacha was a key player demonstrated that appointment to public office is an unbridled license to raid the public till at will without any fear of sanction of any kind."

Here the magazine capitalized on Abacha's rather clumsy attempt to attribute his act of power consolidation to popular opinion rather than his insecurity. Indeed, the theme of illegitimacy underlay most press attacks. Other recurrent themes in commentaries and analyses were ineffectiveness and corruption.

In an interview carried by Tell, a politician and businessman from the North, Abdulkarim Daiyaku, said of Babangida: "No leader so greatly destroyed his country's economy as he has done because he sold everything to himself and his colleagues. Nigerians got nothing."

Continuing on the same theme and arguing that Abacha had refused to probe his predecessor because his administration was as corrupt as Babangida's, Daiyaku remarked: "Those who toppled Buhari, where are they today? They are not better than armed robbers. There is nothing to hide. Everybody can see that they are very rich while the country is in debt." Making very much the same case, an analyst asserted that the military "leadership is the albatross" and "Abacha has no answer."

In an unsigned editorial entitled "The way forward," Tell wrote that: "The ... larger-than-life corruption, the gross ineptitude, the deification of mediocrity as a state policy, the sweeping underground of dissent, the militarisation of political structures and the atomisation of society have all but given rise to a personal dictatorship that is as vacuous as it is sterile and bereft of profit." In an essay on the government's repressive measures against the press, a columnist for The African Concord magazine wrote:

The truth... is that those whom the gods want to destroy they first make mad; when a government, any government, therefore, goes as panicky as the Abacha-Diya administration has done, then, it is better for it to go. When a government is blind enough to gather gangsters as its counsellors and special advisers as their guide, then, it is best for it to quit. The Guardian group was raided and shut down soon after this issue was in circulation, probably not because of this column, but partly because of a cover story that featured interviews of Northern politicians calling for reinstatement of the June 12 election.

As noted earlier, such calls were the starkest reminder to the Abacha regime that it was illegitimate in the eyes of a substantial segment of the Nigerian populace. The cover of Newswatch's March 13, 1995 issue, has centered on it in bold letters, "Corruption Inc.

Anatomy of corrupt practices in Nigeria." The indepth article reported on the practices of various government corporations, among them the Nigeria Airways, Nigerian Telecommunications, and the Nigerian National Petroleum Corporation. It offered anecdotes of specific instances of gross corruption, before finally placing the blame directly on Abacha. During the second anniversary of the June 12 election, a writer for Tell all but called for an insurrection: The military and particularly Abacha have nothing to offer us except suffering and corruption and those they have done with all the weapons at their disposal. Enough is enough. The die is cast. Sometimes God uses us to answer our own prayers. We need to fight for our emancipation....

After the Abacha regime intensified arrests and imprisonment of journalists and opposition activists and charged several with complicity in an ostensible coup plot in 1995, some opposition publishing houses toned down their criticism. However, Tell, TheNews, and Tempo, the latter's reincarnation, remained in the forefront of journalistic opposition, despite repeated and prolonged jail terms for several of their editors and writers.

In this regard, it could be said that the opposition journalists epitomized Merrill's notion of the existentialist journalist. In his sequel to "The Imperatives of Freedom," Merrill writes:

The existential journalist rebels against being buried in ... modern corporate journalism.... He cares little about strict professionalism or institutionalism; more important to him is a sense of self-esteem and self-reliance. He takes stands; he chooses; and he is willing to take the consequences of these choices. This is often quite painful.

DEFICIENCIES IN COVERAGE

Several deficiencies were evident in the June 12 press, and all were noted or acknowledged by the journalists interviewed for this study, though not necessarily with regard to their own publications. As will be discussed later, the deficiencies are rooted in elements of the press system, including political agenda, economic pressures, and professional shortfalls.

Among the specific deficiencies identified were news stories of doubtful facticity; sensationalist covers and headlines that promised much more than the accompanying stories bore out; one-sided coverage of issues; resort to incendiary, rude, or crude language; the fusion of news and commentary; and pandering to the government. Most of the deficiencies come under what Merrill and Odell discuss as constituting "journalistic propaganda."

They also fall short of the standards suggested by McQuail as appropriate for evaluating media performance. These standards are collapsed for discussion as deficiencies in facticity and accuracy, balance and objectivity, and civility in discourse. As will be elaborated on later, the deficiencies reflect the economic, political, and social circumstances of the June 12 press.

FACTICITY AND ACCURACY

The most common complaints regarding facticity and accuracy were about uncorroborated, often conjectural, allegations of malfeasance against public officials. Given the widespread perception of graft in the Nigerian polity, such allegations were readily found credible. They resulted in myriad lawsuits against the press, including by sitting members of the Supreme Court of Nigeria. Some reported incidents appear to be outright fabrications. For instance, in 1994 a magazine carried an account of a fist fight between two well-known representatives at the national constitutional conferences. The participants denied it and there was no corroboration.

Misreporting was also rampant with regard to the government's claim of a coup plot in 1995 and the related arrests, detentions, and trials of several officers and civilians. Reports of battery against prisoners were also rampant and sometimes false. For instance, there were reports that a former military governor arrested in connection with a coup plot had been severely beaten, along with other detainees. However, when he appeared in court subsequently, Newswatch reported that: "His appearance gave the lie to publications that he was battered beyond recognition. There were no signs of torture on his face or body. None of the accused showed signs of torture."

Also, reports of plans to execute notable prisoners, including Obasanjo, were as common as reports of decisions to release them. Similarly, various reports of the imminent release of Abiola turned out to be false.

Given the inconsistency of the Abacha regime discussed earlier and the execution of the activist Ken Saro-Wiwa and others in 1995, the contradictory reports of pending release and execution of prisoners were all plausible. There may have been sufficient basis for them in the particular contexts, or the publications may have rushed to press on the basis of tenuous evidence or stretched the known facts to titillate or arouse the public.

There are indications, indeed, that some of the coverage reflected desired outcomes and was intended to inspire or arouse the faithful, as the mass media often do in wartime. Often stories were packaged to suggest more than was warranted.

Soon after Abacha replaced Shonekan as the head of state, for instance, Tell had on its cover: "Why IBB is on the run." The extensive story inside was captioned, "Flight of a dictator."

Despite the definitive cover and headline, the third paragraph in the story indicated some degree of uncertainty, stating that "more facts are emerging to indicate that Babangida's quiet departure might eventually turn out to be a full-blown exile."

The reasons proffered were Babangida's suspicion of Abacha's intentions toward him and public hostility toward Babangida, including claims that he was accosted in his hometown by young boys who, among other things, called him a thief and threw coins at him.

The most authoritative and definitive claim that Babangida was leaving for exile was made by a former president of the Nigerian Bar Association, Alao Aka-Basorun, who said: "Babangida has gone for good. He fled the country because he knew his enemies are closing in on him". There was no indication of Aka-Basorun's basis for the claim, other than a personal speculation. Babangida did return and was subsequently active in the coalition that had Obasanjo elected president in 1999.

Just before the first anniversary of the June 12 election, Tell declared on its cover, "Abacha's days are numbered." The headline inside stated, "Red Card for the Generals" and is followed by the subtitle, "The Abacha junta seems cornered as the ghost of June 12 roars again in the shape of an ultimatum from pro-democracy forces."

The extensive reportage that followed noted various pro-democracy meetings and declarations, a snub of Abacha by Vice President Al Gore at the inauguration of Nelson Mandela as president of South Africa, and heckling of the Nigerian delegation to the occasion. There was no indication of how these events constituted a mortal and imminent threat to Abacha's power.

Similarly, a March 1994 cover story in TheNews, "Forces That Will Chase Out Abacha," suggested an impending end of the Abacha regime.180 The inside story was, however, an analysis of Nigeria's deepening economic difficulties. The analysis was a well-researched and cogent essay on the Nigerian economy, but it hardly supported the suggested threat to Abacha's power. These instances are particularly suggestive of an attempt to boost the opposition's morale, especially among the populace.

By mid-1995, the major news was about the detention and pending trial of people who were alleged to have plotted a coup against Abacha. A panel, the equivalent of a grand jury, was set up to conduct preliminary inquiries into the allegations.

On the cover of an issue in May, TheNews announced, "Not guilty. Army panel clears coup suspects." Much of the story that followed was a recounting of events leading to the arrests, attempts by some traditional leaders to free the detainees, and comments on the investigations. Just a few paragraphs reported on the "verdict."

One of those paragraphs included the following statements: "On 6 May, the panel turned its report over to the Chief of Defence Staff. The report vindicated government's first position that the coup plot was a mere rumour calculated to cause disaffection." The information is unattributed.

However, several paragraphs earlier, the magazine reported as follows: "The coup panel, according to Colonel Ugbo who spoke to the press during the Sallah festivities, will submit its report the weekend after Sallah.... Immediately after the Sallah, however, Brigadier-General Fred Chijuka at his own press conference said that the panel had not finished its work because they were on Sallah break."

There was no indication as to why the "not guilty" cover more closely reflected the panel's position than the contradictory remarks just quoted.

Tell's cover story on the subsequent trial states: "Death to the generals?...(sic) Abacha held Hostage In Abuja." The bold cover, though suggesting substantive disclosures, merely reflected the general knowledge that executions were possible in such contexts.

The secondary story that Abacha was being held hostage in Abuja noted, in essence, that Abacha had minimized his public appearances, a fact that had to be stretched considerably to amount to a hostage situation, with all its implications of a palace coup.

Tell's cover story on the execution of Saro-Wiwa also includes elements that would seem to have stretched the facts. The account suggests that Saro-Wiwa was supernatural. Tell narrated that the execution pulley failed three times when pulled to execute Saro-Wiwa.

After each failure, one of Saro-Wiwa's colleagues was successfully hanged using the same pulley. Saro-Wiwa was eventually executed in the fourth attempt after he became "weary from seeing his compatriots disappear across the horizon of life [and so] finally chose to go." Tell cited unnamed and unidentified sources for the account. The story is reminiscent of Shakespeare's account of the assassination of Julius Caesar, according to which, Caesar died not because of multiple mortal wounds but only after despairing over the "ingratitude" and treachery of his trusted lieutenant, Brutus.

BALANCE AND OBJECTIVITY

Another evident deficiency in the coverage is the lack of

balance and objectivity. Of course, as McQuail has suggested, objectivity has to be understood as the management and reduction of manifest bias rather than its absence. But the Nigerian press's historical partisanship and the country's political polarization during the June 12 crisis limited the press's objectivity.

For the most part, the government-owned or pro-government press, especially the broadcast press, covered events uncritically, often as though there was no crisis. On the other hand, the dominant opposition print press covered events primarily from an adversarial perspective. For instance, regarding the constitutional conference sponsored after the nullification of June 12 election, Yemi Ogunbiyi, secretary of the Newspaper Proprietors Association of Nigeria and one of the founding editors of the Guardian, acknowledged that the paper gave voice only to critical views.

His explanation was that the paper's editorial stance may have intimidated and dissuaded people with contrary views from submitting articles. That the editorial stance could be so intimidating would, by itself, suggest extreme partisanship in coverage. McQuail has argued that providing access to a diversity of opinion is an important function of the news media.

The government-controlled or pro-government press was also lacking in balance to the extent it minimized critical coverage of the government.

The New Nigerian, for instance, was made to carry a substantial amount of "news stories" and "editorials" written by government officials in Abuja, the federal capital, and faxed to the paper in Kaduna. The practice continued even after the newspaper's editor, Yakubu Abdulazeez, resigned in protest in June 1993.

The resignation reflects the tension inherent in a press system in transition. Before the era of the independent press, politicians and bureaucrats routinely dictated news coverage, and there was little dissension. But the growth of the independent press had apparently influenced journalists working for government-owned news media.

CIVILITY IN DISCOURSE

Under the general topic of media and culture, McQuail discusses issues of "taste and morality." He argues that media adherence to high standards in this regard elevates the quality of public discourse and contributes to general cultural aesthetics.

But coarse tone of attacks emerged as another major area of deficiency in the coverage by the opposition press. Aspects of this deficiency may be evident in some of the comments excerpted above.

They support the claims cited earlier that the Nigeria press is polemical and abusive. Such polemics has been identified as a significant factor in Nigeria's descent into civil war in 1967. However, in contrast with the pre-civil-war press, the June 12 press was much less overt in its ethnic-based attacks. It directed much of its invectives at the military and the "Northern oligarchy," thus emphasizing class rather than ethnicity. Still, the image of the opposition press as abusive was widespread and not without basis.

It should be noted that even existentialist journalism as advocated by Merrill still requires a commitment to facticity and integrity. In clarifying his notion of "the imperatives of freedom" and rejecting criticism that he had prescribed journalistic anarchy, for instance, Merrill wrote that the purpose of his treatise "was to give an emphasis to ethical and responsible journalism as it had seldom been given before: from a philosophical perspective, one which, to be sure, emphasized the virtues of freedom, rationalism, and humanism."

EXPLANATIONS OF DEFICIENCIES

It seems that, more than anything else, the partisan orientation of the Nigerian press is the primary reason for the deficiencies.

The opposition press's commitment to ending military rule, for instance, seemed to transcend concerns for journalism standards. Thus, the news value of precedence was whether the information was damning to the government.

But there are other related factors: concerns for commercial viability, the psychological response of journalists to their victimization, limited resources and trained personnel, and restricted access to government information.

The need to remain commercially viable amidst stiff competition in a depressed economy was strong. Economic imperatives are major factors of news values, even where editorial and advertising functions are separated. It was even more of a factor for the Nigerian opposition press, most of which were founded by journalists who presided over both the editorial and business aspects. For these papers, editorial and business decisions were hardly separate.

And sensationalistic misrepresentations and coarse language appealed to readers, who reveled in public excoriation of the feared military and regarded as heroes those who had the courage to do so. Such tendency to capitalize on public resentment of the government is not unique to the Nigerian opposition press. In a study of the Taiwanese press's role in democratizing Taiwan, for instance, Lee narrated that some magazines published certain materials just to court censorship, "only to hoard [copies] en masse for consumption at a higher asking price."

Dan Agbese, the editor-in-chief of Newswatch, alluded to this economic factor of coverage in a speech on the role of the press in Nigeria's current democracy. Agbese asked, "What sort of press does the new democratic Nigerian nation deserve?.... Is it a press whose commercial imperative, the need to survive in a hostile economic climate, over-rides its responsibilities?" The implied concern was a source of underlying tension in some newsrooms, but the spiral of silence ensured that journalists who disapproved of misrepresentations in their publications often muted their objections for fear of being considered "soft" or "sellouts."

Moreover, as journalists suffered repeated harassment and assault, they became increasingly bitter and their activism took on a more personal dimension. This is consistent with findings of personal influence in news judgment even in nonpartisan press systems. Such a reaction also took place in

Taiwan in the 1980s, when "indiscriminate seizure of. . . magazines bred resentment and inspired radicalism." In the Nigerian case, resentment was reflected in the abusive nature of some commentary and analysis. Thus, the June 12 crisis became a war in which journalists fought with the printed word against a military government that assaulted them with all the instruments of coercion at its disposal.

Also, the rapid expansion of the print and broadcast press during and just before the June 12 crisis caused a shortage of experienced journalists. The shortage was exacerbated by the flight into exile and the imprisonment of several journalists during the crisis. Accordingly, many media houses were filled with personnel with marginal training and skills. Given the important role of education in the inculcation of professional values, it was inevitable that the quality of journalism would be adversely affected.

Limited access to government information also created an atmosphere for speculative and misleading reporting. The extreme tension between the military government and the press caused more than the usual government-press distrust. Thus, even journalists who were competent and committed to professional standards often could not get the necessary facts from the government to report accurately.

PUBLIC AND PRESS PERCEPTION OF THE PRESS

The Nigerian populace, in general, seemed to have reacted ambivalently to the press performance during the June 12 crisis. Such an ambivalence would indeed be predicted in the corollary by Gurevitch and Blumler's complementarity theory given the irreconcilable tendencies of Abacha's exercise of power and the emergent orientation and anomalies of the Nigerian press. Public approval of criticism of the government and especially the combative approach of the opposition press was evident in the popularity of the most adversarial publications, including especially Tell, TheNews, and Tempo.

Despite the weakened economy and the high cost of the publications relative to average purchasing power, the opposition publications fared well - at least better than most others - in circulation. For instance, after Tell in 1993 published a frank interview in which Obasanjo excoriated Babangida and questioned his sincerity in conducting a transition to civilian rule, its circulation doubled from about 40,000 weekly to 80,000. By 1994, Tell had become the first Nigerian "newsmagazine to hit a weekly print-run of 100,000 copies."

In contrast, the New Nigerian, whose content substantially represented government perspectives, plummeted from a daily circulation of about 50,000 before the crisis to about 250 by 1995, much of that being circulated among government officials. This suggests that even middle-class Northerners rejected the paper that had once been the authoritative voice of the North.

However, despite the general public approval of the opposition press, the public was concerned about deficiencies in press coverage, especially misrepresentations.

This researcher first realized the extent of the press's credibility problems in 1995, when he was repeatedly asked by acquaintances who saw him carrying stacks of various Nigerian newspapers and magazines, "Why are you buying those lies?"

The inquisitors cut across class boundaries (there was a student, a petty trader, a civil servant, and a physician) and the questions were without regard to the particular publication. When asked why they held such views, the questioners typically laughed knowingly, shook their heads, and merely said of the publications, "They just carry lies."

General distrust of institutions of Nigeria's public life may have contributed to the press's credibility problems. Rampant corruption and a sense that everyone was out for his/her own good may have, thus, reflected in public perception of the press and compounded the press's credibility problems. However, as has been indicated above, the deficiency in coverage was real and substantive.

The press reflected awareness of the public image and was often critical of itself. For instance, in a foreword that applauded a national award to a reporter for TheNews "as the ethically steadfast journalist of the year," one of the publishers wrote that "Coming at a point when the press is taking its own fair bashing in the crisis of credibility affecting many national institutions, this is no mean feat."

Sometimes the press's self-criticism seems to reflect the rivalry and ideological differences among the various publishing houses. When Newswatch was shut down in 1987 for publishing the report of a government commission before it was made public, The African Concord attributed the shutdown to "serious structural deficiencies in the decision-making process" at Newswatch. When subsequently the Concord, the Guardian, and the Punch groups were proscribed in 1994, a columnist for Newswatch suggested that the closures served some useful purposes.

The rivalry is most manifest in a commentary in the Vanguard newspaper that compares the dominance of the South-West-based news media in Nigeria with Jeremy Tunstall's thesis that "the media are American." The columnist wrote:

Our own variety of imperialism and dominance would have been tolerable if it was subtle and polished and if it pandered to truth, fairness and objectivity. Instead, it is coarse and rough-hewn. And the tragedy is that sometimes it can be whimsically hubristic, tyrannical, acutely constricted in purview and it visits unmitigated mayhem on the truth.

The column did not indicate whether the writer judged the Vanguard, whose headquarters are also in the South-West, to fit this description nor whether the press in other parts of the country were more credible.

In remarks to the press during the height of the crisis, Tony Momoh, the chairman of the Nigerian Press Council's Rights and Privileges Committee, seemed exasperated by the deficiencies and the ineffectiveness of the NPC to prod the press toward higher standards. Though he criticized government repressive measures and said that proscriptions were ill-advised, arbitrary, and ultimately disadvantageous to the government, Momoh said also that dereliction in the June 12 press "cannot be defended anywhere." In a communique issued by the NPC in 1994, the council stated that some publications had "in a bid to sell, rattled the sensibilities of decent people in society, not just by the bold exhibition of lack of finesse, but more unfortunately, by the blatant publication of unverified allegations of a nature even bordering on criminality."

SUMMARY AND CONCLUSIONS

This chapter begins with a discussion of the factors of press systems and their application to the Nigerian context during a turbulent period. It is noted that the press in every country reflects its particular circumstances, including the country's economic system and well-being, the political structure, the people's culture and values, and the press's sources of funds.

Regarding the economic factor, it is noted that the ideology, development, and health of the economy all play vital roles in shaping a press system. For instance, economies in crisis or transition tend to produce stresses in press performance, and the sources of funding for the press determines its editorial orientation.

Regarding the political factor, it is noted that irrespective of the formal ideology, the politics of every country reflects the structural distribution of power. Ethnic pluralism and balance, for instance, militates against despotism and facilitates open expression. This reality is manifest in the interplay of power and authority: Effective exercise of power depends on its authority, which, to a great extent, reflects the consent of those over whom it is exercised. The resulting dynamics necessitate the implicit negotiation of power and affect the efficacy of its exercise. This, in turn, determines the tenor of press freedom. The dynamics of power also reflects conditions external to the country.

Regarding the cultural factor, the paper notes the role of civic values and political culture in shaping the relations of the press to the state. It is noted, for instance, that professional practices in journalism necessarily reflect the nature of civic discipline. Indeed, all of the factors of press systems just summarized give rise to the journalistic practices peculiar to a given country, including journalism professionalization and orientation.

The events of Nigeria's June 12 crisis analyzed in this study well illustrate how a press system reflects the larger forces in the society. Beyond that, this study suggests that care should be taken in categorizing countries by press systems on the basis of generalized characteristics. It is important to examine the interaction of the specifics of the factors and generalize from that. In the case of this study, the specifics of these factors may be summarized to indicate: (1) how they engendered repression, (2) how they facilitated resistance and press freedom, and (3) how they affected the quality of the resulting journalism. The general factor (economic, political, or cultural) that subsumes the specifics should be evident.

The specific factors that engendered the repression were:

- A history of military rule that had come to be accepted as the norm in Nigerian politics and therefore apparently caused the military to misjudge the political climate in wresting power one more time.
- A legitimation crisis resulting from the misjudgment, and the resulting exercise of power in the absence of real authority.
- Sheer opportunism by a military that had for long enjoyed the spoils of power and was reluctant to give them up.
- Real fears of secession and fragmentation, as happened during the country's civil war of 1967-1970.

The specific factors that facilitated resistance and press freedom were:

- Ethnic pluralism and relative balance of structural power among Nigeria's three major nationality groups and the myriad minority groups.
- The perception - and the resulting resentment - that the military largely represented a segment of the population, which through it sought to exercise political hegemony over the rest.

- A history of robust public discourse and a vibrant, if partisan, press.
- The rise of an independent press that was tethered neither to governments nor to political parties.
- The global political climate of liberalization, which was at odds with the nullification of a duly conducted election and the subsequent perpetuation of military rule.
- The growth of new technologies of communication which facilitated stealthy production and distribution of newspapers and magazines.
- Individual courage anchored in resentment and an existentialist orientation.

The fate and performance of Nigeria's June 12 press reflected the confluence and clash of the two groups of specific factors. One could not have accurately classified or characterized the Nigerian press system during this period without careful analysis of the interaction of both groups of factors. Nor could one have predicted the relative robustness of the Nigeria press during a period of harsh censorship merely by examining the general factors of press systems, such as whether the country practiced electoral democracy and had a robust capitalist economy and an independent judiciary. The realities of Nigeria's June 12 press system reflected some of what could be predicted from these general factors but confounded others.

The despotism of the military government, the impotence of the judiciary, and the financial difficulties of the press in the context of a developing and troubled economy were all predictable. But these realities were counterbalanced by the factors summarized above as facilitating resistance. The power of the military to impose its will, for instance, was counterbalanced by its problems of legitimacy, the depth of resentment against it, ethnic loyalties, the acquisition of subversive communication technology, and the sheer courage of journalists, among other factors. The June 12 press system, therefore, demonstrates that under certain circumstances a vibrant press can co-exist with harsh çensorship, albeit at high human cost. Similarly, whereas the military government's despotism and the country's economic difficulties would have predicted substantial reduction in the number of media outlets, there was actually a major expansion in both print and broadcast outlets.

Again, this resulted from countervailing trends. The growth of desktop publishing and online technologies made newspaper and magazine publishing much more viable, allowing independent-minded journalists to establish their own publications. Meanwhile, the global climate of privatization had established a momentum toward the licensing of independent broadcasters in Nigeria. The government had to follow through, albeit with implicit constraints. These developments had the effect of confounding what the political and economic realities ordinarily would have predicted.

Furthermore, the study confirms others' predictions and findings that the growth of communication technologies and the increasing synchronization of global political culture provide pivotal leverage to forces of openness and freedom irrespective of the nature of a country's politics. The military government's frequent gestures to pro-democracy groups within and outside Nigeria, as well as the haphazard and confused nature of its repression suggest this reality.

Recent developments in other countries in political stress also attest to the imperatives of technological and global currents. The popular revolt that forced Slobodan Milosevic out of power in Yugoslavia, for instance, may well be testimony, at least in part, to the effects of global trends and the technology of online communication. The mobilization of thousands of people to besiege the Yugoslav parliament might not have been possible in a short order without such a technology, for instance.

One could predict, therefore, that in a country like Iran - where several of the more liberal papers have been shut down by the Islamic clerics - repression will ultimately be subverted. Although Iran does not have the benefit of Nigeria's and Yugoslavia's structural pluralism, the factors of liberalizing technology and the synchronization of global political culture will likely make up for that. Ultimately, political leaders everywhere will have to demonstrate to their people and the world that they respect human rights and democracy. Such a demonstration puts constraints even on the most desperate of despots, and the constraints give the press some leeway for resistance, as happened in Nigeria.

Regarding the quality of the journalism of the June 12 crisis, the factors contributing to deficiencies may be summarized as follows:

- Financial pressures resulting from a weakened developing economy.
- The relative infancy of the independent press, which was still searching for its financial anchors and ethical bearings?
- Overt partisanship - bequeathed by the press's history and the country's politics - which the independent press had not transcended.
- The usual anomalies of a press in times of crisis.
- Logistical difficulties in obtaining information for accurate reporting.
- And a general breakdown in civic culture and discipline.

Some of these problems were beyond the Nigerian press as an institution to overcome. There was little the press could have done, for instance, to transcend the economic pressures or the severely restricted access to government records and documents for purposes of accurate reporting. However, aspects of the press's professional orientation and practices compounded some of the problems.

This study suggests that adherence to high standards of professionalism and avoidance of an overtly partisan orientation facilitate rather than hinder the work of the press in any context. It seems evident that though the Nigerian press's advocatorial and partisan orientation helped to sustain its stinging voice, the orientation and the resulting deficiencies in coverage also caused credibility problems and provided rationalization for attacks against it.

Though press crusade against Abacha did not succeed in toppling his government, it contributed to a severe image problem for the military and compounded the government's crisis of legitimacy. The crisis was increasingly noted and acknowledged even before Abacha died in 1998. Remarks by two army generals after the institution of civilian rule suggest the depth of the awareness.

In a speech in October 1999, Yakubu Gowon, the retired general who headed Nigeria's second military government and was the second in command during the first, expressed regret that the military ever entered politics. Then during a tour of military commands the same month, the Chief of Staff of the Nigerian Army, Major General Victor Malu, instructed soldiers to shoot, as a civic duty, any officer who undertakes another coup.

Malu said of the military: "We are the most hated in society. And the reason is simple. There is no more discipline among the soldiers and officers.... We did many things wrong. We are being insulted on a daily basis by the civilians. They are right because we don't respect ourselves." By "civilians," Malu was referring for the most part to the press. The comments of the two generals suggest a shift toward systems complementarity, as suggested by Gurevitch and Blumler. That is, the military establishment seems to be redefining its role to be consistent with the standards of accountability demanded by a press that had exerted its watchdog role in the harshest of circumstances.

It could be said then that by discrediting the military, the press facilitated the rapid transition to civilian rule in 1999. When Abacha died in June 1998, it would have been usual for his replacement to further prolong military rule. Rather, Abacha's successor, General Abdulsalami Abubakar, promised and promptly instituted a transition programme that led to the election and inauguration of Obasanjo as president in March 1999.

The discrediting may also have emboldened Obasanjo to promptly retire an unprecedented number of top military officers. Such an act by a civilian government would have been improbable in the past, even imprudent. Thus, it is reasonable to say that the press ultimately contributed to ending military rule and has made its return less likely. This assertion is suggested also by findings that military coups in Nigeria have tended to reflect public yearnings.

On the other hand, the credibility problems of the press - resulting especially from undue misrepresentations and overt partisanship - enhanced the government's rationalization of repression. That Abacha found comfort in the press's own crisis of credibility is reflected in a speech that heralded a massive assault on the press in 1994. After accusing "some sections of our press" of disseminating a "great deal of misinformation,"

Abacha asserted that, "Government would not shirk her responsibility to protect the rights of her citizens against the unsavory acts of junk journalism." The phrase "the rights of her citizens" evidently suggests that the government's impending action was inspired by a spirit of selfless service rather than self-preservation. However, though the reality might be transparently contrary, the deficiencies in press coverage gave Abacha's claim a facade of plausibility. This study suggests that the press in every socio-political system - even in times of crisis - would be strengthened by adherence to the basic professional values of facticity, accuracy, civility, and some degree of balance and detachment in news coverage.

Adherence to these standards is, of course, a relative matter. As Wilcox noted in a comparative analysis of black Africa's press, even in the West, "lofty thoughts" about journalism "often do not match the reality." In the United States, where journalism professionalization may be said to be highly advanced, violations are rampant and credibility low, contradicting Merrill's concerns. Analysis of a given press system in terms of professionalism has, therefore, to be understood in relative terms.

There are also concerns that professional values in journalism are Western in origin and may be at odds with the traditional values of and occupational orientations in non-

Western countries. Peter Golding has argued, for instance, that in traditional African communication, information and opinion are proffered in tandem. One could say the same of traditional Asian or European communication. Moreover, what is at issue here are largely matters of accurate representation, and the standards should hardly vary across cultures. The absence of such standards results in the loss of the protective shield of professionalization.

Chapter 3

Political Activiation: Civic Interventions

The perception that reforms are needed to prevent an erosion of citizenship has inspired an era of experimentation in the use of media, schools, and elections to stimulate participation. By some estimates, as many as 600 newspapers in the United States have practiced "civic journalism" in efforts to guide public dialogue toward problem solving and community building.

Civic (or public) journalism represents, according to Schudson, the most impressive critique of the press in a generation and the best organized social movement. In schools, curriculum innovations incorporate participatory activities such as "mock voting" and service learning; these experiences appear to stimulate adolescent enthusiasm for citizenship far beyond that engendered by traditional civics courses. During election campaigns, programs such as deliberative opinion polling and DebateWatch provide forums for dialogue about issues and candidates.1

These programs share a desire to innovate in strategies that recognize the centrality of communication in the stimulation of citizenship at the grassroots level. They are perhaps more ambitious than campaigns in prior decades such as efforts to "get out the vote" or to increase the diffusion of political knowledge - outcomes in which interpersonal communication and communal engagement were tangential goals. Many contemporary interventions set out to create social environments that might cultivate citizenship, rather than seek to stimulate political involvement restricted to individual behaviour. These efforts reflect the gravitation of recent work in communication and political science toward interactive theories of citizenship in which the press, schools, and election campaigns are called upon to reinvigorate democratic life.

But many reform advocates share as well a curious lack of interest in the political communication that occurs within society's most essential primary group -the family. When considered at all, family life and the responsibilities of parenting are typically described as barriers to citizenship, consuming time and energy that might otherwise be devoted to participation in the formal political system. In describing the ideal newspaper reader, Schroll writes that this citizen "is well informed of events and issues, cares greatly about communal matters, and shares such tightly woven ties to other people in the given community that she or he is willing and able to sacrifice personal and family time, on a regular basis, to attend group meetings hosted by the local newspaper."

The dismissal of the family as an inherently non-political institution has occurred in recent theorizing about civic activation despite evidence demonstrating the family's importance in the political socialization of children and parents; its contribution to the stimulation of political participation among spouses; and the setting it provides for news media use and conversations about politics. For example, designers of interventions rarely consider the dynamics of intra-family interaction when conceptualizing how to generate interest in politics.

Household behaviors such as dinnertable discussions and parent-child co-viewing of TV news apparently do not evoke the luster of grand notions such as the "public sphere," "deliberative democracy," or the "civic culture." Even among scholars who insist that interventions should be based on a nuanced understanding of the sociology of political activation, the family is avoided as a social entity, as if contemplation of its role in civic activation can be dismissed as the intellectual equivalent of changing diapers.

A more troubling trend is the bias against citizens of low socioeconomic status (SES) embedded in contemporary theorizing about civic activation. With gaps in civic involvement continuing to widen, we have no interest in adding to the genteel scholarship on how to create ideal speech situations that engage the already engaged. Granted, low-SES adults are notoriously difficult to reach as individuals, but as we will describe, they are situated within primary groups that can magnify the flow of interpersonal political influence.

We invite theorists and architects of interventions to consider family political communication as a resource for civic mobilization. We will first provide a model of activation that situates the family as a mediating institution in relationship to societal agents that periodically heighten the flow of political information.

The family as a social unit is responsive to stimulation originating from media, schools, and elections, and generative of motivation that leads to voting and other forms of participation outside the home.

Exogenous stimulation sets in motion within the home a process of mutual adjustment and reciprocal influence that is conducive to increased political competence of family members. We will apply this theoretical framework to critique contemporary interventions and reforms designed to promote citizenship. Finally, we will provide an intervention strategy that incorporates family interaction to amplify the impact of political stimulation originating from news media, schools, and elections.

POLITICAL ACTIVATION OF THE FAMILY

Our model of family dynamics adopts a "lifespan development" perspective, which recognizes that socialization processes occur throughout a person's life and do not stop once a child reaches adolescence. This approach traces changes in interaction patterns across lifetimes of family members, and focuses on the continual development of the individual.

Families constitute social systems in which role expectations and patterned, predictable behaviour establish homeostatic balance in various domains of interaction, including communication about politics. But relationships and interactions are inherently dynamic, involving adjustments over time and in response to external factors. A family's response to political stimulation provided by an intervention is inherently social - while a father, mother, or adolescent child might initiate political discussion and more frequent use of news media, the family responds collectively to the increased political communication.

We will describe a sequence of activation using the framework of a functional model of political communication in the family. Sociologists have developed functional models to explain counterintuitive patterns of indirect causation in which the consequences of a behaviour or social arrangement appear to be causes of that behaviour. A process might entail uniformity of consequences despite wide variance of activities producing those consequences. The dynamics by which a social system adapts to change involve three elements: homeostatic balance; the structure of behaviors that tends to maintain balance; and disruptions or tensions that upset homeostasis.

Given a family member's increased interest in politics, her developmental goals might require increased communication at home about public affairs. These goals are not necessarily compatible with the relational expectations of others in the family, particularly in low-SES homes, where political issues and controversies are rarely discussed.

For example, the exposure of a spouse to a political controversy at church or at work might result in a disquieting increase in the frequency and intensity of political debates at home, prompting a partner to familiarize herself with the issue. Or, a child's participation in a highly stimulating civics curriculum could represent a source of tension in homes where parents prefer that children avoid bringing up controversial topics.

A parent who observes a child reading the newspaper

for the first time and initiating political discussions could perceive higher information needs for herself, and might turn to news media for cognitive orientations that facilitate future discussions.

Campaigns designed to promote citizenship can provide a source of exogenous stimulation or tension that disrupts the structure of social interaction in the family, prompting efforts among family members to restore homeostatic balance. This adjustment process constitutes the behavioral dynamic that might stimulate growth in the political competence of family members.

A family's response to an intervention produces interdependent outcomes that involve reciprocal influence even though only one family member might have been initially exposed to the intervention. Empirical research supports the conceptualization of a process of family activation that follows a five-stage sequence. An individual's response to an intervention includes heightened civic involvement as manifest in increased interest and information seeking (step 1).

The resulting knowledge acquisition and opinion formation motivates interpersonal communication about politics within the family (step 2), prompting increased expectations for political competence among other family members (step 3). As family members achieve compatibility at higher levels of competence, they acquire an increased capacity for reciprocal influence that helps to sustain interest in civic affairs (step 4), which also increases motivation for civic participation outside the home (step 5). A description of this process in terms of distinct stages allows us to explicate the dynamics of intra-family political engagement, but we hasten to add that these processes are interactive in nature and are presented as a heuristic framework rather than as a linear, deterministic model.

STEP 1: INDIVIDUAL RESPONSE

The process we describe as a sequence of political activation hinges on the ability of a mobilization effort to engage at least one family member, who acts as a catalyst for changing the structure of the family's political communication. Exposure to political stimuli is largely driven by psychological involvement, conceptualized as interest or concern about political topics. From the perspective of intervention planners, a key concern is whether involvement varies in response to situational increases in stimulation, or whether involvement represents an enduring predisposition.

Prior research identified two situational factors that influence involvement beyond individual predispositions - the level or prominence of an election and discussion about politics. For example, Sears and Valentino reported that preadults adopt partisan dispositions via intensive exposure to episodic events such as election campaigns. Prominent events as occasions for socialization are important to any model of civic development because political topics are otherwise irrelevant to many adolescents, low-SES adults, and immigrants.

Situational increases in political involvement are associated with information seeking via purposeful use of news media, particularly newspapers. Frank emphasizes that political involvement "is more than a biding interest in politics. When it is stimulated by a situation, involvement may describe a `process of activation' that can lead to communication outcomes such as media use, interpersonal discussion, and political learning." These findings offer an optimistic view of the capacity for interventions to generated widespread interest given a strategy that promotes discussion during election campaigns.

STEP 2: INTERPERSONAL COMMUNICATION

Some family members -perhaps not all - might develop a keener interest in public affairs in response to an increase in the intensity and diffusion of political stimulation. The resulting acquisition of knowledge and opinions provides cognitive resources for use in primary-group interactions, including conversations with family members. The most politically stimulated family member is likely to initiates these discussions, as demonstrated in the "two-step" flow of personal influence.

A basic insight of the two-step model is that information diffusion and social influence are dynamic processes that occur within primary groups.

Following in this research tradition, Beck provided evidence that primary groups appear to be the most important setting for discussion about a presidential campaign. Data collected from a survey of the Ohio electorate immediately following the 1988 election showed that respondents were most likely to discuss the campaign with spouses and co-workers.

The family in some respects constitutes an ideal setting for the nurturing of discussions about an ongoing controversy, campaign, or political event. In any group situation, a person's ability to participate in or avoid political conversations is largely determined by the supply of willing discussion partners.

At home, the presence of a spouse and other adult household members should enhance opportunities for political discussion. In comparison to those in formal, public settings, family relationships tend to be intimate, trusting, and long lasting. As such, they provide promising opportunities for interventions to prompt political conversation in light of prior research showing that such conversations involve a certain degree of risk outside of the home.

Politics can be a threatening topic, especially in low-SES groups, where it is rarely discussed and where a conversation might challenge a person's sense of personal efficacy. Political discussion occurs more often when relationships are close, contacts are frequent, and participants share similar social characteristics and beliefs.

Even in the absence of an intervention, married respondents cite spouses as their most frequent discussion partner for politics. And while several studies show that parent-child discussion about politics occurs infrequently, situational increases in family-based media use are associated with increased frequency of political discussion at home.

STEP 3: EXPECTATIONS FOR CIVIC COMPETENCE

A functional approach to family political communication suggests that individual behaviors prompted by an intervention should not be understood as ultimate and discrete outcomes.

Instead, indications of individual involvement are implicated in an interactive process of stimulated family communication. In the context of an intervention, the heightened salience of public affairs results in increased expectations for competence in political communication within the entire family.

The salience of politics as a discussion topic varies over time in families and in other primary groups; when politics does become prominent, members of a group make adjustments in their political competence, apparently in anticipation of future discussions. Straits observed that individuals who are only slightly interested in politics are significantly more likely to engage in political conversations if a spouse is named as a discussion partner. Family discussion appears to be the key process by which family members achieve similar levels of interest and competence in behaviors such as paying attention to news, acquiring knowledge, expressing opinions, and voting.

But the increased political interest of one family member might create tension in homes where politics is rarely discussed. The social roles inherent in spousal, sibling, and parent-child relationships involve expectations for communicative competence, and in some cases these expectations involve compatibility if not superiority of some family members in certain areas of knowledge, opinion, and behaviour.

Thus, a parent should know more about politics than a child, according to societal convention, and in many homes, spouses might come to expect that they are more or less equal in expertise about public affairs.

An understanding that these expectations should not be violated can be a particularly strong norm in low-SES homes, which are characterized by authoritarian parenting styles and adherence to traditional gender roles. And while the gap in political participation between men and women has narrowed in recent decades, men are on average more likely to know about political topics. In families in which traditional gender roles are valued, a politically activated wife or daughter could violate family norms.

Disruption of prior communication patterns provides impetus for other family members to increase their own competence, stimulating information seeking, knowledge acquisition, and opinion formation. For example, a spouse might disagree with the opinions expressed by a partner who is suddenly inspired by a campaign, but to successfully counter those views she must pay greater attention to politics.

We are assuming here a positive systemic adjustment, as we are articulating a process by which civic interventions can succeed. But a family system will restore balance following disruption of communication norms by one of two routes - the growth we have described, or regression to previous low levels of civic competence. Step 3 is thus the linchpin in this overall process of family activation, as it triggers either an upward or a downward spiral of citizenship. In response to a politically precocious child, a father might exert cognitive effort via media use to maintain a leadership role with respect to knowledge of public affairs. Or he could admonish the child to keep quiet about politics, and thereby maintain role expectations through coercion instead of expertise.

STEP 4: RECIPROCAL INFLUENCE

Compatibility at higher levels of communicative competence provides family members with opportunities to engage each other in ongoing activities that sustain interest in politics. Theorists in developmental psychology characterize the home as a locus of reciprocal influence in which family members affect the behaviour and cognitions of each other. While a reciprocal interaction approach has been applied to spousal and parent-child relationships, this view has not taken firm hold within the literature of family-based political behaviour. Studies in political socialization and related areas tend to assume a topdown flow of influence, from parents to children, or from the most politically competent spouse to the less competent.

Interventions designed to cultivate citizenship generally focus on individuals, but scholars in health communication have demonstrated the effectiveness of targeting families as opposed to individual family members. Rimal and Flora, for example, reported that a campaign directed at the dietary behaviour of households modified not just the eating habits of adults and children, but the impact that the two had on each other.

While the campaign provided a degree of independent influence on the two parties, it also strengthened the capacity of children and parents to influence each other's health behaviors.

Studies on the political involvement of spouses support the contention that family interaction is characterized by mutual adjustment and that changes in the political interest of one member have consequences for the involvement of other family members.

Jennings and Niemi documented a strong pattern of homogeneity among eleven indicators of husband-wife politicization. Among the criterion measures and correlations were knowledge (.58), reading newspapers (.50), watching television (.50), election activities (.52), and participation in community affairs (.45). While assortive mating accounts for much of the similarity, the authors controlled for demographic variables in the statistical analysis, and showed how correlations increased over the history of a marriage.

The capacity of family members to influence each other's behaviour thus establishes the family as mechanism for political activation, suggesting strategies for interventions to tap into this social energy. An intervention does not have to reach every family member at once to trigger behavioral changes; the stimulation of one member can result in the politicization of the family as a social system. This outcome is reminiscent of "the strength of weak ties" principle, in which an infrequent interpersonal connection might, when activated, lead to a major change in a person's life.

STEP 5: CIVIC PARTICIPA TION

The activation of political interest is thought to occur prior to participation in the formal political system. "The higher the level of psychological involvement, the greater the expected number and variety of political acts in which citizens will engage". But as we will argue in a subsequent section, attempts to explain political involvement using individual-level variables and purely psychological models tend to ignore the micro-social processes that engender civic competence and motivation.

Granted, an increased flow of political information originating from schools, media, and elections induces many individuals to pay attention to public affairs. Social interaction in the family, however, provides a crucial intermediate stage in a sequence of civic activation, translating individual interest into interpersonal communication, heightened expectations for civic competence, and the capacity for reciprocal influence within relationships.

Membership in the family as a kind of domestic sphere, in which individuals provide each other with continuing stimulation about political topics, should also increase motivation for civic participation outside the home.

Research on the antecedents of voting demonstrates that interpersonal communication in primary groups is a particularly important stimulus for persons who are only marginally interested in politics. Married people are more likely to vote than similar individuals who are single, separated, or divorced. People with little autonomous motivation may well respond to political stimulation - such as discussion or co-use of news media - from those with whom they have continuing daily relationships. A change in marital status can affect life-space factors such as occupation, residence, and routines of daily life, but Stoker and Jennings argue that even long-lived marriages have evolutionary tendencies with implications for political involvement.

Prior research has demonstrated the importance of the family in the stimulation of voting. In a secondary analysis of turnout for the 1956 presidential election, Glaser compared the actual turnout of couples with what the expected turnout would be if husbands and wives voted independently. Collective turnout behaviour exceeded the expected distribution if the voting of husbands and wives were independent, and marriage was particularly beneficial for low-SES couples in the stimulation of voting.

Glaser noted that similarities in voting in part reflect similar motivations, outside stimuli, and social norms that affect husband and wife simultaneously. But he argued that joint voting and joint nonvoting occur so much more often than they would if husband and wife were motivated independently that interaction within the family is probably an additional force that supplements other predispositions.

The implications of family influence, however, extend far beyond the recruitment of individuals for participation in the formal political system.

By acquiring discursive habits in the home - such as reciprocity, tolerance for diverse views, turn taking in conversations, and daily discussion about the news - parents and children prepare themselves for participation in civil society. The family's role in boosting civic efficacy deserves more attention from scholars in light of the increasing interest in studying involvement outside the contexts of voting and partisan politics.

TRICKLE-UP INFLUENCE

While we have highlighted prior studies that describe isolated components of this sequence of family activation, our evaluations of a school-based intervention illustrate the entire process at work.

This programme of studies began as a straightforward assessment of the capacity of a school intervention in San Jose, California, to stimulate political communication among students in fifth through twelfth grade during the election campaign of 1994.

The results we will describe here were replicated in evaluations of school intervention effects during election campaigns in 1996, 1998, and 2000. These findings are summarized, which organizes them in concordance with our model of political activation.

We interviewed a student and one parent from 457 families immediately following the November election of 1994. The main independent variable was exposure to a participatory curriculum known as Kids Voting. The programme was conducted in conjunction with the fall campaign, allowing social studies instructors to draw upon a series of heavily publicized electoral contests and ballot propositions.

Student participation in the curriculum was independent of demographic characteristics such as family SES, gender, ethnicity, age, and academic achievement, creating the conditions for a quasi-experimental field intervention. An initial study concluded that exposure to the curriculum prompted students to actively seek information outside of the classroom setting.

In a correlational analysis that controlled for the demographic factors along with the parent's level of behaviour for each indicator, we found that curriculum exposure stimulated students' attention to news, acquisition of knowledge about ballot propositions and candidates, and the formation of political opinions and partisan identification. The curriculum was particularly influential for low-SES students, narrowing communication and knowledge gaps between them and their high-SES counterparts. These results provide evidence for the first step in the sequence: the activation of situational political involvement of individuals despite prior patterns of disengagement.

The second step involves the initiation of interpersonal communication at home by the family member who is most easily exposed to an intervention. While low-SES adults tend to be unresponsive to media-centered campaigns, their children are part of a captive audience at school, creating the possibility for indirect influence on parents. Student participation in the San Jose curriculum prompted child-parent discussion about candidates and campaign issues. Students at school brought home their enthusiasm for the campaign, initiating conversations with parents, and this "trickle-up influence" on parents was strongest within low-SES families - the families least likely to talk about politics in a non-intervention setting.

In the third stage of political activation, discussion and other manifestations of a family member's heightened political interest increase expectations for communicative competence in the family. In response to conversations initiated by their children, parents in the San Jose school districts read newspapers more frequently, paid more attention to televised news, acquired more knowledge, and developed stronger opinions.

A subsequent path analysis outlined the dynamics by which the knowledge gap closed between parents of high and low socioeconomic status. We confirmed that influence flowed from student curriculum exposure, to student-initiated discussion, to parent media use, and finally, to parent knowledge gain.

This third step in the sequence should be accompanied by evidence of tension in family relationships as some members - in this case parents perceive a need to adjust their behaviour in keeping with a more politicized environment at home. While low-SES parents paid more attention to campaign news, they also admonished their children to avoid bringing up controversial topics.

We incorporated measures of family communication patterns (FCP) to illustrate how tension in the parent-child dyad motivated adjustment on behalf of the parent. In developing the FCP model, McLeod and Chaffee found at least two distinct dimensions of communication structure in families.

In homes characterized by concept-- oriented discussion, parents encourage children to express political opinions, including controversial views. In socio-oriented families, parents stress to children the importance of deference; parents impose social harmony by insisting that children give in on arguments that might offend others. In comparison to children from socio-oriented families, children in concept-oriented homes are more likely to read the newspaper, to form partisan opinions, and to discuss politics.

In response to political conversations initiated by the students, parents in San Jose tended to increase their frequency of socio-oriented communication. For example, the parents were more likely to tell students that they should "give in on political arguments rather than make people angry." The increase in socio-oriented responses suggested two phenomena: parents were being confronted with greater frequency and intensity of adolescent political expression, and the parents perceived this new behaviour as unpleasant or threatening.

The increased socio-oriented responses of the parents, accompanied by increases in both the child's and parent's political involvement, demonstrate this third stage of political activation, in which a politicized family member disrupts prior patterns of family communication, motivating efforts of other family members to increase their competence.

The fourth step describes a state of family interaction characterized by increased capacity for reciprocal influence as family members - now compatible at higher levels of competence - engage each other in political communication activities. Our research team conducted a second wave of student interviews six months after the civics curriculum, which ended with the November election in 1994. In comparison to families not exposed to the curriculum, the Kids Voting students and their parents continued to talk more frequently about politics, showing that the intervention exerted a long-term effect on family communication.

We then re-interviewed many of the parents two years later, immediately following the 1996 election. This study sought to demonstrate the specific dimensions of child-parent interaction that might sustain child-to-parent influence in the longterm. The authors developed three measures of child-parent interaction: child-initiated communication, co-exposure to televised news, and discussion about news. The analysis used partial correlations to control for parents' levels of behaviour in 1994 prior to assessing the stimulative input of the children's influence in 1996.

The researchers found that child-initiated communication was correlated with parents' "active reflection" on news, which refers to the parent's attempt to make sense of a story by trying to figure out its political significance. Meanwhile, child-parent co-exposure to TV news and discussion about news was correlated with parents' attention to news and active reflection on the news.

A subsequent evaluation of curriculum effects illustrated how student-- initiated conversations influenced family communication patterns long after the school intervention ended. Stimulated by lessons during the 1998 campaign, students encouraged parents to pay attention to news, tried to influence their opinions, and asked them questions about election issues. Six months later, these behaviors predicted adolescents' and parents' increased perceptions of concept--orientation in the home.

These panel studies suggest that both adolescent children and their parents benefit in the longterm from political discussion and media use at home. Compatibility of political communication at higher levels of competence appears to increase the capacity of family members to influence each other, and thereby sustain civic interest as an enduring family norm.

In the final stage of activation, interest stimulated by the reciprocal influence of family communication provides motivation for voting and other participatory activities outside of the immediate home environment. The direct curriculum influence on students in 1994 extended beyond communication behaviors to both attitudes about voting and actual participatory behaviour.

Curriculum exposure accounted for variance in students' normative support for voting beyond variance attributed to demographic factors such as SES, gender, age, and ethnicity. Kids Voting students were also more likely to report that they participated in activities such as handing out campaign materials and going to see a candidate they liked. As for the parents, student-initiated discussion at home increased the likelihood that the adults would discuss politics with friends. Many of these parents also accompanied their children to the polls on Election Day as part of a "mock voting" programme encouraged by the teachers. In other research on Kids Voting effects, Simon & Merrill reported that voter turnout increases by up to three per cent in voting districts in which the curriculum is taight.

AGENTS OF POLITICAL ACTIVATION

We have argued that families are capable of generating political communication that promotes civic competence and interest, but this can occur only to the extent that they are exposed to exogenous stimulation. In providing a macro-societal environment conducive to political involvement, news media, schools, and elections are commonly understood to function as agents of political mobilization. But declining rates of civic participation have led many to conclude that these institutions do not provide sufficient stimulation and opportunities for engagement.

NEWS MEDIA

News media in normative conceptions of democracy should provide cognitive resources and mobilizing information that engage audience members as citizens rather than as passive observers.

That media should be able to exert this influence is not surprising in that "the combination of television, newspapers, radio, and magazines represent an extraordinary capacity to inform the public rapidly and in considerable depth about major political news".

Apparent resistance to civic involvement, however, persists in the lower strata despite the increased capacity for information diffusion. The potential for widespread diffusion, accompanied by persistent lack of participation among a large sector of the citizenry, led scholars to conceive of the "chronic know-nothings", people who appear to actively avoid political stimulation.

This notion of resistance promoted conceptions of a permanently alienated underclass of people who prefer to remain uninvolved. Refinements in theory and method have improved our understanding of how news media contribute to political involvement, but Hyman and Sheatsley's pessimism endures in contemporary models of stratified media effects.

The attempt of media-based interventions to create forums for civic deliberation derives from the assumption that contemporary society lacks public spaces where citizens routinely meet to forge a sense of community and a common will. The lack of communal interaction instills a feeling of isolation and political alienation, according to this widely accepted view. Reform advocates frequently cite research on the relationship between the extent to which citizens feel connected to their community and indicators of civic engagement such as voting. In reform efforts such as civic journalism, news media are urged to provide content that encourages a feeling of community, along with forums that might engender social connections conducive to citizenship.

Formal instruction in civics in the United States is based on the premise that schools should play a prominent role in preparing young people for citizenship. This training should include the transmission of knowledge about the country's political history and the formal structure of governmental institutions and processes.

Instruction should promote as well civic values such as an appreciation for the importance of voting as a right and a responsibility of citizenship. Evaluations of curriculum influence, however, have reported miniscule correlations between the number of courses taken and longitudinal indicators of civic engagement. The only consistent and appreciable effect appears to be the direct transmission of knowledge from teacher to student.

Shermis and Barth lament that in many schools, civics courses are reducible to the notion that learning is what happens to children. Curriculum in these schools consists of students memorizing the formal decisionmaking structures of government. While civic education has traditionally sought to directly transmit knowledge of the political system and the citizen's role, social studies theory has recently explored informal learning experiences that more directly serve the developmental needs of students.

Reform movements such as "service learning" seek to involve students in activities outside the classroom to foster a sense of empowerment and connections to the civic life of a community. As demonstrated by recent research of Niemi and Junn, adolescents do appear responsive to civics instruction when they are invited to participate in activities that afford them a chance to express themselves. Based on interviews of 4,275 twelfth graders, they found that classroom discussion was a strong predictor of political knowledge.

ELECTION CAMPAIGNS

Elections provide opportunities for formal participation in the political system, and the campaigns that lead up to Election Day are intended to generate interest and excitement that might translate into actual voting. And yet a steady decline in voter turnout since the 1960s has occurred despite increased access to news media, an expansion of literacy and civics instruction in schools, and the liberalization of procedures for voter registration.

News media and schools are implicated in efforts to stimulate voting given the presumption that these two institutions should provide knowledge and motivation for voting. Critics of conventional news coverage, for example, urge avoidance of overly negative campaign coverage, which is thought to induce cynicism and lethargy in the citizenry. Schools are likewise urged to implement curriculum reform that breaks down the barrier of adolescent indifference to political participation.

With respect to voting laws, the belief that registration procedures inhibit turnout has led to a series of reforms at the state and national levels. Beginning in the mid 1970s, several states implemented changes to liberalize voting laws, providing researchers with "laboratories" to assess the impact of various reforms.

Michigan, for example, established the first motor voter law in 1976; Tennessee mandated an early voting system in 1994 to allow voters to cast ballots during the two weeks prior to an election; and Oregon experimented with a vote-by-mail provision for the 1996 election. Comprehensive reform of the federal election law was enacted in 1993 with the National Voter Registration Act. In reviewing effects of eliminating requirements associated with time, place, and manner of voting, Calvert concluded that permissive rules marginally enhance turnout.

But in light of the dismal turnout for the 1996 presidential election, the success of these reforms was deemed less than overwhelming. Referring to the National Voter Registration Act, Knack observed that, "The most dramatic liberalization of voter registration procedures in American history coincided with not only the lowest level of turnout since 1924, but with the largest single four-year decline since 1920.

The theory that registration barriers are the chief cause of the gap between turnout rates for U.S. and other developed democracies suffered a devastating blow, as turnout in North Dakota - where voters aren't even required to register - was a mere 56 per cent of the voting population in 1996."

RETHINKING ASSUMPTIONS ABOUT POLITICAL ACTIVATION

Many mobilization efforts that rely on media, schools, or elections have failed to adequately address micro-social processes that generate motivation and competence for political involvement. This section critiques the activation strategies associated with each institution with respect to four themes: a presumption that low-SES groups are permanently disengaged; a restricted and unrealistic conceptualization of citizenship; a tradition of thinking about political involvement in terms of individual behaviour; and a top-down approach to activation. These interrelated tendencies in the way reforms are conceptualized and implemented help to account for the neglect of the family in efforts to stimulate citizenship.

NEGLECT OF LOW-SES GROUPS

Hyman and Sheatsley provided "some reasons why information campaigns fail" in what became a landmark article cited by scholars to justify pessimism about mass media interventions. Subsequent research has consistently shown the power of demographic variables to predict levels of political interest and behaviour, with education in particular strongly associated with nearly every indicator of civic involvement. Studies in mass communication suggest that campaigns designed to promote equality in citizenship are not only bound to fail, but are likely to exacerbate "knowledge gaps" between individuals of low and high socioeconomic status.

Survey research on political behaviour has tended to view SES as an individual disposition, despite the paradoxical and problematic implications of this theoretical construct. The assumption is that indicators of social status represent individual differences in terms of the ability to process information, of motivation to pay attention to political information, and of frequency of exposure to political discussion or news stories.

The level of a person's formal schooling might in fact be fixed, but the consequence of educational attainment for an individual varies across situations, in response to the flow of political stimulation within that person's social network. Media and schools have the potential to increase political interest in low-SES groups by stimulating political discussion during highly salient events such as election campaigns.

The shadow of Hyman and Sheatsley's pessimism, however, still appears to evoke images of "know nothings" among the planners of intervention campaigns. The failure to even attempt the engagement of low-SES groups is often evident in the goals of news media reforms. Efforts in civic journalism to create ideal speech situations - characterized by what might be considered elitist expectations for the rationality of discourse - will involve some sectors of a community but leave out citizens who are less skilled in public deliberation. Pauly observes that "Public journalism works within a thin and unconvincing account of the communities it hopes to serve.

Taking its cue from a variety of contemporary upper-middleclass reform groups and the language of sponsoring foundations such as Pew and Kettering, it uses terms such as `civic culture,' `civil society,' and `social capital' with a breezy selfconfidence."

Rosen argues that journalists should acknowledge that they represent a "political institution that has a legitimate stake in whether politics works for all or becomes the professional playground of a privileged few," but this rhetoric of inc fusion is rarely matched by practical suggestions for engaging low-SES groups.

Rosen, for example, suggests methods for newspapers to convene with highly motivated voters so they can add to their knowledge of ballot issues. Charity describes the ideal reader, one who "would be eager to organize deliberative forums" if only she could get a little training. He provides practical tips and points to accessible resources useful for organizing a meeting among similarly motivated citizens.

We suspect that the lack of interest in programs that might politicize low-- SES groups stems from the longstanding assumption that dispositional barriers in the lower social strata create an enduring resistance to political stimulation. The preference for strategies aimed at the highly educated and already interested - or perhaps the "why bother?" approach to engaging the lower social strata - is reflected in the design of several recent innovations that derive from discursive models of deliberative democracy.

These programs provide blueprints for how to organize conversations among citizens during election campaigns; examples include deliberative opinion polling and the use of interactive media to create electronic town meetings. An emphasis on deliberative democracy in the design of interventions is not necessarily compatible with more inclusive approaches to participatory democracy.

The failure to engage low-SES groups has also been a persistent problem in the reform of voting laws. Constituencies in which there has been a relatively high proportion of non-voters are the ones least likely to take advantage of curtailed voting procedures. A more effective approach would involve the stimulation of motivation to vote by targeting primary groups as resources for political mobilization. Early field experiments demonstrated how interventions increase turnout among those least likely to participate by treating voting as social rather than individual behaviour. Eldersveld conducted an experiment in Ann Arbor, Michigan, concentrating his efforts on 500 election "apathetics" - people who did not vote in prior local elections.

His goal was to determine the comparative effectiveness of personalized contact and impersonalized canvassing via mail. The results showed that voting was higher for those personally contacted, particularly among those with only a high school education, those who lived in small households or lived alone, and those who had recently moved to Ann Arbor. In all three cases, these were people who tended to lack "social connectedness" and interpersonal political stimulation.

The effect of person-to-person pressures, Eldersveld concluded, was to compensate for the absence of social interaction that would otherwise encourage voting.

In educational reform, a prominent theme is the desire to alleviate disparities in schooling opportunities and outcomes. While a substantial body of research has documented how differential opportunities in education generate job-market disparities, less scholarly attention has been paid to inequality in educational preparation for citizenship. We do know from empirical studies, however, that SES-based gaps in knowledge and other indicators of civic competence emerge during adolescence.

Low-SES children, for example, read the newspaper less frequently than their high-SES counterparts, and this gap widens during the formative years of adolescence. This differential pattern in developmental strides toward citizenship poses a challenge to civics instruction in the United States, which is intended to provide equal opportunity for participatory citizenship.

Findings from the Kids Voting studies provide reason for optimism about the efficacy of curriculum reform. As envisioned by Dewey, schools can function as laboratories for civic preparation, allowing young people to practice civic skills such as opinion expression in peer-group settings. Students represent a captive audience at school, which creates the possibility for widespread diffusion of political stimulation. As demonstrated by the scenario of "trickle-up influence," students can function as "opinion leaders" who extend classroom stimulation to low-SES parents.

Parent involvement, in fact, has become the focus of efforts to understand and alleviate the inequalities in educational outcomes in the United States. A plethora of policies and programs have been implemented across the country to enlist parents in children's formal education. But in the realm of civics instruction, low-SES parents are likely to remain disconnected from a child's schooling unless specific efforts are made to involve them.

Along with the tendency of low-SES parents to avoid discussion about politics, these parents might feel less welcome in the middle-class school culture. They are more likely to have inflexible work schedules, preventing involvement in school activities; and parents without prior success in school would tend to lack confidence in performing tasks such as helping with homework.

Desimone argues that despite the national attention focused on parent involvement, the social mechanisms needed to translate policies into effective practice are missing. The mediating effects of family interaction need to be identified, studied, and incorporated into practice. "It is imperative that we increase our understanding of how parent involvement best can be employed for all children, especially for those at risk of educational failure". We concur, but add that theorists of curriculum reform should extend their view of family influence beyond topdown effects of parents on children.

Students have the capacity to activate the entire family as a setting for political involvement.

RESTRICTED VIEW OF CITIZENSHIP

In most daily interactions, the political self is confined to primary-group interaction. Political competence acquires social utility in intimate settings in which civic growth serves developmental and relational needs. By contrast, many traditional models of political participation seek to show how private interactions in the home, the church, and the workplace provide opportunities to develop and try out civic skills - such as public speaking and social networking - that are transferable for use in the formal political system.

That is, scholars are usually concerned with how private life recruits citizens to serve the needs of the political system. Our interest here is essentially the opposite - we are trying to understand how politics serves the family as a dynamic system, and how it serves the developmental needs of its individual members.

We view citizenship as a manifestation of human growth. It is a far broader concept than a sense of civic duty, or rational attempts to influence public policy. Citizenship in liberal democracy, however, is nearly always conceptualized in terms of self-governance. Communication campaigns should consequently prepare and motivate citizens for participation in the formal political system, according to this view.

For example, several civic journalism projects have set out to boost voter turnout by providing in-depth coverage of issues that help voters decide among candidates and ballot propositions. The liberalization of voting laws in many states, meanwhile, is intended to make registration and actual voting as easy as possible.

According to the model of political activation presented here, individuals are motivated to acquire civic knowledge, skills, and communication habits that make them competent for social interaction within their families and primary groups.6 Political behaviour outside the home is obviously important in any conception of participatory democracy, but increased political competence is most immediately useful within the context of an individual's primary groups, rather than being functional for participation in the political system, an activity that is for most people an abstraction or a remote possibility beyond the ritual of casting a ballot.

An intellectual tendency to extract individuals from their immediate if perhaps mundane - social environments, and to imagine them as participants in idealized participatory forums, is evident in the scholarship of both empirical research and normative conceptions of democracy. The reification of participation in constructs such as the "public sphere, " for example, while important in normative conceptions of democracy, describes participation at high levels of abstraction without explicating engagement in micro-social contexts.

If events such as an election campaign or a school intervention are to influence individual behaviour, such effects are contingent upon interactions of individuals within primary groups. The family is thus situated as an intervening agent that mediates the effect of exogenous influence on individual outcomes. Unfortunately, theorists' restricted view of citizenship as activity that occurs outside of the family has prevented the development of models that might effectively incorporate the dynamics of intra-family communication as a strategy for civic mobilization.

We urge an expanded view of citizenship in which political competence is manifest in political communication that serves relational and developmental needs of family members. Interrelated behaviors such as media use, knowledge, opinion formation, and discussion of politics are systemic to an individual during periods of heightened involvement, and systemic at the level of family interaction.

These mutually supportive activities constitute a single condition of the person and the family in that the behaviors are all part of the same structure of family communication. Citizenship consequently has an important intra-family function, apart from the more traditional understanding of involvement as participation in the formal political system.

From a developmental perspective, we understand citizenship as an integration of political communication behaviors within the evolving structure of family interaction. Political involvement thereby allows for growth in family relationships as children and parents take advantage of opportunities to practice communication skills and develop competence.

This view of citizenship is consistent with recent critiques of liberal democracy that question traditional conceptions about the self and its relation to politics. Standard liberal democracy, as articulated by Madison and James Mill and incorporated into American pluralism, presumes that democracy is primarily of instrumental value for protecting interests that belong to individuals or groups prior to - and independent of- political life. Conceptions of liberal democracy, consequently, do not necessarily require theories of communicative competence or self-transformation through social interaction.

In contrast, theories of "expansive democracy" refer to conditions that enhance self-development and personal expression. Under this view, political preferences and identity are formed in social contexts in which individuals are required to make choices: "Individuals choose in order to become, and the nature of the opportunities given for the expression of choice affects the formation of the will". This broad conception of citizenship is reminiscent of Thurgood Marshall's assertion about the purpose of free speech: "The First Amendment serves not only the needs of the polity but also those of the human spirit - a spirit that demands self-expression".

INVOLVEMENT AS INDIVIDUAL BEHAVIOUR

Studies on civic behaviour usually conceptualize the individual as the unit of observation and analysis. While suitable for experimental and survey design, this approach limits the theoretical frameworks that can be used to develop intervention strategies. By focusing on political involvement as essentially individual behaviour, reform advocates fail to appreciate that the social networks surrounding people constitute resources for activation.

This tendency is evident in contemporary critiques of the press, which describe political involvement in terms of psychological engagement with news media content. Modern trends in political journalism are blamed for initiating what Pinkleton and Austin refer to as "a spiral of disaffection." Media-induced cynicism about politics and government is thought to result in a lack of motivation to obtain information, which leads to further cynicism, low levels of political efficacy, and ultimately, alienation.

Cappella and Jamieson, for example, criticize journalists' use of strategic frames, arguing that they activate cynicism that results in decreased political participation. Sabato and Patterson contend that unrelenting negative coverage of politicians, including the periodic "feeding frenzy" of attack journalism, encourages readers' cynicism and disgust.

Empirical studies on the relationship between news exposure and political involvement, however, indicate that purposeful use of media is associated with high levels of participation. McLeod and McDonald found that even as newspaper users were more likely to blame politicians, they also participated more in the political process. But the belief that media contribute to psychological disengagement is prevalent among academic critics, providing a misguided rationale for news media reform.

We do not believe that civic disaffection - or activation for that matter - can be explained by focusing exclusively on an individual's cognitive or affective response to media content. In the context of a mobilization effort, news media use is only an initial stage in a process of activation that requires the expression of political interest in primary-group interaction. But given a conviction that journalistic practices are responsible for the pathology of disengagement, it is only natural to assume that media-centered reforms will be sufficient to engage individuals.

Civic journalism, for example, advocates that the press become a partner with citizens and with local institutions to alleviate political disaffection while forging connections that might establish synergy to solve community problems.

This prescribed outcome, we note, does not explicate the process by which citizens become motivated for civic involvement in social environments. Advocates and critics of this reform movement have begun to address a missing link in the theory of civic journalism -the process by which press innovations activate citizenship at the micro-social level of grass-roots participation.

Civic journalism has thrived as an ongoing critique of traditional journalism, and as a debate among academic and media elites, but with respect to theory, the movement lacks a political sociology in which citizen behaviour might be explained in terms of media exposure and use.

TOP-DOWN ACTIVATION

By a top-down approach to political activation, we mean an attempt to impose or transmit civic orientations that promote regime stability and other needs of the political system. A democratic system functions by virtue of the consent of the governed, and in this regard, schools, media, and election campaigns act as societal agents to encourage voting, to affirm normative values, and to transmit knowledge of issues, candidates, and political traditions.

Research in political socialization has been criticized, however, for focusing on the functional requirements of the macro-political system instead of the developmental needs of the citizens themselves.

The liberalization of voting laws in the absence of efforts to generate motivation for voting reflects this top-down perspective. The intent of legal reform is not necessarily relevant to the lives of people who have personal priorities more pressing than political participation. Efforts to lower voting registration barriers share an assumption with many media-centered reforms, that the problem of anemic citizenship can be alleviated by increasing the "supply" of easily accessible experiences that stimulate political involvement.

The expectation is that by making voting easier - or by increasing the flow of political information via mass media -

citizens will take advantage of the many opportunities for involvement. But these efforts are likely to fail without concurrent programs to stimulate "demand" for political stimulation within the context of social interaction. Supply-side strategies for activating political engagement invite an unflattering comparison with the nation's "war on drugs," a deployment of resources routinely criticized for focusing on the supply of drugs rather than addressing demand as the root cause of the problem.

Whether the behaviour is something to discourage such as drug use, or something to encourage such as voting, successful strategies hinge on the capacity to intervene in social settings that influence a person's motivation. Recent studies on voting behaviour show that turnout will increase despite restrictive election rules when political parties and advocacy groups make serious efforts to mobilize voters by reaching out to them in their homes and neighborhoods.

A top-down perspective is reflected in the failure of media interventions to recognize the potential for civic activation at the grassroots level. According to advocates of civic journalism, local media can function as the means through which citizens come to know parts of the community they do not regularly interact with. Because the community rarely comes together as a whole, a surrogate is needed to advance public life.

It is difficult to resist pointing out the irony of this seemingly democratic appeal to press reform - the elitist assumption is that people at the grassroots level - in their homes, schools, workplaces, and peer networks - are not capable of sustaining political engagement for themselves. Civic journalism proponents advocate that the media become more inclusive in drawing people into civic spaces, but missing from this perspective is the acknowledgment that citizens are already embedded in primary groups that periodically undergo episodes of heightened political involvement.

The notion of a functioning linkage between the press and the public originates from John Dewey's argument for the creation of conditions by which people could routinely participate in public life. Haas asks the pertinent question: "In what capacity, then, should journalists engage citizens in the democratic process? No one has so far addressed this issue in detail, although the literature of civic journalism suggests that journalists should engage citizens in their capacity as members of specific communities."

A common theme of press criticism is that news media should not only stimulate the political involvement of existing institutions, but should strive to create communities of civic engagement where they do not currently exists. One manifestation of this goal is the creation of "focus groups" in which strangers are brought together at the urging of local media to discuss issues of the day.

Glasser argues that interventions of this sort are too often conducted as patronizing gestures rather than serious attempts at civic activation: "Focus groups, town meetings, salons, and other attempts to convene the community amount to at best a contrived and artificial response to the need to cultivate citizenship. They create at most an ad hoc venue for discussion, a small and temporary site for a debate managed by and too often only for the press."

Schools in recent years, meanwhile, have been criticized for a top-down approach to civics instruction. In the traditional model of didactic learning, students are placed in the passive role of simply absorbing knowledge of the country's political heritage and governmental structure. Empirical research provides evidence that patterns of classroom interaction, rather than transmission of substantive information, predict outcomes conducive to citizenship.

Ehman demonstrated effects of an "open classroom environment," which occurs when students engage freely in making suggestions for structuring the classroom environment, and when they have opportunities to discuss all sides of controversial topics.

In this longitudinal study, Ehman concluded that perceived freedom to express opinions in class is a strong predictor of interest in politics.

These findings are consistent with Dewey's philosophical model of the democratic learning environment as elaborated in Democracy and Education. Dewey contended that schools educate for citizenship indirectly, by means of the environment they create. He believed that the most effective learning occurs when student activity is carried out in a social context characterized by free expression, peer interaction in cooperative activities, respect for diverse viewpoints, and equal participation in democratic decision making.

The participatory focus of the Kids Voting programme reflects this philosophy of civic education and provides a model for future efforts at curriculum reform. The goal of civics instruction as competence in political expression serves most immediately the social and developmental needs of the students themselves rather than the systemic requirements of the political regime.

A STRATEGY FOR POLITICAL ACTIVATION

Family-based interaction constitutes a valuable resource for mobilization efforts, but to appreciate this potential requires a reconceptualization of activation as a micro-social process. According to our functional model of family political communication, the family constitutes a social system that tends to maintain homeostatic balance in various domains of social interaction, including civic competence.

A civic intervention such as a school curriculum or a mass media campaign can heighten the political interest of the family member initially reached by the intervention, which might create tension if other family members perceive a need to increase their own civic competence. Developmental gains in citizenship occur when the family system adjusts to reestablish equilibrium in response to exogenous influences that create tension.

This framework contrasts with a tendency toward reductionist thinking in which campaign effects are evaluated in isolation to each other, and in the absence of social context. Interventions should strive to influence the structure of communication within primary groups rather than try to coax behavioral change from an individual independent of her social environment.

A family's response to an intervention takes the form of "endogenous feedback", whereby behavioral outcomes are interdependent in response to an exogenous influence. While any given member might be initially exposed to political stimulation, the family as a system responds by way of interactions that reflect mutual adjustment and reciprocal influence.

We have modeled this process as a sequence of five steps: stimulation of a family member who is most easily reached by an intervention; initiation of interpersonal communication; heightened expectations for political competence; a resulting increase in the capacity of family members to influence each other's political interest; and greater motivation for participation outside the home. With this process in mind, interventions should be based on two distinct but related strategies. The first challenge is to coordinate public institutions that normally operate in isolation to each other, so that they provide sufficient stimulation for families.

As a model of institutional integration, Kids Voting incorporates influences of schools, media, and elections, while simultaneously engaging the family as a social context in which the increased flow of political information is used in interpersonal communication. Students and parents become immersed in a social environment in which exposure to political communication is nearly unavoidable. Students essentially act as a conduit from the school to the family, allowing the programme to overcome social structural barriers that would otherwise prevent an information campaign from reaching low-- SES adults.

An integrative approach takes advantage of what each agent has to offer while avoiding the temptation to assume that any single reform will be sufficient to activate citizens. An integrative strategy also alleviates the tendency to miscast institutions in roles they are unable to perform. Much of the controversy surrounding civic journalism, for example, is stirred by disputes over what the press can realistically contribute. Critics contend that the press is not equipped to provide forums such as neighborhood focus groups, and neither is such a role appropriate given a need to preserve press autonomy. An integrative intervention bypasses this controversy by enlisting the press to focus on what it does best - providing stimulation at the macro-social level - in coordination with agents (such as schools and families) that are better suited for interactive citizenship.

Recognizing that no single institution creates conditions necessary for widespread civic participation, McLeod, Eveland, and Horowitz argue that for interventions to succeed, "There needs to be not only mobilization, but also cross-mobilizing of community institutions and organizations. The synergy of organizations that typically work separately can have a greater effect when these organizations work together." Ideally, an intervention would be comprehensive and integrative in scope to engage families, news media, schools, and elections to take advantage of symbiotic interactions among the various agents.

At a practical level, we are not calling for the invention of new programs for civic activation, but for strategies that incorporate the family. The Newspaper Association of America, for instance, sponsors Newspapers in Education to promote discussion of current affairs in classrooms. Educators should consider takehome assignments in which students ask parents about news topics.

The emerging popularity of media literacy also represents an opportunity to design curricula that would engage family members in co-use of traditional media and the Internet. For example, together a child and parent might dissect a political ad to identify its persuasive strategy, and thereby empower each other as sophisticated users of political content.

DebateWatch organizers could design programs in which each family as a social unit watches presidential debates, along with the conventional approach in which strangers or neighbors are brought together. Meanwhile, election officials and civic organizations could work with local school districts to establish "mock voting" programs so that children can vote alongside parents on Election Day. Programs that encourage voting as a family activity might be more effective at boosting turnout than recent efforts to remove legal restrictions to registration. Indeed, prior research has shown that voting turnout tends to be a joint household activity, with adult family members either voting or staying home as a social unit.

The second challenge for intervention strategists is to identify the intrafamily motivations for acquiring political competence. Media-centered campaigns represent information control processes in that sponsors attempt to influence the information environment so that as many individuals as possible are exposed to a particular topic. But an intervention strategy should go beyond efforts to merely saturate a social environment so that everyone is exposed. Such an approach might result in a certain amount of passive learning as individuals gain knowledge despite minimal effort.

A more powerful strategy would be based on a careful analysis of how communication experiences are used in family interactions to serve relational needs or developmental goals. Information will be processed, knowledge gained, and opinions formed when these cognitive resources are functional in interactions that are meaningful to the individuals involved.

The scenario we describe as "trickle-up influence" took advantage of two developmental tendencies - the need for adolescents to assert independence via opinion expression, and the need for parents to maintain their leadership role in the family. The politicization of low-- SES parents becomes possible because of a particular stage within the family life cycle, in which teenagers are beginning to engage in "adult" conversations. Political communication might be functional for other stages in family development, such as when young adults enter the formative years of marriage and desire increased knowledge of a community while setting down roots.

And when their children eventually leave the home for college or work, retired couples might have more time for political discussion as they pursue other interests.While the genesis of political habits and orientations can be traced to family interactions and other socializing experiences, family life is routinely dismissed by reform advocates as private behaviour that individuals must transcend to pursue citizenship. Hays notes that "In the past, scholars have attributed low levels of political participation among voters under thirty to such distractions of youth as getting an education, finding a spouse, or having fun with friends." The description of acquiring education and entering marriage as "distractions" illustrates the failure of scholars to theorize about the relationship between family life and civic competence.

In response to institutions that periodically heighten the flow of political information, the family acts as a mediating agent that translates the raw material of political stimulation into motivation for civic participation. Far from being a barrier to involvement, the family constitutes a setting that amplifies intervention effects by translating individual involvement into interpersonal communication that politicizes the entire household. In the future, reforms incorporating the family as a social unit might demonstrate why interventions can succeed despite the dismal predictions of chronic disengagement.

Chapter 4

New Model for the Asian and the World Press

In the study of the global media, there is abundant literature about the dominance of the Western media. Much less prominent as a research subject is the dominance of Western perspectives in building media theories, such as the four theories of the press, which have been used as a universal guide to the understanding of the press systems around the world since they were created in 1956.

It is interesting to address the issue of the dominance of Western scholarship in media research in view of the ancient civilizations of the East, especially India, where several of the world's religions originated, and China, where paper and the printing press were first invented. Pi Sheng, a Chinese metalworker, invented the movable-type printing press in 1045, more than 400 years before Gutenberg did when the latter reinvented the printing press in Europe. But in some of the American media history textbooks, only the name of Gutenberg was introduced.

Since the fall of the Iron Curtain, the further opening-up of the economies in China and India, and the arrival of the Internet, the meeting of the minds of the East and West has been accelerated. More and more media researchers from both the East and the West have come to re-examine the four theories of the press as the dominant paradigm in studying world press systems. Jiafei Yin encountered major difficulties in using the theories as a guide in describing press systems in Asia because the four press theories were built primarily on Western perspectives. When theories fail to serve as an effective guide to the understanding of the subject of inquiry, it is time that new theories were developed, theories that would be based on cultural values not only from the West but also from the East.

The Asian civilization is as different from the Western civilization as any two civilizations can be. Moreover, Asia is a politically and culturally diverse continent, where reforming and developing communist countries are right next door to some of the most successful capitalist countries in the world. And no one or two religions dominate the continent. It is hard to lump sum Asia together in any kind of description, and it is even harder to pigeonhole the vastly diverse Asian media systems into the four press categories developed by Western media scholars, who failed to include media experiences from the East in building their theories.

This chapter debates the applicability of the four press theories in the Asian media context and the reliability of press freedom ratings of each country given by the Freedom House. The chapter starts with a review of the well-established press theories and continues with an analysis of representative media systems in Asia. As Asia is a vast and diverse continent with dozens of countries, it is not feasible to analyse every media system in the region.

Therefore, representative media systems were chosen in analyzing the applicability of the established press theories while more countries were included in brief discussions where common characteristics make the analysis also apply. Discussions focus on comparisons of the theories with the media systems in Asia and on identifying the difficulties in trying to match the two. The second part of the chapter proposes an alternative press model based on an analysis of Eastern and Western philosophical thinking and cultural values relevant to the media.

THE DOMINANT FOUR THEORIES OF THE PRESS

The seminal work Four Theories of the Press established the dominant paradigm in analyzing global media systems and, in particular, in assessing levels of press freedom in countries and regions throughout the world. Other theories on press systems followed, such as development journalism in developing countries, revolutionary media, and democratic-participant media. However, the newer theories were mostly complementary to the established four theories of the press.

Of the four theories, "the authoritarian system has been most pervasive both historically and geographically," according to Siebert. The goal of the media under such a system was to support and advance the policies of the government so that it could achieve its objectives. Werner J. Severin and James W. Tankard, Jr. in summarizing the major characteristics of the four theories wrote that the authoritarian concept was based on the sixteenth and seventeenth century English history and philosophy of the absolute power of the monarch.

Contrary to the authoritarian theory, libertarian theory held that man was rational and an end in himself. The happiness and the well-being of the individual was the goal of society. The social responsibility theory was an outgrowth of the libertarian theory and was first developed in the twentieth century United States by the Commission on Freedom of the Press, which emphasized social responsibility of the press.

The last of the four theories was the Soviet communist theory, which was based on Marxist ideology and value of unity - unity of the working class and unity of the Party. For the sake of unity, there should be only one right position and only one truth, the absolute truth. Under the Soviet system, the government had a division of censorship.

CRITICISM OF THE FOUR THEORIES

Dominant as the four theories have been, there is no lack of criticism of them. Critical of the social responsibility theory, John C. Merrill, who strongly argued for the independence of individual journalists in his writings, asked his students: Who should be the authority in defining what responsible journalism is? Shouldn't journalists themselves be allowed to make that judgment?

The most comprehensive criticism of the four theories came almost forty years after the theories were first published. In "Last Rights: Revisiting Four Theories of the Press," published in 1995 and written by a group of media scholars from the same school where the four theories originated, the authors found the overall theoretical framework of the four theories flawed.

The book, edited by John C. Nerone, pointed out that the four theories were not value-free despite their valuefree appearance. The theories were based on a pro-capitalist bias and were the products of capitalism and of the Cold War era. Because of such bias, the authors contended that while the four theories were critical of the Soviet communist media, they ignored the concerns of the libertarian media, especially the concentration of media ownership.

The authors argued that the theories focused only on the political control of the media, state power, but were silent on other kinds of power and restraint on the media. For example, the theories only discussed media's political freedom, not economic freedom from the market forces and ownership ties. Another problem with the theories, the authors argued, was that it allowed only two media environments - libertarian and authoritarian - the other two being only the derivatives of the free and the controlled media environments. The book also listed "internal inconsistencies and inadequacies" among the four theories.

In a study examining the press systems in China and Japan, Betty H. Winfield et al. (2000) found that Western scholarship on press systems tended to disregard the cultures, philosophies, and traditions that distinguish Asian mass media. She said studies such as the four theories of the press keep a Western emphasis while ignoring political foundations and beliefs in Asian societies.

Shelton A. Gunaratne (2005) conducted research on West-centrism in communication theories. He believed that the four theories "ignored the dynamic diversity inherent in complex dissipative social systems" and found them "static" and "deontic".

WESTERN PRESS THEORIES VERSUS EASTERN PRESS SYSTEMS

In an attempt to research and categorize press systems in Asian countries, Jiafei Yin (2003) found major difficulties or misfits in trying to pigeonhole Asian media systems according to the four press theories, which were developed by Western media scholars and were based on Western philosophies and the analysis of Western history, politics, and culture. The following section discusses why the dominant press theories could not satisfactorily describe the realities of media in Asia.

THE "LIBERTARIAN PRESS" IN ASIA

SELF-CENSORSHIP IN THE ASIAN PRESS

The Japanese press is considered the liveliest in East Asia and was ranked the freest in Asia by the Freedom House for 2005. Reporters Without Borders gave Japan the second-highest ranking in Asia in press freedom after South Korea for its 2005 report. Japan's press industry is the largest in the world. It has five national daily newspapers, each claiming a circulation in the millions.

That compares with the top two dailies in the United States -USA Today and The Wall Street Journal - each of which has a circulation of around 2 million. Yomiuri Shimbun, the paper with the largest circulation in the world, has a circulation of 14 million. Asahi Shimbun has a circulation of 12 million. These two Japanese national dailies are the only two newspapers in the world with a circulation surpassing 10 million. The circulations of the other three range from 2.7 million to 5.6 million.

Japanese journalists are well trained and well informed. They have to study for months to pass rigorous exams to even get hired. The exam includes a ninety-minute general intelligence test, a ninety-minute writing test, and a ninety-minute foreign language proficiency test, usually in English, Spanish, French, or Chinese.

Even if a candidate gets good scores, he or she has to pass three to four interviews. Special schools help prepare university students and graduates for the test. But Japanese journalists may find their training and skills wasted under a press club system.

To understand the nature of the Japanese press system, the economic system in Japan has to be examined first. Democracy describes Japan's political system, but freewheeling capitalism is out of the question in Japan although, theoretically speaking, Japan practices free market capitalism. The Japanese economy has thrived and become a dominant force in the global economy under state-guided capitalism.

Instead of regulating the industry, the government helps the industry to grow and compete on the global market. Government and big corporations in Japan are partners in nation building. Political freedom and rights do not translate into economic liberalism in Japan, which has much to do with the Japanese culture, or the Asian culture.

In Asian societies, especially those under the influence of Confucian thought, the strength of a country is regarded as more important than the profitability of a company, and the well-being of a family is more important than individual rights and freedom. For a country like Japan with limited arable land and scarce resources, the survival and prosperity of the nation take priority in national life. The royal family and often the government are symbols of the nation, and they command respect.

Such a cultural tradition contradicts the Western concept of media as a watchdog and the ultimate goal of libertarian philosophies - man as an end in himself. In Japan, media keep cozy relations with the government and the big industries through the press club system, or "information cartels," which comprise press clubs, industry associations, and media conglomerates, which Freeman (2000) calls "the unholy trinity."

The press clubs channel information from government offices to media organizations. Such a club system discourages independent reporting and thoroughness in journalistic investigations and results in "uniformity of content" and "pro-establishment style of journalism". The information cartels ensure no competition among media outlets and no scoops. In Asian societies, the motto promoted is not Darwin's "survival of the fittest," but the survival of all, which may explain why in many Asian countries, such as Japan, China, and Singapore, comparative advertising is banned.

The club system works well for the Japanese press, which profits from large circulations, high advertising revenue, and exclusive information access from the government. But it is a system designed by the industry to serve media companies' economic interests, a system that has frequently led the press to support state goals. It is in this sense that the media can be understood as collaborators with the state in the management of society, Freeman said. Such a system discourages investigative reporting and places a premium on relying on official sources rather than alternative information. It interferes with the public's right to receive relevant information in a timely manner.

As a result, all the high-profile political scandals that emerged in the first half of 2002 were not uncovered by the vernacular dailies, but by the non-mainstream weeklies. Because of its less than rigorous reporting, the Japanese press fails to act as a watchdog of the government and is called a lapdog, which was blamed for failing to keep the public informed of the irregularities within the financial industry and the corruption within the government. When the Asian financial crash hit Japan in 1997, the magnitude of the crisis took the public by surprise.

An in-depth analysis of the Japanese press system makes it clear that the ideas available at the "marketplace of ideas" are rather limited. Free competition that is at the very core of the libertarian theory is stifled under the press club system, which also bars reporters from foreign and non-mainstream media outlets from attending exclusive press briefings and getting official press releases. While government control of the press in Japan is not a major issue, control by professional associations and the media organizations themselves is still very effective and produces the same result of a less informed public. The reason why the Freedom House rated the Japanese press as the freest in Asia may be because of the fact that the Japanese government seldom takes direct actions against the press or journalists. In Japan, there is hardly such need, as the press polices itself rather diligently.

Like Japan, South Korea is a newspaper-rich country. South Koreans get their news primarily from daily newspapers. The country has ten national dailies, which are in circulation wars in the millions. In addition, there are 100 free dailies, 314 specialized dailies, 1,999 weeklies, 2,319 monthlies, and 1,245 other periodicals. All newspapers print forty-eight to fifty-six pages for advertising space. In South Korea, each household subscribes to two or three national papers and one local paper, a dream for newspaper owners in any country.

For 2005, the Freedom House rated the press in South Korea "free." And the Reporters Without Borders described the South Korean press as opposite of that of North Korea: "diverse, privately owned and critical of the government". South Korea is a relatively new democracy. After decades of fighting for democracy, South Koreans started to enjoy their political rights in 1987 when a civilian government was sworn in after a general election.

But until Kim Dae Jung, a freedom fighter and folk hero, became president in 1998, the newly found press freedom in South Korea had been contained by its press club system like Japan's, by the common economic interests of the government and big business in South Korea, including the media, and by the influence of Confucian values.

South Korean industries, like those of Japan, used to be guided and supported by the government. The press in South Korea has allied itself with the government and big businesses and is widely seen as "pro-business," "pro-government," and "conservative".

Chong-Hyuk Kim, a reporter for the Joong Ang Ilbo in South Korea, told a Freedom Forum panel that South Korea's ostensibly democratic government barred publishing the size of foreign reserves and foreign debt. He said, "It has become traditional practice between government and media in South Korea not to report critical and important information. The government insisted if that kind of information were revealed, it would be harmful to national security and the national reputation.

The media accepted that kind of assertion". The result of such secrecy was the unexpected Asian financial crash in 1997, which hit the South Korean economy hard and caught its people unprepared.

A reader of the Chosun Ilbo, one of the largest papers in the country, wrote: "Korean journalism still is a superficial observer of the events and does not carry a torch for the righteous social and ethical standards in a rapidly transforming materialistic society. It still is timid and not impartial and indifferent to power politics".

The press system in South Korea had many similarities with that of Japan until Kim Dae Jung became president in 1998. Since then the South Korean press has started to develop in a new direction, and the press club system is being phased out.

Press freedom in South Korea improved noticeably during the tenure of Kim, when the press became more aggressive in covering the government and more vocal in criticizing government policies. But the unprecedented press freedom in Korean history under Kirn's government was overshadowed by government's crackdown on the major papers with charges of tax evasion in 2001.

Press freedom is still fragile in South Korea, and its press system is in a transitional stage. It remains to be seen if the South Korean press is finally breaking away from self-censorship or if it still wants to maintain good relations with the government and big businesses by avoiding coverage of critical issues.

Self-censorship is not only a major issue in Japan and

South Korea but also a major concern in Hong Kong and Thailand. The media in Hong Kong and Thailand are in a category of their own. They are among the freest in Asia when they resort to sensationalism to survive the intense competition.

In Hong Kong, tabloids represent the mainstream press. Practice of yellow journalism, including sensationalized reporting, price wars, and stealing talent from competitors, reached its climax in 1995 and again in 1997. In both Hong Kong and Thailand, the press exercises a high degree of freedom when it is dealing with non-political topics, but starts to be cautious when news stories concern politics, the government, or the royal family.

Before Hong Kong was returned to China, many of the newspapers in the former British colony were pro-British. Since the sovereignty changed hands, more papers are now pro-Beijing. Self-censorship is considered a major concern and the main threat to an independent and free press in Hong Kong despite a great deal of aggressive reporting. Part of the problem of press self-censorship was due to the fact that after Hong Kong was returned to China, the ownership of some of the major newspapers changed hands, including the South China Morning Post. The new press owners have investments on the Chinese mainland and do not want to offend the officials in Beijing.

BBC News introduced the media in Hong Kong as editorially dynamic, free, and diverse, but it cited increasing self-censorship and pressures on editorial policies. In Hong Kong, direct government intervention of the press is minimal. However, pressure from the central government in Beijing and new owners of the press makes many editors and reporters wary of how to handle sensitive information or topics.

A public opinion poll found that 48% of the people in Hong Kong believed the local news media practiced self-censorship. The study showed that 62% believed the local news media had qualms when criticizing the central government, while only 34% believed it had concerns in criticizing the local government. "The number of respondents who said the media practices self-censorship has significantly increased, mainly because they think the media has become apprehensive when criticizing the central government," a survey organizer said.

Newspapers in Hong Kong adopted specific strategies in the politics of self-censorship. Francis L. F. Lee and Angel M. Y. Lin argued that in transitional societies such as Hong Kong when political pressure on the press is added to a commercial media system and a professional journalistic culture, the politics of self-censorship often becomes a strategic contest between the media and political actors.

The Ming Pao daily constructed the debate as a factional rivalry in order to position itself as an arbitrator, according to Lee and Lin. In contrast, the popular Apple Daily presented the story as a sovereign people's fight against a powerful entity, which was much more critical toward the central government. "Nevertheless, it also appropriated the dominant discourse, constructed internal contradictions, and decentralized the Chinese central government to smooth out the radicalism of its criticisms".

Jasper Decker, a former staff member at the South China Morning Post, also observed less obvious characteristics of self-censorship, such as the tone and attitude in news stories concerning China. Reporting became less aggressive. Management emphasized the virtues of writing to allow readers to read between the lines. In 1997, the New York Times noted that Ming Pao had "reduced the space given to columnists critical of China and has toned down its previously aggressive reporting of China".

Other newspapers avoided devoting space to politically sensitive topics by assigning their reporters to cover other, non-controversial topics. A content analysis of 1997 editorials of major newspapers in Hong Kong found that 56.2% of the editorials addressed local issues in Hong Kong, while only 8% of the editorials discussed issues in China and 7.6% dealt with topics related to the ties between Hong Kong and China.

Self-censorship was an issue even before 1997. Jim Sciutto,

a former Hong Kong journalist, claimed, "Self-censorship is nearly epidemic in Hong Kong, affecting the entire media hierarchy from publishers to beat reporters. A free Hong Kong press is already eroding." In a 1990 survey of Hong Kong journalists, 5% admitted fear of criticizing China in their work, and 54% believed that their fellow journalists felt the same way. The anxiety was not alleviated in the following six years as a similar survey in 1996 found that one in every four journalists expressed concerns over criticizing China.

As much of the self-censorship in Hong Kong was the result of pressure from newspaper editors and owners, some local journalists and researchers argued that it was censorship, not self-censorship on the part of the reporters. Carol Lai, a former chairwoman of the Hong Kong Journalist Association, believed that the influence of editors might have impacted journalists' writing more than any threats from the government. She believed most of the reporters wanted integrity in their reporting, tried to report accurately and objectively and seldom censored themselves. Some editors, however, watered down criticism or killed stories they deemed offensive.

Media owners and editors censored their reporters in the hope of preventing interference from the central government so they could keep their papers in business. Others might wish to expand their investment on the mainland. The Hong Kong Journalist Association noted that the South Chin Morning Post had reduced and diluted its coverage of China since Robert Kuok became an owner in 1993. "In Hong Kong, pro-Beijing forces don't fight the media, they buy it".

In order to be successful, the media in Hong Kong have learned to remain apolitical. Since the late 1960s, major newspapers in Hong Kong have become increasingly less partisan and have avoided taking less popular stand on issues, and instead, have focused more on the market and middle-class liberalism in order to increase profits.

Self-censorship in Hong Kong prompted one Hong Kong journalist to compare Hong Kong tycoons, who toned down their coverage of China, with mainland media outlets, which became more aggressive in their reporting as they sought market share. In the near future, Hong Kong may have to learn a thing or two from the mainland press when it comes to press freedom, according to Mark Simon of the Apple Daily.

In Southeast Asia, the Thai press enjoys a considerable degree of freedom. Its 1997 constitution protects media freedom, freedom of expression, and access to information. Even under the media-unfriendly prime minister Thaksin Shinawatra the media were free to criticize government policies and cover cases of corruption and human rights abuses, but journalists tended to exercise self-censorship regarding the military, the monarchy, the judiciary, and other sensitive issues.

Press freedom is deep-rooted in the Thai culture. However, the tradition of self-censorship in Thailand is as long as its history of a free press. Despite the freedom they enjoyed in the 1980s, Thai editorial writers and reporters censored themselves, mindful that there were unwritten government rules regarding the coverage of the monarchy, government affairs, internal security matters, and Thailand's international image.

"Self-censorship is probably a perfect form of political control. Politicians in power don't have to risk creating public ire by openly bullying the media. Media proprietors and journalists know exactly what the 'invisible rules' are". The degree of press freedom and selfcensorship in Thailand is often dependent on the kind of government that is in power. The Thai government under Prime Minister Thaksin provided a telling example.

Since Thaksin came to power, the majority of media outlets were forced into submission. Some journalists lamented that truly independent journalists were now "a rare and endangered species" as too many members of the media were influenced by the lure of political favour, or in fear of political power. The government rewarded media outlets, supportive of its policies through the allocation of advertising by telecommunications firms and state enterprises, which resulted in an increasing level of self-censorship. More sophisticated media outlets included mild criticism of the government in their coverage but avoided more serious issues or pursuing issues further.

In such a media environment, anyone in the broadcast media speaking more than "30% of the truth" could get into trouble. The media were thus forced into three categories - government partisans, government mouthpieces, and those that engage in self-censorship. Most mainstream newspapers were won over by the government either through friendly persuasions sweetened with advertising deals or through political pressure, and all television stations were pressured into practicing self-censorship in covering the government.

Using sharper words, The Nation wrote, "...the majority of those who own media outlets sense Thaksin's political invincibility and are prostituting themselves voluntarily. The broadcast media are the most obvious, acting in collusion with the government.... Nowadays, broadcasters are considered strategic partners with the government. Lump-sum financial rewards have made parts of the media into circus dogs that are ready to do summersaults." The print media were no exception, the article said. Publishers were more willing to follow the government line to ensure their business future. Self-censorship was increasingly becoming the normal code of conduct for editors and journalists under Thaksin.

Under a climate of fear and self-censorship within the media community, the Thai media have morphed into the "custodian of the government". In one particular case, the owner of the newsmagazine, Siamrath, exercised self-censorship by canceling the distribution of 30,000 copies of an issue that contained reports critical of the government. In another case, the management of the Bangkok Post removed its editor Veera Prateepchaikul for "irritating" the prime minister by using the word "arrogance".

Concerned over the retreat of press freedom, The Nation argued, "The professional integrity of the media should never be conditional on the political power or popularity of a leader, much less his power of patronage to throw financial benefits their way". Two recent court rulings upheld the constitutional rights to freedom of expression in the country, one vindicating former iTV journalists, who were dismissed for refusing to compromise their professional integrity, and the other in favour of media-freedom advocate Supinya Klangnarong and the Thai Post, who were sued for defamation.

Also in 2006, all the free TV channels covered the anti-Thaksin activities, with the exception of only one channel. That was unprecedented under the government of Thaksin. The Freedom House can rate the Thai press as "free," such as in 2002, or "partly free" since 2003. But it is certainly a different kind of free press even though its self-censorship practices are much less systematic than Japan's.

SELF-CENSORSHIP VERSUS SOCIAL RESPONSIBILITY THEORY

There are fundamental differences between press self-censorship in Asia and the Western social responsibility press theory. First, as discussed earlier, the social responsibility theory derived from the libertarian theory, which emphasizes the freedom of the press and pluralism in the marketplace of ideas. Therefore, the basis of the social responsibility theory is still press freedom, even when the press is urged to use that freedom responsibly. Press self-censorship in Asia, however, is based either on control by the press clubs in the case of Japan and, formerly, South Korea or on fear of government retribution in the case of Hong Kong and Thailand. In either case, freedom of the press is being severely curtailed.

Second, the goal of the Hutchins report, A Free and Responsible Press, is to recommend ways in which a free press can better serve the society at large. The report proposed five standards in improving the quality of news reporting, including the comprehensive coverage of news events to ensure its accuracy, representation of different demographic groups in society in news reports, and the provision of service to all the constituencies of society. But the primary goal of press self-censorship in Asia is for self-preservation. It is to protect the business interests of the press rather than to better serve the public. Newspapers in these Asian countries are highly profitable; thus, the management does not want to offend the government or big business.

Third, ideally speaking, if the social responsibility press theory is implemented in the newsroom, the result will be a better-informed public and a more ethical and responsible press, whereas press self-censorship in Asia can only result in uniform content, suppressed information, and a poorly informed public. If the ultimate goal of the press in these Asian societies is the pursuit of profits, it will be difficult for the press to be socially responsible or professionally ethical.

ANARCHISM IN THE ASIAN PRESS

Although Asia is rarely known for press freedom, there are some rather free press systems in the region, particularly transitional press systems such as the ones in Taiwan, the Philippines, and Indonesia, where the whole control system was torn down when martial law was ended or strongmen overthrown and where there was tremendous backlash against press control.

But often the enthusiasm for newfound press freedom in these countries leaves the press bordering on a state of anarchy. After decades of government suppression, the press in Taiwan, the Philippines, and Indonesia was enjoying unprecedented freedom and explosive growth when the rules, regulations, and bans were lifted, licenses for starting up newspapers became easier to obtain, and the enthusiasm for starting up newspapers was high.

Such outpouring energy overwhelmed the governments in these societies after decades of authoritarian or military rule. These governments had yet to establish trust and credibility among the people and construct new frameworks in regulating the press without the suspicion that democratically elected governments were reintroducing government control over the press. The booming press industry tipped the balance between supply and demand. Intensified competition combined with new press freedom drove many of the papers in these countries to "freakdom" of the press, meaning sensationalism in news coverage.

In Indonesia, now that the press is finally free, the main problem is a lack of professional standards and ethics among journalists. More and more journalists are violating the most sacred principle of the profession: tell the truth. Journalists today are accountable to no one but themselves and their proprietors because of the sweeping deregulation of the media.

The ministry of information was abolished, and gone also was the licensing system. In 1999, a new press law was passed to guarantee freedom. But excesses and abuses of press freedom have ironically prompted calls from the public for the government to restore some control of the press.

Freedom of the press is a double-sided sword, which can expose corruption and injustice but can also hurt the freedom and media if the freedom is abused. Media in Indonesia has changed its role from being a mouthpiece of the government under Suharto to being a critical watchdog today. "Barking headlines, hard-biting editorials, sharp commentaries, satirical cartoons and investigative exposés are now common features of our media".

But the media in general failed to promote the basic principles of journalism, such as accuracy and balanced reporting. Syamsul Muarif, the state minister for information and communication, a new government agency, listed five diseases of the press: pornography, character assassination, false and provocative news, misleading advertisements, and unprofessional journalists.

Media hold up a mirror to the society they cover; in the case of Indonesia, what is reflected is pervasive corruption, which poisons the soul of journalism. Indonesia was rated as the fifth most corrupt country in the world, where corruption spread from the central government to local governments. This culture of corruption gave rise to "envelope journalism" and "bogus journalism". With "envelope journalism," journalists receive cash from news sources to compensate for their low salaries, compromising the integrity of the press.

"Many people are willing to provide bribes for journalists to ensure that the press will cover or blow up good stories about them or stop publishing bad news about them." And this is a common practice for almost all private and state organizations. Every day no fewer than 2,000 journalists make their fortune by asking the members of the parliament for money.

The amount offered was so enticing that it attracted fake journalists to news conferences for the enveloped cash, resulting in "bogus journalists," who reached hundreds in Jakarta alone. Some of these bogus journalists were laid-off journalists, while others had no previous connections with the media.

"Envelope journalism" brought about public complaints that news stories were inaccurate and failed to cover both sides of a story. Ulin Ni'am Yusron, chairman of the Jakarta Independent Journalists Alliance (AJI), said, "It is too much to ask them to make impartial, quality news if they are underpaid".

In Indonesia, only 30% of about 1,200 publishers in the print media were financially healthy. Therefore, not only journalists can be bought, media organizations can be bought as well. A 2005 survey published by the Alliance for Reform and Democracy in Asia found that 40% of the respondents in Indonesia did not perceive the media to be free and independent of the government and "other sources". Respondents cited widespread bribery of journalists, the buying of air time on talk shows and other forms of advertisements by public figures, and the efforts of both political parties and big business in establishing their own media or buying into media in order to influence public opinion.

Blame was laid on the lack of professionalism and increasing competition from both the local and foreign media. Nurbaiti contended that the immediate future did not look bright either. The outlook for 2006 was that "the Indonesian media will continue to compromise in the search for balance between profit and quality journalism".

Advocacy journalism sells papers too. During the height of the brutal communal conflict in Maluku province, the Jawa Pos media group was accused of profiting immensely from the conflict, which split up the community along ethnic and religious lines. The group's new paper launched during the middle of the conflict, the Ambon Express, was labeled a "Muslim" daily, and the group's established paper, Suara Maluku, was considered a "Christian" paper. Almost all media outlets in Maluku at that time were accused of taking sides.

The same kind of "provocative reporting" was used during the tension between Indonesia and Malaysia over the disputed Ambalat offshore oil block in the Sulawesi Sea. In their coverage, the Indonesian media failed to promote peace; instead, it contributed to the tension. The national media focused on the possibility of war rather than advocating a peaceful settlement, and the local media preferred to cover the deployment of soldiers or the recruitment of volunteers to attack Malaysia.

In the Philippines, the press claims to be the freest in Asia even though broadcasting is still subject to regulation. Sheila S. Coronel (2000) described the Philippine press as "rowdy," "vibrant," "pluralistic," and "anarchistic." She said Filipino journalists are noisy and powerful. Media exposes have caused the resignation of officials and raised public awareness about important issues. Because of their recent history, Filipino journalists protect their freedom fiercely and are firm believers in the watchdog role of the press.

In post-Marcos days, the Philippine media were able to publish information with few restraints. But with few principles of ethics or responsibility to guide them, journalists followed their own set of rules. As a result, accuracy and truth were compromised. Many Philippine journalists believed that journalism was mostly instinctive, and that theories and principles were not much more help than as mere guidesthat there existed no rules specific enough to constitute applicable and reliable standards. "Never has the profession been so cheapened-and cheapened yet by its own practitioners". This belief led to the general deterioration in the quality of the profession. Part of the problem was due to the mushrooming of news media outlets and the growing demand for journalists. The proliferation of news media outlets depleted the supply of qualified journalists and "opened the profession to invasion by pseudo-journalists, resulting in widespread malpractice".

The news media were criticized for irresponsible and sloppy reporting, for checkbook journalism, and for using its freedom to commercially exploit the public's taste for the sensational. Television bore the brunt of criticism. In the words of a print journalist-turned TV journalist, "Philippine TV has not reached the point of maturity, where we can say that it is really doing things in the service of Filipinos. At this point, it is more of the service of business, making money, fighting the ratings game, and being No. 1". Journalists were eager to present to the public every possible news source without checking his or her credibility. "Anything that would raise the decibel of noise (was deemed to be) good".

A TV reporter who covered the police beat wrote an article in the Philippine Journalism Review, introducing his work. It seemed the most important story to him that day was an action-packed exclusive. The kind of exclusive he was referring to was stories like a fight in a bar between two groups of men. He described that as his "most memorable" story - "The protagonists hurled chairs and exchanged fierce blows (one had his nose bridge badly broken; the other had his face bloodied) until police on patrol intervened. We had everything caught on tape, and my crew and I went home happy with an action-packed exclusive".

Other scoops the reporter and his crew chased included a fire that gutted a car after it crashed into a ten-wheeler, a holdup incident, carjacking in a tunnel, and a fake kidnapping case. Such stories were the focus of his news coverage and the theme of his article. Given the rampant corruption, the high profile problem of murdering journalists and other challenges the country is facing, can the freedom and the power of the media be put to better use?

The news media have also used their freedom to outdo

rivals in the race to peddle newspapers and television programs. When members of the First Philippine Mount Everest Expedition scaled the world's tallest mountain, crews from both ABS-CBN and GMA-7, two TV networks, followed the team to cover the event. Both were exclusive broadcast partners, each network sponsoring its own climbers. Both networks wanted to break the news first and have better videos. And both networks denied that they tried to dictate the pace of the ascent. The competition was viewed as a "ratings war," or "a network war," which the networks denied.

The race in ratings sometimes resulted in tragedy. More than seventy people died in a rush to get inside a sports stadium, where a TV extravaganza sponsored by ABS-CBN was to take place, and the network found itself the subject of news. The motivation for staging the event was again fierce competition between ABS-CBN and GMA-7.

Media ownership pattern, on the other hand, is hardly representative of the interests of different sectors of the society when anybody can buy into the media as long as he or she has money. Media in the Philippines remain an elite enterprise, and newspapers operate in the vested interests of their owners. Media owners sometimes use their newspapers to defend and advance their businesses and political interests. And political patronage in the press is not unusual.

Similar to the situation in Indonesia, money corrupts individual journalists as bribery gets in the way of reporting the truth. "There are many journalists who allow themselves to be used as tools of the government". One reporter wrote about a typical case where a highranking government official was trying to buy her silence with a thick envelope of cash. The reporter was investigating bribery charges against the official and his wife. The reporter was "stunned" and "humiliated" by the matter-of-fact manner in which the bribes were delivered. The case showed the prevalence of corruption in Philippine journalism.

The chase after profits and mounting libel suits against the media prompted growing criticism against the media and calls for improving professionalism. The establishment of

Citizen Press Councils and calls for appointing media ombudsmen to keep down libel suits were part of the efforts by the media industry to use the power of a free press more responsibly.

In Taiwan, the press started to enjoy press freedom after martial law was lifted in 1987, and political discussions are much more open in the press since. According to the 2005 Freedom House report, Taiwan is well known for having one of the freest media environments in East Asia because of its firm commitment to judicial independence and economic freedom. Today's media in Taiwan are among the freest and most competitive in Asia.

The media in Taiwan are free and powerful. "For all its shortcomings, the press is free, bold and aggressive". Like their counterpart in the Philippines, the news media in Taiwan play a critical role in exposing government corruption, which would have remained hidden from public view without investigations by the media. Media exposés of corruption cases and scandals involving high-ranking officials resulted in devastating defeats in local elections and resignations of high officials.

However, the media in Taiwan are often criticized for abusing that power and freedom. They are often regarded as a source of social chaos and accused of stirring up disorder by making "unfounded reports" and spreading stories that were not true. Some media organizations tend to be biased or sensationalize their reports. As Taiwan's democracy is sometimes ridiculed as "rambunctious," its media are also considered as lacking accuracy and accountability. To win sympathy and support, the island's embattled president Chen Shui-bian trumped up his family troubles, and the media dutifully sensationalized the story as soap operas.

For circulations and ratings, the media spent too much energy on sensationalizing crime stories and the private lives of public figures. One recent example involved a police investigation of a death. For two weeks, the media provided excessive coverage of the case on a daily basis, including the daily activities of the suspect and the police's pursuit.

In another extreme case, the Scoop Weekly, a tabloid magazine, enclosed a VCD of an alleged sexual encounter of a female legislative candidate in one of its issues. The magazine defended itself by saying that the VCDs were enclosed in the magazine as "evidence" supporting the veracity of its investigative reporting.

Some reporters, in the rush to be the first to get the story out, sacrificed accuracy in their reporting rather than tried to find credible sources to check out the facts. And sometimes police complained that newsgathering and reporting got in the way of solving criminal cases. "The freedoms that were so hard to obtain, ironically, now threaten some parts of a society that considers the press the enemy because of its influence and power".

The excesses of press freedom in Taiwan, the Philippines, and Indonesia are typical of press systems in transition from being tightly controlled to almost completely free. The new democracies in Eastern Europe have encountered similar problems, such as the boom of tabloid journalism, the withering of quality press, bribery, and corruption.

The media systems in transition reflect the problems of those societies undergoing major transformations - rough politics in the fight for the power vacuum, partisan press, intense competition because of the new freedom, corruption for lack of a strong and independent judiciary system, weak financial foundation for the media, and lack of training of the journalists.

Democracy is still young in these societies; it will take time for a democratic system to mature. Because of traditions and culture, press freedom in these countries will still have its ups and downs. The newfound press freedom in Asian societies has its own distinctive social and cultural contexts.

THE "AUTHORITARIAN PRESS" IN ASIA - THE INFLUENCE OF CONFUCIANISM

The press in Singapore and Malaysia is often regarded as the prototype of authoritarian press in Asia. In both countries, the means to control the press are very similar to those used in sixteenth or seventeenth century England, including government censorship, suspension of license, legal actions against the press, and even shutdown of the offending publications. But that is where similarities with Western authoritarianism end.

The authoritarian press theory was based on the historical analysis of sixteenth and seventeenth century England while the authoritarian press in Singapore and Malaysia is shaped more by the Asian cultural tradition and the practical needs of the countries' geo-political realities.

While government authority came more from the absolute power of the monarchy in sixteenth and seventeenth century England, in Asian societies, especially in Singapore, which is under the heavy influence of Confucius's teachings, governments regard themselves both as parents and as rulers, which helps explain why even gum chewing and flushing toilets are regulated.

According to the Confucian hierarchical order of political system, government is the paternalistic figure of the land. "The ruler is the wind. People are the grass. When the wind blows, the grass is sure to bend," Confucius said. But Confucius was also a philosopher. He said, "Authority springs from morality, not force". He believed that people should accept authority, but authority must be just. Confucius asked: "When government leads by the right example, who dares to go astray?" In contrast, authoritarian theory does not address the quality of a government or the morality of the rulers.

Singapore is a society where a no-nonsense government promotes Confucian values of education, hard work and clear moral principles. The Singaporean government is one of the very few in Asia where corruption is rare. The government is as clean as the streets in Singapore, which is often considered the cleanest city in the world. The government in Singapore prides itself on its system of meritocracy and efficiency. Different views are tolerated to a certain extent, but if the press publishes articles the government takes offense to, the government pursues the press relentlessly all the way to the court, which often has a chilling effect on the press.

Confucianism extols cooperative and harmonious relations, which are what the Singaporean government hopes to cultivate both at home and abroad. The government keeps a watchful eye on the press for any stories that address race relations, religion, or problems in neighboring countries. Such stories are banned in the Singaporean press because of the mixed racial and religious makeup of its population and its often-sensitive relations with its neighbors. Violence and chaos caused by racial and religious differences in neighboring countries put the Singaporean government on high alert. Former Prime Minister Lee Kuan Yew said that any journalist who did not support Singapore-Malaysia relations would be sent to jail.

Malaysia has many similarities with its neighbour, Singapore, in its treatment of the press, as the two countries were once merged into one for a brief period in their history. Both governments are unequivocal promoters of "Asian values" and loud critics of Western culture.

Asian values in Malaysia include emphasis on the social role of the press, which is for development, and on morality, which in part might have resulted from the Islamic influence in the country. Confucian influences are not as heavy in Malaysia as in Singapore, where Chinese account for about 75% of the population. In Malaysia, Muslims make up about half of the population.

Malaysian leaders, especially former Prime Minister Mahathir, have the government-knows-best attitude. The government has set the goal of making Malaysia a developed country by the year 2020, and it wants the press to help in that endeavor, which means highlighting government development plans, promoting racial and religious harmony by suppressing coverage of racial and religious issues, and controlling Western influences by limiting overseas TV programming to 30%. While the Singaporean government is often criticized for trying to silence dissent and punish the press for negative coverage, the government in Malaysia has promoted positive press coverage on such topics as "Asian values" and national development.

In some aspects, Malaysian media seem to border on the communist system not only in promoting positive news coverage, but also in media ownership. Party press sets the trend in Malaysia, where political parties own major stocks in media agencies.

The ruling political party UMNO owns media giants the New Straits Times and Utusan Malaysia. The Chinese and Indian parties in the country also have acquired major stocks in media agencies that cater to their ethnic groups. The government has a direct stake in the media too by owning the national news agency, Bernama, which has the right to distribute foreign news reports.

Under authoritarian rule, governments do not own the media; they punish the media when they are not happy with the coverage.

One salient feature of the authoritarian press system is government's various ways of punishing and controlling the press when the press is defiant. Even though the Malaysian government punishes occasional rebellious papers, the Malaysian press, especially the mainstream press, mostly saves the government's wrath through compliance with very restrictive press laws.

The Printing Presses and Publications Act of 1984 gives the minister of home affairs the power to revoke publishing licenses without judicial review.

As a result, the Malaysian mainstream press has become so tame that its credibility has been questioned. Zaharom Nain wrote, "... The Malaysian mainstream media - the press and broadcasting - have never aspired to be the guardians of the freedom of speech."

"... The mainstream newspapers' failure to be a credible source of information is a reflection of a journalist's failure in performing her duties professionally," a member of the National Union of Journalists said. The inaction of the press against government suppression of press freedom came under fire too. "The credibility of Malaysian journalists has been damaged as much by dilution of professional standards and ethics as by passivity in tackling legal and administrative restrictions".

THE "COMMUNIST PRESS" IN ASIA - SWEEPING REFORMS

Today's Asia hosts the majority of the world's remaining communist countries - China, Vietnam, Laos, and North Korea. Trying to understand the press systems in these countries using the Soviet communist press theory as a guide would be misleading.

The communist press theory was based on the model of the Soviet press system, which can't satisfactorily describe the varied press systems in these remaining communist countries today, especially the Chinese press system after more than twenty years of sweeping economic liberalization and opening to the outside world.

The Freedom House rated China 7 for political rights and 7 for civil liberties, not free for 1997-98 (on a scale of one to seven with one being most free and 5.5+ being not free), the same ratings for 1972-73, which meant that for the twenty-five years in between, political rights and civil liberties in the Chinese society remained the same. For its 2005 survey on press freedom, it ranked China the 177th out of a total of 197 countries studied.

The Freedom House rating was in sharp contrast to the 1998 U.S. State Department report, which stated that Chinese citizens benefited from "(h)igher disposable income, looser economic control, greater freedom of movement, increased access to outside sources of information, greater room for individual choice, and more diversity in cultural life". Emmons wrote that, "There are those who believe that the media and freedom of speech, in general, never have been as uninhibited as they are today...". Emmons cited in his paper, "Surprisingly, the average Chinese citizen enjoys significantly more personal freedom today than ever before".

When China is undergoing economic reforms, what exactly does "media reform" mean? It meant the public's right to know according to late premier Zhao Ziyang; it meant commercializing Chinese media and building a stronger media industry according to late reform architect Deng Xiaoping; and it means the relevance of the media to the people according to current Chinese leader Hu Jintao. Reforms bring choices, and freedom means having choices.

Since the reform started, China's media outlets proliferated. Today China has around 2,000 newspapers, more than 9,000 magazines, 1,000 radio stations, and 200 TV stations broadcasting 2,900 channels. The choices and competition on the media market today stand in sharp contrast to the one voice on the media scene in the past when every city had only one Party paper. Choices, instead of one voice, symbolize the major changes Chinese media consumers have experienced.

Introducing the profit motive, which is absent from the Soviet press model, into the media sector was another reform measure that caused sweeping changes to the industry-it changed the nature of the media in China. Economic reform of the media in China began almost as early as the overall economic reform.

And media commercialization becomes an important part of the development of the market economy as the government has adopted a policy of gradually cutting subsidies and encouraging commercialized financing. Advertising, the capitalist genie, has returned to the world of communist media.

To meet the new challenge, the press, including the ones directly under the control of the Party, is becoming increasingly commercialized. Even the official Xinhua news agency and the Party paper, People's Daily, are diversifying their product line to increase profits. To be competitive on a booming media market, where the number of journalists has doubled in twenty years, media in China have to appeal to the readers, some of them by resorting to sensationalism.

To speed up the reform, the government announced in June 2003 that it would end subsidies to all the newspapers in China except three papers and one journal, and all the publications in China had to sever their ties to government departments and stop mandatory subscriptions.

Those titles earning less than 50% of their revenues through voluntarily paid subscriptions had to be shut down.

By November that year, a total of 1,452 Party and government newspapers had been affected, 673 of which had been suspended from publication.

The overhaul of the Chinese press system has substantially changed the economic and administrative relationships between the government and the press. From then on, the press has been financially independent of the government, even though the state remains the owner of the press. The biggest challenge facing Chinese editors today is to strike the right balance between being politically correct and economically viable.

In fact, one of the major problems hampering the development of the Chinese press today is the low ethical standards held by some local and commercial papers. Hunan TV, a challenging rival of China Central TV (CCTV), developed a huge following with a series on an orphaned woman looking for her biological parents.

In its reporting, the network turned an old rape case into a love story, resulting in being sued. Some media outlets were given warnings and reporters detained for extorting large sums of money from people allegedly involved in wrongdoing. It is no longer rare in China today that newspapers are exposed for their sensationalism, fabrications, or staged news, which are commonplace in a free press environment but seldom occur under a tightly controlled communist media system. Orthodox communist papers are serious and "clean."

The Soviet press model mostly prescribes a promotional role for the press - the press should be an agitator, an organizer, and propagandist for the socialist cause, but never a watchdog. In the Chinese press today, there is no lack of exposés or negative news, which is a taboo in the rigid communist media model, as bad news is perceived as demoralizing.

Given the rampant corruption among government officials in China, some high-level government officials encouraged the press to play the watchdog role by engaging in more investigations. Zhang Baoming, head of the State

Administration for Production Safety, called on the media for more active participation in the investigation of major industrial accidents, almost every one of which, he said, was connected with corruption. Caijing, a financial magazine, made a name for itself for its investigative reporting of the financial sector. Who would have imagined that the communist press would engage in investigative reporting?

Former Chinese Premier Zhu Rongji tried to promote the watchdog role of the media. Commenting on a popular talk show on China Central Television, "Focal Point" (Jiaodian Fangtan), which routinely exposes official corruption and mismanagement, Zhu praised the programme as "a mirror and watchdog of the government and a supervisor of the government through public opinion". Wu Guanzheng, secretary of the Central Commission for Disciplinary Inspection, also urged the media to play the watchdog role in the national campaign against corruption. He said media publicity was vital to the campaign, and the authorities should listen to "the voice of the media."

The Zhejiang provincial government encouraged the news media to provide tips directly to its inspection department as the government found it effective to follow and prosecute corruption cases exposed in the media. The government even offered rewards of up to 20,000 yuan ($2,500) if the tips were verified and led to prosecution. In contrast, the municipal government of Nanjing was widely criticized for stipulating that all corruption exposés be signed off by the person exposed in the story.

In Qijiang County, Chongqing municipality, hidden cameras were installed to monitor the performance of government officials. The Southern Metropolis Daily and the Beijing News both carried editorials, arguing that the watchdog role of the media would be much more powerful and effective than the hidden cameras, as it is a bottom-up rather than a top-down approach.

In many cases, the news media are playing such a vigorous watchdog role that a "Witness Protection Law" is being proposed as investigative reporting invites reprisals.

Some news sources were detained, jailed, or sent to labour camps. In one case, an editor was beaten to death by Taizhou city police for an embarrassing exposé.

Attacks against journalists have increased in China in recent years as reporters have become more aggressive in reporting sensitive social issues. At least 100 journalists were physically attacked in 2003.

In 2002, the central government was investigating provincial government officials in Jiangxi and Zhejiang provinces for punishing journalists who exposed problems in their jurisdictions. The Soviet communist media did not carry exposés. In China, exposés of high-ranking officials, though allowed, still have to be approved by the government however.

One other important feature of the communist press system is the state ownership of the media. The majority of the media outlets in China today are still owned by the state. However, foreign investment is entering the Chinese media sector, and such investment as mandated by the rules of the World Trade Organization is increasing with the deepening of press reforms.

Interest in China among international media groups surged in 2005 after the Chinese government issued rules allowing foreign investment in joint-venture television, radio, and film production companies. News Corporation, Viacom, and Sony Pictures were among the big names involved in joint ventures with Chinese media companies.

The current policy stipulates that investors are denied decision-making power in the media outlets' editorial content. But in practice, the situation is getting murky. The editorial staff of the China International Business, a monthly economic review, gets its salaries from Ringier AG of Switzerland. Such business arrangements are not rare. Many foreign publishers sign deals in media advertising or consulting but actually help produce content.

Under the Soviet press system, there was tight control of information and very limited access to government information, resulting in more propaganda than information in the news media. In China today despite government control, access to information has gained substantial progress in recent years.

In 2000, the government of Anhui Province took the unprecedented step of issuing a regulation banning its officials from refusing interviews to the press. Other provinces and cities followed suit. Such regulations were unimaginable before the reforms or under the Soviet media model. The central government now has also installed a spokesman system to meet the needs of the press, both national and international.

In Shanghai, a reporter, based on a city ordinance mandating the disclosure of public information, sued the city planning department for repeatedly declining interviews. This was the first such case in China where a reporter sued a government department for violating his rights to reporting. The reporter complained that city government departments often denied interviews to him. The city ordinance required city departments to disclose information concerning the economy, city management, and public services. Such ordinance was listed as top priority in the legislative plan of the State Council. It would make disclosure as the principle and non-disclosure as the exception rather than the other way around as in the past.

China is opening up. It has opened up its market to the world, including the media market, even though it is only the entertainment media for now. It is not difficult today to find popular foreign consumer magazines on the newsstands in China. International Data Group, a Boston publisher, alone has invested $20 million in China, publishing twenty-eight titles and planning another four.

These operations are either in the form of joint ventures or through licensing the titles and content for publication in China. China is also working on an international media centre with a total floor space of 130,000 square meters, which will serve as an office building for more than 100 foreign media organizations in Beijing.

And in 2001, Reuters's Qing Niao website, a site for trade

information and e-business, made a low-key entry into China. The Soviet communist media model was a closed system. But China has opened up, and it wants to reintegrate itself into the world community.

The one medium that provides a public forum for the ordinary Chinese and connects the Chinese people directly with the rest of the world is the Internet, which claims about 137 million users in China by the end of 2006, the second largest in the world after the United States. China has witnessed the fastest growth of Internet use among countries whose annual per-capita is less than $2,000, and the number of net users is expected to increase by at least 15% annually before 2010.

The Internet is breaking through the silence of traditional media by posting stories rejected by official newspapers. With its power of reaching millions of people at the same time, the Internet has directly helped in effecting legislative changes in the country by exposing police brutality, which brought about public outrage on an unprecedented scale and caught the attention of legislators and the government.

The Internet, with its public forums where people can discuss topics shunned by the traditional media, is producing a better informed, more vocal public and a more open society. Inadvertently, it has ushered in a public discourse that has been absent for almost half a century. It also enabled direct communication between ordinary citizens and government officials. The acceptance of the Internet in China itself is one important indicator of the passing of the rigid communist media system in China, as Internet, a revolutionary medium, defies total control.

Some media researchers argue that as long as there is government control, the media in China should be categorized as communist media. It is true that there is still government control of the media in China - there are news topics on which diversity of opinion is not allowed, there are websites that are blocked, and there are newspaper editors that have been fired. However, since the start of the reforms, the changes that are occurring in China have substantially reduced government controls. These changes are happening because of the intention of the government to open up, the new financial independence of the press, the proliferation of media outlets, and the availability of the Internet.

Sometimes the sheer size of the country poses a challenge to effective control. For example, when the government could not effectively implement a ban on satellite dishes in 1994, it changed its policy by licensing them instead. A year later the government also specified permissible programs and viewing hours. Foreign affairs used to be an area off limits for public discussions in the media. The advent of the Internet with its convenient online forums has made it a hot topic for public debate.

Government control of the press is a universal phenomenon. The issue is the degree of control. In the age of the Internet, total control is out of the question. And in the case of China, that control is being relaxed and challenged from all sides. More recent examples include the suspension and the return of the supplement of a major newspaper in Beijing and the debate over a section of a draft law on managing disasters and accidents.

The weekly "Freezing Point" published by the popular China Youth Daily, which stands out from other newspapers in China for its aggressive reporting and biting commentary, was shut down in late January 2006, and its editors removed to its research department because some government officials were not happy with one article.

The case was widely publicized by the media worldwide. The supplement resumed publication one month later following public outcry against such heavy-handedness against the press, including staff letters protesting the actions and an open letter to top Party officials signed by thirteen prominent scholars and former officials who were contributors to the supplement.

The writers of the open letter included Zhu Houze, a former Central Propaganda Department official; Hu Jiwei, a former editor-in-chief of the People's Daily, and He Weifang, a law professor from Peking University, who said, "The purpose (of the letter) is to change the current incorrect policies on freedom of speech" (f 3), The letter said although not all signatories approved of the article, they all supported Freezing Point's right to publish it.

They quoted Chinese leader Hu Jintao as saying no organization in China has special legal privileges. The letter said that the newspaper suspension was neither legal nor sensible and it violated citizens' basic rights to speech and freedom of information, which are their constitutional rights.

Another controversy arose over a draft law on emergency management, which included industrial accidents, natural disasters, and health and public security crises. Part of the draft law addressed the news coverage of emergency situations by the media, stipulating that media outlets could face fines between 50,000 yuan and 100,000 yuan if they reported the emergency situations without authorization or released fraudulent reports and if such reports led to serious consequences.

The law was drafted following the aftermath of the outbreak of SARS, when health department officials hid the facts from the public, resulting in rampant rumors in the press and in the streets. Government officials said the purpose of the law was to ensure timely release of accurate information by local officials.

Opposition to the draft law was loud and clear. A legislator, He Keng, said journalism had its own rules and argued that the watchdog role of the media was not strong enough in China.

The New Express, a commercial newspaper published by the Yangcheng Evening News, carried an editorial arguing that the law would diminish the watchdog role of the media, that there was no guarantee that the information released by government departments was accurate and that some "natural disasters" were man-made. In a column in the outspoken Southern Metropolis Daily, Changping pointed out that in the case of coal mine disasters, often local officials and mine owners colluded with each other in covering up the facts of accidents as both profited from the mines. In such situations, how could the media wait for the local government to release accurate information? Changping argued.

One often ignored issue is the self-censorship in the newsrooms in China, which sometimes applies tighter control than the government does for the interests of the media organization or the management. For a lack of laws and regulations, the new media are trying to police themselves.

Nineteen websites jointly issued a set of self-disciplinary rules against bloggers' personal attacks, fabricated stories, plagiarism, and pornographic and violent content . Hosts of the sites said they were ready to delete such materials once they appear on their sites. Min Dahong, a journalism professor said that many big websites in the world have explicit written rules on deleting or editing users' messages that they regard as abusive, defamatory, offensive, obscene, or in violation of a specific law.

Ultimately how much freedom or control the Chinese media will experience is not only up to the government; it is also up to the editors and reporters of the media, especially those leading media organizations in Beijing, as to how far they will push. So far the most vigorous push comes mainly from local media outside of Beijing.

Following China's example, Vietnam started its own economic reforms in 1986 and "remains wedded to the Chinese model of reform". Its press system is also undergoing similar changes. The liberal economic reforms eroded the pervasive authority of the Party. As a result, "Vietnam is no longer as tightly controlled as it used to be although it does remain an authoritarian one-party system". Facing a rise in corruption like China, the government encouraged the press to expose corruption, made new laws to facilitate news gathering, and warned against officials trying to obstruct journalists.

Even though strict censorship still exists in Vietnam today, meaningful independent journalism is possible on certain occasions. There are instances where journalists successfully challenged the police and the court in violating reporters' rights in newsgathering and forced the police and the court to back down. "In terms of freedom, the press here in Vietnam has been getting better and more aggressive". One editor at Lao Dong (Labour), Nguyen Due Tuan, said, "There is no question we have more freedom today.... Now, reporters like to see how far they can push and still get their stories published". Similar to the situation in China, editors in Vietnam now have more discretion in deciding the content of their publications.

The press in Vietnam is surprisingly lively in terms of the types of newspapers and magazines. Since the reforms, both the quantity and quality of the press have improved. The press today is becoming more information oriented than ideology dependent, as the importance of information is generally recognized in a more market-oriented economy.

The Internet entered Vietnam in 1997. By the end of 2006, the number of Internet users had reached 14.5 million. Despite government announcement that access to the Internet would be unrestricted, the Freedom House reported that in 2004 the Vietnamese government suppressed dissent on the Internet with new guidelines of government control and censorship, including a permanent monitoring system aimed at the country's privately run Internet cafes.

Despite the reforms, the majority of the media outlets in Vietnam are still state-owned. But the government has permitted some form of private ownership of periodicals, a bolder step than China's. The condition for ownership is that the publication should be a joint undertaking between the owners and the relevant state agency. An example is the Vietnam Investment Review, the first foreign-owned, Western-style periodical in the country.

The government also abolished direct subsidies to the press even though some form of state funding is still continuing. As a result, the press is forced to become more commercialized, and the survival of the press is subject to market forces, which seems to dictate a success formula of tabloid journalism. Some papers publish uncommon crime stories gathered from police records, all in the name of exposing social problems.

In the pursuit of profits, newspapers in Vietnam start to face criticisms about their low ethical standards. Some journalists in Vietnam now claim that they are having more debates on "responsibilities and morals of journalists" than on press freedom.

Early in the reform, the sensationalism and the increasingly aggressive investigative reporting alarmed the Party leaders, who worried that the state was losing control of information flow and wanted to rein in this threatening trend. The government began clamping down on the press in 1989 and tightened control of the media by establishing a new press department aimed at monitoring and controlling press coverage about security matters, issuing new rules regarding passing information to foreign news organizations, amending the 1990 press law, requiring compensation if news coverage leads to losses to the business interests of organizations or individuals.

The government also reminded the press to champion the fight against corruption and other social evils instead of seeking profits alone, but questioning Party rule remains expressly prohibited.The Vietnamese leaders are still ambivalent about the degree of control and the liberal reforms, which help with the country's economic development but threaten the power and control of the Party.

North Korea may be the only communist country in Asia left with a press that could still fit the Soviet media model. There has been very little change in the country despite the fact that other remaining communist countries in Asia are undergoing major reforms to open up and revive their economies.

Perhaps because of the poor performance of its economy, the widespread and chronic famine, and tremendous external pressure to change, the government is exercising strict control of information flow across its borders. As a result, information about the country is scarce even with CNN's 2006 documentary, which was shot inside the country with a hidden cell-phone camera.

North Korea is the most censored country in the world.

Its people experience the world's deepest information void, and the country has no independent journalists. The main role ascribed to the press is that of spreading the viewpoint of the government. All newspapers and broadcasting stations are under direct government control, and all news is positive.

According to the 2003 annual report by Reporters Without Borders, all the news media in the country focused on the personality cult of Kim Jong Il. The report said three subjects dominated the coverage in the print media: the personality of Kim Jong II, praise of the army, and criticism of the country's foes, especially South Korea, the United States, and Japan. In a story, the official Korean Central News Agency reported that Kim Jong Il was so beloved that after a deadly munitions train explosion in a populated area, people ran into buildings to save the ubiquitous portraits of the "Dear Leader" before they rescued their own family members . Nothing was mentioned in the news media about the malnutrition among children and urban populations or the failure of the government's "self-reliance" policy.

In the leading Party paper, the Rodong Shinmun, commentaries carry greater weight than news stories, and reporters do not compete for scoops among themselves, who are given instructions from the Central Party Committee's propaganda and agitation department on what to cover and in how many pages. Anyone disobeying the instructions is severely punished. Reporters may be jailed for a commentary that deviates from the Party line. Harassment, psychological pressure, intimidation, and round-the-clock surveillance are routine.

The North Korean newspapers do not carry any advertisements except a handful of government notices. For the mass media in North Korea, there is neither private ownership nor market competition. North Korea's revised 1998 constitution guarantees citizens' rights of freedom of speech, of the press, of assembly, demonstration, and association. But the government prohibits the exercise of these rights in practice. There are strict controls to prevent access to any kind of news coming from abroad. Radios sold in

North Korea can receive only domestic programming. Radios obtained from abroad must be altered to work in a similar manner. The national news agency has Internet sites hosted in Japan. Direct access to the web is limited to the privileged few. And to prevent Western influence, very few journalists in North Korea receive training in the West.

It is also hard for the foreign media to do reporting inside the country as they are all portrayed by the regime as liars seeking to destabilize the government. Foreign journalists visiting North Korea have to be on guided tours. However, in 2006, the Associated Press became the first Western news organization to have a permanent bureau in the country.

AP Television News's full-time office in Pyongyang operates in association with the country's state-run broadcaster and is staffed mainly by local reporters. With the increase in international trade, even North Koreans have started to have greater contact with foreigners, which might result in greater access to information from the outside world.

The press in North Korea seems to be the prototype of the communist press, but it does not represent the trend where the press in other communist countries is heading. It is misleading to put the press systems in China, Vietnam, and North Korea in the same category. To do so, media researchers have to disregard the sweeping changes in the Chinese and Vietnamese press.

THE "DEVELOPMENT MEDIA" IN ASIA

Neglected by the authors of the four press theories were media in the poorer countries of the world-development media. The press in South Asia may best be described by the concept of development journalism, a concept developed later to supplement the four theories, as the development of communities and giving voice to the underprivileged are major goals of many of the local media in the region.

The development press is popular in the region perhaps because South Asia is the least economically developed region on the continent. More than half of the world's underweight children lived in India, Bangladesh, and Pakistan, said a recent

UNICEF report on the global progress on children's issues. In India, approximately 47% of the under-five population was underweight. The report found that South Asia was the only region that showed a gender bias with regard to child nourishment, with girls more likely to be underweight than boys. The issue of undernourishment points to the problems of poverty, lack of education, and inequality in the region.

In India, communication not only means the transfer of information, but also includes the participation in the society and in the community. The Indian brand of development journalism "focuses on the needs of the poor, the deprived, and the marginalized and emphasizes their effective participation in developmental planning". It motivates the participation of the people and advocates for their interests instead of the views of the policy makers and the planners. And it promotes social justice for all.

Journalists in the country believe that the media should not only carry stories about health campaigns like the one against AIDS but also discuss issues that are important for a civil society because only the mass media can reach the vast rural population and give them a voice in debates affecting their lives. The mass media can also play a crucial role in social progress, as any transitional society will encounter new attitudes, a new mindset, and a new value system.

Development journalism enthusiasts in India conducted workshops for social activists to train them to write stories about development issues and workshops for local editors and journalists to familiarize them with realities and issues in local communities.

Commercial newspapers also play a role in development journalism. The Jharkhand-based Prabhat Khabar had been doing development journalism by giving people information on science, information technology, economics, and the comparative financial progress of different states. The paper also conducted "readers' courts," where readers could interact with journalists and discuss ways of improving the quality of the paper, much like the role of the focus groups in civic or public journalism in the United States.

Radio plays a special role in development journalism in South Asia because of its easy and wide reach in the vast rural areas, where literacy rate is still relatively low. The Indian communications NGO (non-government organization) had been highlighting the importance of community radio in India for over half a decade and called for the extension of community broadcasting.

In India, awards are given to mentors of development journalism for encouraging and nurturing journalists to investigate and write on development issues and for supporting journalism initiatives towards "a common social good".

Journalists and media researchers in India and Pakistan criticized some of the mainstream media for their elitist approach, focusing on the prominent while ignoring the plight of the underprivileged in rural communities by following Western news values.

The degree of press freedom in South Asia, however, varies considerably from country to country. Once the largest colony in the world, India is the largest democracy in the world today. Only under Prime Minister Indira Gandhi was an attempt made to curtail press freedom by declaring a political emergency to suspend civil rights. The government of Narasimha Rao tried to prevent exposés of government corruption under the pretext of protection of privacy. Despite such government attempts at control, the press in India has largely remained private, free, and vibrant.

Cushrow R. Irani, editor-in-chief and managing director of The Statesman, said that India's press today is as free as it chooses to be. N. P. Chekkutty, editor of Media Focus, wrote, "The Indian media works in an atmosphere of freedom. We are the purveyors of free thoughts and opinions. We do reflect the freedom of expression the Constitution guarantees to our citizens, and we, therefore, are the epitome of a free, liberal society".

With the freedom it enjoys, the press in India often plays its watchdog role seriously. "Newspapers in India are completely free, as free as the newspapers in the United States, as they are privately owned and free of censorship". It is the newspapers that have exposed corruption in India, though some journalists are attacked for their investigative reporting. The Indian press has always been vigilant about protecting its freedom and aggressive in reporting.

Free as it may be as the press in the United States, the Indian press clearly differs from the Western libertarian press system in the perception of its mission. For its social role, the Indian press may be closer to the civic or public journalism in America, which also prescribes an advocacy role for the press. However, in India development journalism represents the aspirations of many journalists, while in America the ethical implications of civic and public journalism are still being debated.

In India, press freedom is guaranteed by the Constitution and the independent court system, which is very similar to the situation in neighboring Pakistan, formerly a part of India before its independence. Behind India, which has a relatively low literacy rate of 65%, Pakistan's literacy rate is even lower at 38%, which limits the growth of its press industry. There are about 1,330 newspapers in print in Pakistan, but only 1% of the population buys a newspaper.

The press in Pakistan is independent of the government and mostly privately owned. Major public issues are debated in the press, which has become an instrument for change. In Pakistan no law governs the registration of publications. In recent years, Pakistan has been moving toward greater press freedom, and its press is among the most outspoken in South Asia. In both India and Pakistan when the government tries to crack down on critical press coverage of the government, the courts often strike down government charges in support of press freedom.

There are exceptions to the constitutional guarantees of the freedom of speech and of the press in Pakistan, the most important of which is the "reasonable restrictions imposed by law in the interest of the glory of Islam". The Constitution prohibits the ridicule of Islam, of the armed forces, or of the judiciary.

Development journalism is perhaps less developed in Pakistan than in India. Circulation of newspapers in the rural areas of the country is one of the lowest in the world because of the urban orientation of the papers and the cost of subscription in addition to a low literacy rate. The rural market is largely untapped. The dramatic increase in the number of publications in recent years is not supported with trained staff. Many journalists, especially rural ones, lack the basic skills to cover the complex issues important to their communities.

However, electoral politics has increased the importance of rural centers in the emerging democracy of Pakistan. Supporting development journalism, the Pakistan Press Foundation (PPF) was established to help raise the standards of journalism, particularly of the vernacular and regional press, and to promote greater awareness of social and development issues through the media. In 1999, PPF restarted the rural journalists' skills development project.

By 2002 hundreds of Pakistani rural journalists have attended the workshops. The emphasis of the workshops is on improving basic skills of newsgathering and news writing, as participants are given exercises using actual issues, such as violence against women, environmental issues, child labour, bonded labour, and crime rates.

The end of monopoly of the electronic media in Pakistan provides new hopes of reaching a rural audience as radio is acknowledged to be a more suitable and affordable means of providing local communities with a voice of their own. It is more interactive and more suitable for community development. In less than six years, between 2000 and 2006, the broadcast sector completely changed the monolithic landscape that existed for about fifty-three years. But the proliferation of radio stations has created the co-existence of robust liberty and open lawlessness, and commercial interests dominate the airwaves while development journalism still needs time to take hold.

Research on the topic, however, is several steps ahead of the media industry. Development journalism is regarded as an Asian model of journalism, stemming from the dissatisfaction with the Western news values that do not serve the cause of national development ated). Western news values of timeliness, prominence, proximity, conflict, and the bizarre exclude the ordinary people in the news unless they are involved in accidents, violence, or catastrophes.

Development journalism, on the other hand, should focus on the educational function of the news, stories about social needs, self-help projects, and obstacles to development. In the exploration of the development journalism model by Asian media researchers, the watchdog role of the media was emphasized, and the media were urged to remain vigilant against government involvement.

In Sri Lanka, three newspaper groups dominate the island's newspaper scene - the ANCL, the Upali Newspapers Ltd. and the Wijeya Newspapers Ltd. The ANCL has been under government control since 1973, while the other two are privately owned but have close family connections to political parties.

In the broadcasting sector, Sri Lanka (formerly known as Ceylon) was perhaps the first British colony to introduce radio broadcasting a few years after its inauguration in Europe in 1920s. The country liberalized its radio and TV sectors ahead of the rest of Asia. It permitted the establishment of more commercial radio stations than any other country in the region and put the state-controlled Sri Lanka Broadcasting Corporation under considerable competitive pressure. It also allowed private radio stations to broadcast news and current affairs, unlike some of its neighboring countries.

Efforts at setting up community radio have never stopped in Sri Lanka. Universities in Sri Lanka and UNESCO played host to regional workshops on community radio for participants from South Asian countries. The goal of such workshops was to make community radio a reality in South Asia and encourage- cooperation among community radio advocates in the region. Radio still is a popular medium in South Asia, particularly in rural areas. In Sri Lanka telephone boxes, where a radio station button is installed, allow listeners to contact a station without paying a fee. The system makes it easier for listeners to participate in the programs and solve problems in the communities.

The mass media in Sri Lanka also play a role in environmental education. Most people in both urban and rural areas use different media outlets as their primary source of environmental education, especially the print media. Television is the next major source of information for the urban population, while radio for the rural population. The media cover environmental issues in the form of news, editorials, investigative stories, entertainment, and educational programs.

Development journalism in the country can have a bigger potential if the government allows even greater participation by the public in media discussions, which is often limited when there is an increase in guerrilla warfare in the country.

It is evident from the above discussions that the degree of press freedom under the development concept varies from country to country, and that is where the controversy with the concept lies.

While one scholar describes it as "the pursuit of cultural and informational autonomy" and "support for democracy" among other goals, another scholar criticizes it as "a rationale for autocratic press control" and "guided press".

Where do all the discussions about the press systems in Asia leave us theoretically? When theories encounter major difficulties in serving as a guide to the understanding of the realities they are supposed to describe, new paradigms are needed. So are the criteria of the Freedom House for assessing global press freedom and civil liberties when their rankings fail to reflect changing realities. Obviously, more factors should be taken into consideration than the current criteria.

The Last Rights concluded that the four theories were a "durable" but now "questionable" map and that a "more adequate" map is needed. The book presented inspiring criticism of the four press theories but stopped short of proposing a new paradigm.

CONSTRUCTING ALTERNATIVE PRESS THEORIES AND MODELS

Both Eastern and Western media researchers have tried to redress the deficiencies of the four-theory model by creating their own models. Three more theoretical concepts-development journalism, democratic-participant media, and the revolutionary media-were developed to accommodate the progress and changes in press systems and to supplement the dominant paradigm's four press categories.

Of the new theoretical concepts, development journalism has caused more controversies because the degree of press freedom varies greatly from society to society, and the very concept may imply a role for the government. The controversy also seems to stem from the fact that the deciding factor in creating the four press theories was the presence or absence of press freedom, which was defined mainly in terms of government control. Based on such a criterion, how can one type of press system allow vastly different degrees of press freedom in different societies? When a new concept cannot be fit into the established paradigm, it becomes "controversial."

Progressive, insightful, and creative as these new theories are, they are mostly supplementary to the established four press theories. Ralph Lowenstein developed a "progressive typology," according to which, "press systems evolved from authoritarian to libertarian, to social libertarian or social centralist, and then to a big futuristic question mark". This typology seems to have the same tendency as the established four theories of basing its discussions mainly on the development paths of Western press systems, which makes it less relevant to the evolution of press systems elsewhere in the world.

J. Henry Altschull proposed three basic media models - market, Marxist, and developing. To make the concepts value free, Altschull described them as market, communitarian, and advancing. In trying to reclassify media systems, Altschull brought in the element of culture and belief systems.

He explained that the market system emphasized the

"individual" while the communitarian system focused on the "communal life" or the "collective." Altschull also analyzed the role of the media - preserving status quo under both market and communitarian models and advocating change under the advancing model. He explained that there were variations within each model, giving the classification much flexibility.

With the exception of the advancing model describing press systems in the South, Altschull's models were also based mainly on the analysis of Western media systems even though he classified his models also as East, West, and South, where East refers to Marxism and the former Soviet communist bloc in Eastern Europe rather than to Asia.

The only Eastern society mentioned in the analysis was Japan. Altschull explained that despite the variations within the market model, the basic belief systems - hostility to a communitarian belief system - remain intact. "Discord notwithstanding, the broad sweep of the first movement of the symphony is heard throughout the industrialized capitalist world, in Japan as in Denmark and Canada".

Despite Western influence, the Japanese society, steeped in Asian culture and Confucian traditions, has no such hostility. As discussed earlier in this chapter, the press club system in Japan dictates communal behaviour within the industry by discouraging competition and scoops and encouraging collective reporting. A mixture of the East and the West, Japan proves to be a difficult case to be classified.

John C. Merrill's circular model shows that individualistic press systems gravitate toward libertarianism and more collectivistic systems are at the authoritarian end. Merrill said, "... the basic model is a simple spectrum, with authoritarianism at one end and libertarianism at the other. All press systems fall somewhere along this continuum". Merrill's model resembles Altschull's models without the "advancing" or "South" element. Men-ill's model has the merit of built-in flexibility.

The classification of a press system depends on in which direction the system gravitates. But it is still difficult to place

Japan on Merrill's model. The Japanese press is mostly free from government control, but it is not individualistic. The press club system emphasizes collective action, but it cannot be described as authoritarian.

The models proposed by Altschull and Merrill represented major improvements over the four-theory model - AltschulPs model moved away from the exclusive emphasis on government control, and Men-ill's model had the merit of built-in flexibility to accommodate different types of press systems and changes within those systems. Despite Men-ill's inclusion of the communitarian factor, the two models still seem to largely rely on Western philosophies, scholarship, and examples of Western media performances.

Jiafei Yin (2003) called for the construction of a new model, which would be based on a broader foundation of both Western and Eastern philosophies and cultural influences, but did not produce an actual model.

Shelton A. Gunaratne brought in both Eastern and Western philosophical, religious, and cultural traditions in building his model-The Dao of the Press. There are two parts to Gunaratne's model: one part is the libertarian-authoritarian (L-A) continuum with varying shades of social responsibility across the continuum, and the other part is a centre-semiperiphery-periphery world system with individuals and groups, nation-states, and the world system at different levels. And all the three levels "autopoietically adjust the degree of free expression" along the L-A continuum.

Gunaratne's model emphasizes both Eastern and Western cultural values in the definitions and interpretations of the term "social responsibility," giving the model much needed flexibility in accommodating different shades of social responsibility found in world cultures. Merrill also addressed the relativity of the concept of responsibility among societies and even within a society.

Similar to many of the previous press theories and models, Gunaratne's L-A continuum also focuses on the libertarian-authoritarian dichotomy, reflecting Western emphasis on freedom and liberty. With the rich heritage of

Asian philosophies and cultures, can a new model reflect diverse global cultural values and describe and explain press systems around the world without bias either from the West or the East?

After all, different cultures prioritize values differently. Therefore, press theories that are supposed to address global press systems should have a wider base to reflect a broader, more balanced global view. With adequate attention to factors such as world history, global cultures, and economic pressure, the problems inherent in the four established theories because of the authors' Western bias and their sole focus on governmental influences can be addressed.

For a new paradigm of press theories, the optimal balance between specificity and universality should also be considered. The four theories of the press have the beauty and elegance of a very simple but clear structure - four categories under a dichotomy, which aimed to describe and explain press systems in the whole world. Conveniently general as they are, the four or five theories have difficulties in providing a reliable guide to the global press systems. The universality of the theories is limited. However, if categories are too specific and accurate in describing particular press systems, there may be too many categories for the model to be an effective guide.

One other important factor that needs to be paid attention to in building a more reliable press model is that the model should be dynamic so that it can accommodate the changes in the press systems around the world. Obviously, press systems in the new democracies in Eastern Europe are very different from the press systems in the West even though they all operate under democratic systems now.

The press systems in the new democracies in Asia, such as Indonesia, Cambodia, the Philippines, Taiwan, and South Korea, vary from those in Eastern Europe despite the fact that they are all new democracies and share some similarities.

And the press system in China today cannot be compared with the Chinese press system two decades ago, or the press system in North Korea. It would defeat the purpose of having models if every time any changes occur, new models have to be created.

A DICHOTOMY OF VALUES, EAST AND WEST

A new paradigm of press theories requires new ways of thinking in order to broaden the foundation. In this section, an examination is conducted of the dominant Eastern and Western cultural values, which are by no means exclusive to either the East or the West but rather reflect the quintessence of each.

To summarize Asian, or more particularly the Confucian, culture, leading Confucian scholar Tu Wei-ming said: "Industrial East Asia, under the influence of Confucian culture, seems to have developed a different kind of modern civilization, less adversarial, less individualistic, and less self-interested. One sees there the coexistence of market economy and government leadership, democratic parity with meritocracy and individual initiatives with group orientation."

THE INDIVIDUAL VERSUS THE STATE AND FAMILY

Western libertarian philosophy values the independence and rights of each individual. John Stuart Mill's On Liberty spelled out classic liberal individualism-it "set out the limits to the legitimate interference of collective opinion with individual independence". Mill wrote that the only warranted interference with the liberty of an individual is for mankind's self-protection, that is, to prevent harm to others, and that no power should be exercised over an individual for his own good. "Over himself, over his own body and mind, the individual is sovereign."

The Confucian thought, however, focuses on the state and the family. Confucius believed that only when the state and families are strong can the well-being of individuals be guaranteed. In the equation of the state, family, and individuals in Confucian societies, individuals are often encouraged and expected to sacrifice their own rights and interests for the sake of the state and family if contradictions should arise, which is in sharp contrast to Mill's belief that the individual is sovereign. In Confucian societies, the state is sovereign. In Western culture, individualism is extolled, but in Eastern culture, people are taught to think about "us."

In the West, ideal societies are composed of free individuals while in Confucian societies the individual "is not viewed as an isolated individual but as a centre of relationships". The Chinese tradition has largely been influenced by a Confucian-based relational and social definition of person instead of by any concept of discrete individuality. "Under the sway of this relational understanding of human being, the mutuality and interdependence of personal, familial, societal, and political realization in the classical Chinese model can and has been generally conceded."

FREEDOM AND RIGHTS VERSUS RESPONSIBILITY

John Locke, an early libertarian, believes that freedom is essential to the full development of a human being. Merrill summarized Locke's philosophy as "Each person has a natural right to be free and not to be subjected to the will of another." Freedom, for Locke, is a "natural" right. "Besides being bound by natural law, humans possess natural rights, in particular the right to life, self-defence, and freedom. They have also duties; in particular, the duty not to give away their rights".

The Enlightenment in eighteenth century Europe led to the rise of classical liberalism and capitalism. It also led to the French and American revolutions, which uprooted the power of religion and the aristocracy in France and heavily influenced the most distinguished leaders of the American Revolution-Jefferson, Washington, Franklin, and Paine. "The language of natural law, of inherent freedoms, of self-determination, which seeped so deeply into the American grain, was the language of the Enlightenment,..". "Give me liberty or give me death." Patrick Henry's rallying call meant that there was no compromise over liberty-to be free is the precondition to live.

In the East, the emphasis is on being responsible and loyal rather than on being free. Western libertarian philosophers' focus of attention falls on the welfare of the individual, so it is only logical that these philosophers advocate that these individuals should be equal and free to pursue what they want. Confucian thought lays emphasis on the group; hence, there is the concern of being responsible and loyal to the group. In his research, Tu pointed out the Asian focus on the ethic of service and obligation.

INDIVIDUAL FREEDOM AND HAPPINESS VERSUS PUBLIC GOOD AND RESPONSIBILITY

Mill, a defender of personal and political liberty, said in his On Liberty: "The only freedom which deserves the name, is that of pursuing our own good in our own way, so long as we do not attempt to deprive others of theirs, or impede their efforts to obtain it".

Mill's "sovereign self" echoed the U.S. Bill of Rights and the Declaration of Independence in upholding individual freedom and rights and the pursuit of happiness, not individual or collective responsibility. So when President Kennedy demanded, "Ask not what your country can do for you; ask what you can do for your country," it was refreshing to the American youth as their civic education focused mostly on the value of equality, freedom, and rights embedded in the Constitution when they grew up.

Confucius teachings emphasize a strong commitment to the world and encourage sacrifice of self-interest to be ethical. The Confucian concept of the ethical links up directly with the public good. And Confucius believes "self-realization is fundamentally a social undertaking, therefore, 'selfish' concerns are to be rejected as an impediment to one's own growth and self-realization".

In Western democratic societies, the legal system is very well developed as the law embodies the ideal that everyone is equal before the law. And citizens have a strong sense of the law, which sets the boundary of people's behaviour, including what parents legally can or cannot do in disciplining their children.

In Asian societies, especially more traditional and less

developed societies such as China, the legal system is much less well developed. With the opening up of the country's economy, China's legislative body, the National People's Congress, has been busy making laws as conflicts in the past were resolved mostly through mediation based on judgments of who was right and who was wrong.

And a major part of Confucius's teachings comprises moral guidelines, which is why he was also considered a moralist. Confucius firmly believes that children are the responsibility of their parents and that aging parents are the responsibility of their grown-up children whether it is legally required or not. As a result, Chinese press occasionally exposes cases of mistreating aging parents by their grown-up children even though it is a private matter.

Likewise, Confucius believes that it is parents' fault if a child goes astray. Even today some immigrant Asian parents are surprised by the child abuse laws of the United States, where children are encouraged to call the police if they are spanked by their parents. Such laws would shock Confucius.

Confucius's teachings also place emphasis on being just and public minded. It would be unimaginable to Confucius that one country could have billionaires the same time it had a trillion dollars of national debt. According to the moral teachings of Confucius, those who pursue only personal interests (li) are the "little men" (xiaoren), people of no character; only those who think about what is appropriate and beneficial to all concerned (yi) are the "gentlemen" (junzi), people of noble character.

TO BE FREE TO EXPLORE VERSUS TO KNOW RIGHT FROM WRONG

Western libertarians advocate for a free marketplace of ideas, where the public should be left free to explore and discover the truth on their own. In his pamphlet, Areopagitica, John Milton argues that truth would emerge victorious over falsehood should the two be locked in a grapple. John Milton also wrote about the importance of diversity of opinions and perspectives.

In Asian societies influenced by Confucian thinking, especially in the case of China after almost 5,000 years of civilization, truth seems to be self-evident. In such cases, the focus is on teaching the people what is right and what is wrong rather than the freedom to explore what is right and what is wrong. The real challenge becomes the task of convincing the people, or in an ideal Confucian way, for people to convince themselves, to always make the right choice. Confucian scholar Tu Wei-ming phrased the contrast as "the right to think" versus "right thinking."

In Western democracies, the emphasis is on the process-if decisions are made with public input. In Confucian societies, the emphasis is on the result-if the right decision is made. The process often is deemed less relevant.

DEMOCRACY VERSUS MERITOCRACY

The U.S. Declaration of Independence states unequivocally at the very beginning, "all men are created equal." The conviction in the equality among men forms the basis of Western democratic governments-government of the people, by the people, and for the people.

Such libertarian thinking has deep roots in the history of Western philosophy. In Two Treatises of Civil Government, Locke maintains that before there were any states to make statutes, men were aware of a natural law, which taught that all men were equal and independent. "These men, with no earthly superior above them, are in a state of liberty, but not a state of licence."

In his book, A Theory of Justice, John Rawls promotes the adoption of a "veil of ignorance," which would ideally eliminate all the personal identifiers of each individual-male or female, black or white, rich or poor, intelligent or not-and return everyone to his or her original position of being equal with everyone else. "Rawls believes that justice will come forth from a discussion by rational and equal people concerned with their own interests but without anyone being advantaged or disadvantaged".

Western societies are democratic and horizontal,

emphasizing public participation in the government, while Confucian societies are hierarchical and vertical, believing in meritocracy instead of democracy.

For more than a thousand years in the history of China, only top scholars after rigorous national exams became government officials. In Singapore today, the brightest young people are selected for education in world's top universities supported with government funding so they will become the next generation of worthy leaders. "Statecraft is an integral part of Confucian learning". The ideal Confucian officials are people with "inner sagehood and outer kingliness."

Equality in human relations is a foreign concept in Confucian thinking as he decreed three sets of subservient relationships: subjects should obey their kings, sons should obey their fathers, and wives should obey their husbands. Confucius was not a democrat as some Confucian scholars tend to believe.

CIVIL LIBERTIES VERSUS SOCIAL ORDER AND STABILITY

The concept of human rights was developed during the Enlightenment. The Bill of Rights as amendments to the U.S. Constitution marked a milestone in mankind's fight for civil liberties. Western democratic societies keep a watchful eye on the government to prevent it from encroaching upon those rights. The most recent example was the heated U.S. Congressional debate on the Bush administration's domestic spying programme.

In contrast, a salient feature of Confucian thinking in government is the primacy of political order. In China, the traditional assumption has been that personal order and the order of a society entail each other. Thus, in Confucian societies, governments expect respect and obedience to keep social order.

Social stability often takes precedence over civil liberties and is regarded as vital to the strength of a country and the welfare of its people. The Confucian order was built on traditional values and norms. Confucius's unwavering focus on social order and stability might have been the result of the endless wars China was embroiled in during his lifetime.

Thousands of years later, some Asian leaders could not agree more with the ancient Chinese philosopher. Fighting back criticism about too much control in his country, Lee Kuan Yew, first and former prime minister of Singapore who led the city-state for thirty-one years, said, "Without order and stability, nothing can be achieved". Lee was responsible for turning Singapore from a fishing village at the end of the Second World War into one of the cleanest and richest countries in the world today.

COMPETITION VERSUS HARMONY

Capitalism thrives on free competition on the market, which is supposed to drive economic growth even though such growth may be achieved at a social cost. Competition presupposes freedom and equality, but competition spawns conflicts as well-disputes between management and labour, hostile business takeovers, smearing political campaigns, fights in sports arenas, and even the constant race to be the most popular teen in high school. As a result of competition, people are labeled as winners and losers.

And the rule of competition decides that there are often more losers than winners, resulting in many unhappy people. In some Asian societies such as China and Singapore, and even in some European countries such as Germany, comparative advertising is banned. In Japan and South Korea, state-guided capitalism softens real competition.

"Harmony is at the core of the Chinese culture". Preferred methods of resolving conflicts are building consensus and making compromise rather than many voices competing. "A pertinent contrast can be developed between the western liberal commitment to many voices and the traditional Chinese concern for a communitarian consensus as a social good". One values pluralism; the other harmony.

The "promotion of harmony and goodwill among individuals and their families and community in the context of the five constants: ran, yi, li, zhi, and xin (humanity, righteousness, decorum, wisdom, and trust) is a social responsibility from the Confucian point of view".

However, the ancient Chinese sage would be flabbergasted to witness the transformations China is going through today. Since China ushered in the market economy and private enterprise, competition is becoming a new way of life, bringing relentless assault on traditional values and leaving the conservatives lamenting the decline in moral standards.

"POWER CORRUPTS" VERSUS A TOOL FOR NATION BUILDING

Press in the West takes pride in being a watchdog of the government. The uncovering of the Watergate scandal has inspired young journalists to follow the footsteps of Bob Woodward and Carl Bernstein. Dan Rather's dogged pursuit of the truth in Bush's service in the National Guard cost his career. To deal with an inquiring press, government officials hide behind press secretaries.

In traditional societies, people tend to be in deference to their governments. In Confucian societies, the government is supposed to take care of the people, and the people are expected to respect the government. "Confucianism holds that man is born for uprightness, and that people's goodwill is essential for good government in the context of an intellectual democracy headed by a benevolent ruler". Chinese "benevolent despotism" fascinated Western thinkers. In Confucian societies, the press becomes a tool for nation building. Even in Japan and South Korea, both democratic societies, press tends to keep cozy relationships with the government and is, thus, reduced to a lapdog.

The dichotomy of dominant Western and Eastern values does not imply that there are no overlapping areas between Western and Eastern cultures. There are Western philosophers such as Plato and Rousseau who put emphasis on the state and the collective rather than the individual and preferred rule by the elite, which is very close to the Confucian ideal of government.

In The Social Contract, Rousseau promotes public good and common interest instead of interests of individuals. In the East, there are also philosophical schools such as Taoism that focuses on individuality and extols the virtue of being free, free from the constraints of governments and institutions for the full and free development of the potential of each individual.

But these philosophical schools in the East or the West have not become the dominant influence in their respective cultures. By and large, contemporary Western societies extol freedom and individuality, while Asian societies emphasize interests of the collective and the concept of responsibility regardless of political systems.

Some critics may contend that few Asian societies today including China can be described as Confucian societies because of the influence from the West. Indeed, modernization has inevitably had an impact on Asian societies, especially the young, who are much more accepting of what is Western. Tu Wei-ming said: "The Westernization of Confucian Asia, including Japan, the two Koreas, mainland China, Hong Kong, Taiwan, Singapore, and Vietnam, may have forever altered its spiritual landscape. But its indigenous resources, including Mahayana Buddhism, Daoism, Shintoism, Shamanism, and other folk traditions, have the resiliency to resurface and make their presence known in the new syntheses."

Confucianism is neither a political system nor a religion; it is a way of thinking and a way of life. It is deep-rooted in the cultures of Confucian societies, and it is reflected in the decisions people make in their everyday lives, including the value of family ties, education, and hard work. A recent media farce in China provides a glimpse of the undisputable respect Confucius still enjoys in China today. A Peking University professor was quoted in the media as saying that Zhang Ziyi, an internationally known Chinese actress, who was featured on the cover of an issue of Newsweek in 2005 and at the Oscar award ceremony in 2006, was greater than Confucius.

The statement, perceived as an insult to the Chinese culture, sparked a public outcry on the Internet condemning the professor. Bombarded with interview requests from the media, the professor had to post an article on his blog, claiming that he was misquoted by the media for sensationalism.

He explained that Confucius represented China's elite culture, while Zhang Ziyi represented its pop culture. The professor hoped that with the actress's international appeal, she could attract more worldwide interest in Confucianism. An examination of dominant Eastern and Western values helps provide a more balanced foundation for building a new press model.

THE TWO-DIMENSIONAL FREEDOM RESPONSIBILITY COORDINATE SYSTEM

THE SYSTEM

Based on earlier press models and on an analysis of the salient values of the Western and Eastern cultures, a new press model is proposed here, which is a two-dimensional coordinate grid with the horizontal axis denoting the degree of freedom in a press system and the vertical axis indicating how responsible a press system is.

The system illustrates that a free press can be responsible or irresponsible, and that a press that is not free can also be responsible or irresponsible. Merrill also believes in the possible existence of responsible authoritarian systems and responsible libertarian systems.

The Two-dimensional Model

The major difference between what is proposed here and most of the theories and models before it is that this proposed model has departed from the traditional one-dimensional models, which focus mainly on the degree of freedom in a press system, reflecting Western philosophical emphasis on the concept of freedom. The proposed two-dimensional model, instead, has broadened the foundation of theory building to include a key Asian cultural emphasis on the concept of responsibility.

The Asian emphasis on the concept of responsibility is not only a result of Confucian moral influence, but also a result of the socio-economic realities of Asia, where development journalism originated and is still being pursued and where guerrilla warfare or religious and ethnic rivalries can flare up as a result of provocative news articles. And even in Hong Kong, where dominant discussions tend to focus on the survival of press freedom, Chief Executive Donald Tsang encouraged journalists to think about what was important to society rather than what was popular to readers at the 2005 News Awards ceremony.

Confucius's teachings mesh well with the aspirations of development journalists in Asia, who see the role of the press as agents for social change. Through their work, they want to improve the quality of life of their people. Pakistani media researcher Owais Aslam Ali (undated) analyzed the major differences between Western news values and Asian news values, which he summarized as elitist press versus press for national development.

He pointed out the futility of Western news values in "the monumental uphill struggle" of the Third World toward economic progress. Given the diverse economic and social realities of the countries of the world, it is not difficult to see why different philosophies of journalism and news values exist around the world.

Some Western libertarian thinkers also addressed the issue of responsibility, rationality, or limits in exercising freedom. Locke gave impetus to the concept of "responsible individualism," predicated on a love of reason and the importance of natural law. According to Locke, individuals live in a social context and need order, not anarchy, for their own well-being.

"Therefore, reason serves as an automatic limitation on freedom. In order to guide themselves in living an orderly and moral life, which is the essence of humanity, rational people voluntarily give up much freedom". Even though well known for his libertarian ideas in his pamphlet On Liberty, Mill held an elitist view on entitlement to freedom. "Mill felt that his freedom principle was appropriate only in societies of relatively high educational standards in which people could rationally exercise freedom".

In the field of journalism, debates on press responsibility and accountability have never stopped, such as the work of the Hutchins' Commission, which gave rise to the social responsibility press theory, and the ongoing experimentation with civic or public journalism in the United States. If there is public concern over press responsibility, the concern should be addressed in building a new theoretical model.

The newly added dimension of press responsibility adds balance to existing press models by bringing in cultural values important not only to the West but also to the East, presents a fuller description of a press system, and helps address an important public concern over press responsibility and accountability.

Defining and Measuring Press Responsibility

The immediate question that arises is the definition of responsibility as what is considered responsible in one culture may be viewed as irresponsible in another culture. The notion of responsibility is always culture-specific. Similar to the argument that all concepts of responsibility are relative, the concept of "a free press" is also relative, as there is no absolute freedom of the press in this world, not even in the United States. Addressing press freedom worldwide, Merrill said, "... in fact, there are no free-press nations".

Because of the challenges in setting the standards of a responsible press that can be universally accepted and in deciding who should have the authority in setting the standards, and because of media's aversion to the concept of "a responsible press" imposed from the outside as illustrated by the fate of the Hutchins' report and by the "survey methodology" section of the 2005 Freedom House report that practically equates press responsibility with government control, discussions about press responsibility often hit a dead end. They do not have to be. Ali (undated) emphasized the watchdog role of the media in development journalism, warned against the discussions on Asian values in journalism being hijacked by government officials as justification for the control of the media, and urged Asian journalists, "who have been struggling to reduce government involvement in the media," to create a form of journalism relevant to the needs of their societies. Only then will the concept of Asian values have credibility, Ali wrote.

UNIVERSAL VALUES IN JOURNALISM

A starting point in exploring the standards of a responsible press can be the search for universal values in journalism, and the Hutchins' report can serve as a helpful reference, such as being accurate and providing balance and diversity of opinion in news coverage, acting as a watchdog of the government, businesses and all other powerful social institutions, addressing issues of public concern, covering all sectors of the society instead of just the prominent, and avoiding invasion of privacy and sensationalism.

If the list continues to include the elimination of hate speech, which is banned in Germany, and pornography, which is banned in the Muslim world, most of the Asian countries, and perhaps some African and South American countries as well, the exploration for universal standards of a responsible press will soon become controversial. And questions such as what is balanced to one may not seem to be balanced to another remain.

CURRENT COMMUNITY STANDARDS

To deal with such tricky issues in setting the standards of a responsible press, the standards used for deciding what is obscene can be borrowed-current community standards. If the majority of readers believe their press is responsible, then they have a responsible press.

Vice versa, if the majority of readers believe their press is irresponsible, then they have an irresponsible press. As the concept of responsibility is highly cultural-specific, the best solution is to let the local population decide instead of imposing standards from the outside.

INDEX OF PRESS RESPONSIBILITY

Based on accepted universal values in journalism, which may include truth, accuracy, and balance, and results of public opinion surveys on press responsibility, an index of press responsibility can be compiled for each country to help media researchers and students better analyse the characteristics of a particular press system.

If survey results distort reality such as in a controlled society, where a survey of honest public opinion is not feasible, universal values in journalism can serve as primary checkpoints.

In the meantime, despite the fact that they sometimes serve as a helpful reference, the criteria of the Freedom House in determining the ratings of press freedom in each country should be revised to add balance to the current standards, which do not take into account media content. The current methodology examines the legal, political, and economic environment of the media, but not the results of those environments-media content.

The survey questions are predominantly negative. Data are not collected through systematic or scientific method but through arbitrary answers by a small group of hand-picked interviewees, including "correspondents overseas, staff and consultant travel, international visitors," and "specialists in geographic and geopolitical areas." Such data collection methods raise serious questions about both the reliability and validity of the results.

THE FOUR CORNERS AND FOUR QUADRANTS

If a pair of dotted diagonal lines are superimposed on the coordinate grid, four corners of the grid will appear, representing four extreme types of press systems-free and responsible, free but not responsible, not free but responsible, and not free and not responsible. As the four corners indicate maximum or minimum degrees of freedom and responsibility, very few press systems fall exactly on those four corners; most of the press systems will fall somewhere within the four quadrants.

Free and Responsible

While it may be hard to find a perfect example of a free and socially responsible press, some media endeavors are definitely directed toward that goal, such as public broadcasting in Britain and the United States, the civic and public journalism in the United States, and community and development journalism in India and Pakistan. Even though these types of journalism do not represent the mainstream media in their respective societies, they are the free press's attempts to be responsible and relevant to its readers.

The press in this group is mostly free and chooses to avoid sensationalism and play a positive role in society on its own. With or without public funding, it provides mostly quality information and often a public servicefighting crime in neighborhoods, boosting voter turnout, and educating and empowering the poor rural population. Depending on events of the day, its content can be a mixture of negative and positive stories.

In well-developed and free media markets, the press can afford to choose to be responsible because such a press would be assured of market support if there is public demand for a free and responsible press. Even in underdeveloped societies such as those in South Asia, press responsibility in the form of development journalism can exist because of support from the vast rural audience. For the press to be free and responsible, the market has to demand it and has to be well developed enough to finance it.

Free and not Responsible

It is not very difficult to find free but irresponsible press around the world, press that chases profits or power under the name of press freedom. Under such press systems, the press is free to pursue whatever story sells on the market with little concern for the consequences of such reporting. In the race to be the first on the market, accuracy in reporting and ethical standards are often compromised. If criticized for their low professional standards and lack of accountability, journalists in such media environment often invoke the defence of freedom of the press. Such press systems tend to exist in intensely competitive media markets, such as new democracies in Taiwan, Indonesia, the Philippines, and some East European countries, where media outlets mushroom and bring immense pressure on the media market and where new regulations are still taking shape. Even in China where the press is becoming increasingly commercialized, tabloids, sensationalized news, or even made-up news stories are not hard to find.

Such press systems may also exist in well-developed, saturated and consolidated media markets where it is very challenging to expand market share such as Hong Kong and Thailand.

Because of the profit-oriented nature of such press systems, media companies are regarded as moneymakers, regulated by market demand only. Circulations and ratings become the only measure of success. Whatever sells is repeated in the media, resulting in over-coverage of some topics and events, such as celebrity journalism and press conferences, and the undercoverage of other less glamorous topics and events, such as poverty. Under such systems, the media spend far too much time covering and far too little time uncovering. As they become pure businesses, such media are financed mostly with advertising dollars and subscriptions.

Another form of press irresponsibility is the partisan press or political patronage of the press, in which case some press allows itself to be used as political tools especially when the democratic system is still young.

With a political power vacuum as a result of the dismantling of control mechanisms, political families, parties, or organizations often rush to take control of the media and use the media to advance their particular agendas, often employing such tactics as personal attacks or smear campaigns. Such a press tends to exist in free but less developed media markets as political patronage provides much needed financial support for the media.

Under such press systems, media content is often

negative, full of political attacks in partisan press, or sex and violence in tabloids instead of stories about progress, which is often a long and less dramatic process. Tabloids and partisan press are typical products of such a press system.

Responsible But not Free

The very term seems to be an oxymoron. Critics may ask how a press can be classified as responsible if it is not free. The answer can depend on the definition of responsibility according to local community standards.

Such press systems tend to exist in more traditional societies where the emphasis is on the group rather than the individual and where cultural traditions or religions have a major impact on public life. Press in this group tends to stress the importance and interests of the country, society, community, and families rather than freedom and rights of individuals. It tends to follow moral or religious principles and societal goals in news coverage rather than follow market demand because to publish what is perceived to be responsible is more important than to publish what sells. The emphasis is on publishing what is right versus the right to publish, which is the difference between what is ethical and what is legal.

The goals of such a press may vary from country to country, including social order and stability, economic development, or reinforcement of religious values. The press in this category tends to support these societal goals under government or public pressure, or both.

For example, in Saudi Arabia and much of the Islamic world, newspapers devote sections to the teachings or discussions of Islam while criticism of Islam is forbidden. And in most of the Islamic press, the content is very clean, free of pornography. Elsewhere in the world, many of the developing countries in Asia, Africa, and South America see national development as the top priority and expect the media to serve as a tool for nation building. In Singapore, because of the fear of ethnic and religious riots and the importance of its relations with its neighbors, the press cannot report on issues concerning race, religion, or its neighbors to maintain order and stability.

If the majority of the people in these societies support those goals, then the press is responsible. However, in some cases, especially when a country is involved in a war, current community standards may prove unreliable when the public is caught up in a patriotic frenzy. When that happens, it would depart from the universal values in journalism, such as accuracy and balance.

Because it has special roles to play in society, press in this group may obtain financial support from the government, public or social institutions, or the church even though a major part of its income may still come from the market.

Not Free and not Responsible

The press in this group does not enjoy much freedom of operation, and the controls applied unilaterally by the government are most likely not supported by the people. The most typical examples are perhaps the press in North Korea and Turkmenistan, where there is very little information but plenty of glorifications of the state leaders in the press. Hardships endured by the people can hardly be found in the news media. The press in this group is also prohibited from criticizing the government or exposing corruption. The press in this group does not have the freedom to make its own editorial decisions, and public opinion is suppressed.

After a review of the different types of press systems, where should the Japanese press be plotted on the coordinate grid? It should perhaps be placed somewhere close to the origin of the coordinate grid as being partly free and partly responsible. It is free from government control but not free from industry control.

And if the press refrains from uncovering high-level scandals in the government or big corporations, it cannot be described as socially responsible. But until the Japanese people start to reject their press, which is opposite to the fact that Japanese newspapers enjoy the highest circulations in the world, the press in Japan cannot be described as irresponsible either. A responsibility index as discussed earlier plus a more accurate press freedom rating can help determine the position of the Japanese press on the grid and the positions of the press in other countries.

A DYNAMIC MODEL

The proposed two-dimensional Freedom-Responsibility coordinate system attempts to provide a more balanced press model in explaining press systems around the world, measuring not only the degree of press freedom but also the level of press responsibility. The validity of the new model will be determined by how many press systems in the world it can satisfactorily describe and explain.

But societies are constantly changing, and so are their press systems. One of the advantages of the new model is that it can accommodate such changes in the system. For example, the American press seems to be trying to be more responsible and relevant to its readers while having some of its freedom curtailed because of the War on Terror. Comparing with the press elsewhere in the world, the American press is best known for being free but not necessarily for being responsible. The low credibility of the news media in repeated public opinion polls shows public dissatisfaction with media performance. Civic and public journalism seems to be pushing the American press toward more press responsibility when the press tries to be more relevant to its readers and more conscious of the role it can play in society, such as helping crime-fighting and boosting voter turnout.

And in the age of war on terror, the Bush administration is tightening up press access to information, citing national security concerns. It also launched an investigation into the leaking of the National security Agency's domestic spying programme to discourage such disclosure of information. During the war in Iraq, the government controlled reporters' access on the battlefield with a system of embedded reporters. And the concentration of ownership also reduces the independence and freedom the press once had.

The press in China seems to be moving slowly in the opposite direction-freer but messier even though sometimes more relevant to its readers. The press in China used to follow only Party lines. Now it also has to follow market demand by addressing public concerns. Some local papers target rural poverty by providing tips on how to grow better crops or how to generate cash by engaging in non-farming businesses. Competition, unheard of before the economic reforms, has given rise to diversity in the media.

The Internet has provided a channel for news stories turned down by the traditional media. These changes are clearly pushing the Chinese press toward more freedom and responsibility. However, competition also drives down the quality of news coverage and the ethical standards of journalists as sensationalism and bribery are prevalent. The Chinese press is in a state of flux as different factors are pulling it in different directions with deepening economic reforms. The most important factor, however, is still government policies.

The press in Russia presents perhaps the most intriguing case for study as the degree of press freedom and responsibility shifted dramatically with the changing political climate of the country.

Described as the prototype communist media, the press in the former Soviet Union was a political tool, following Lenin's ideal of press's functioning as collective agitator, propagandist, and organizer. After the fall of communism, the press in Russia changed overnight from not free to completely free. Then under the presidency of Putin, press freedom in Russia was once again being curtailed. With a new president coming into the Kremlin, the status of press freedom in Russia is yet to be determined.

The proposed new Freedom-Responsibility model is dynamic not only because it can accommodate the changes within particular press systems, but also because it can reflect changes in the structure of the model. In the debate on press freedom and press responsibility in the West, the concept of press freedom often trumps the concept of press responsibility. The same is true on the global scene as free news media in the West dominate the global information flow.

The call for the New World Information and Communication Order from developing countries was drowned out in the West's battle cry for the free flow of information. And the Freedom House measures press freedom, not press responsibility. Given the dominant position of press freedom in the coordinate system, the press freedom axis represents the yang arm of the coordinate system while the press responsibility axis stands for the yin arm of the system. The yang and yin axes complement each other, forming a balanced system.

However, the pendulum of history never stops swinging. Laozi, an ancient Chinese philosopher, sees reversal as the way the natural order operates: "everything that has gone far in one direction will move in the opposite direction, and to be in a low or weak position is to be in a state in which one will thrive". That is the law of the dialectics. If the abuse of press freedom becomes a global issue and the world's press is forced to be more responsible because of public pressure, there can be a paradigm change within the coordinate system with the concept of press responsibility becoming the dominant feature of the model and thus, the yang axis of the system, and the concept of press freedom becoming the yin axis of the system. But that may take a long time to occur even though such changes will never stop.

Confucius advocated the "middle path" and Aristotle promoted the "golden mean," each avoiding the extremes at either end. The same principle applies to press performance-there is neither absolute press freedom nor absolute press responsibility. The desirable middle path would be the optimal combination of press freedom with press responsibility, a blend of the West and the East.

The two-dimensional system proposed in this chapter is an attempt at exploring a more balanced model in studying press systems around the world. The major challenge in the application of the model would be the measurement of press responsibility in a press system. So far no effort is ever made in that regard, given the expected controversies it is bound to draw. If media observers and researchers can agree that development journalism and press responsibility do not automatically translate into government control of the press, measuring press responsibility does not have to be a forbidden task.

The compilation of a global press responsibility index can provide a helpful guide in studying the characteristics of a press system. A good starting point can be the identification of universal values in journalism as discussed earlier. The more universal values societies can agree upon, the more reliable the index can be. "Current community standards" in the form of public opinion surveys offer a way of accommodating values specific to local culture. Debates on universal values in journalism can be messy, but the results can be crystallizing and enlightening. With more research, media researchers from the East and the West may find more common ground than they expect.

One weakness of the model is perhaps that Western and Confucian philosophies and values tend to dominate the discussions even though there are so many other religious and philosophical influences in the world. Therefore, this study is only exploratory in nature. It can be enriched and improved with perspectives from more cultures or serve as a starting point for future research.

In future research, alternative concepts or dichotomies can be explored in building new models, such as an observer-interventionist/activist dichotomy, or commercial-ideological dichotomy. The point of departure will depend on the angle of analysis and on the perspectives and approaches of researchers.

Chapter 5

Global Media Events in India

This focuses on perceptions of televised global beauty pageants among business and media professionals in India who organized, sponsored, and supported the Miss World beauty contest. The 1996 Miss World pageant, which was held in Bangalore, a cosmopolitan city in South India, proved to be highly controversial due to protests expressed against the pageant by religious leaders, conservative women's groups, feminist activists, and political parties.

My analysis of discourses on Miss World that circulated among professionals in the Indian culture industry is based on data gathered from ethnographic fieldwork in Mumbai and Bangalore. Informants' statements about the televised Miss World revealed that categories of nation and gender deeply influenced local producers' interpretations of the benefits that accrue to India through the practice of hosting global media events.

In selecting a logo for Miss World, organizers and sponsors had to carefully negotiate local religious and gender politics as well as global fashion and beauty standards. Organizers' motives in holding the pageant in India demonstrated the launching of new configurations of global cultural flows that highlight Third World culture industries' desires to manage and control their own projects of globalization.

The study shows that the selection of a venue for Miss World was shaped by struggles to challenge regional hierarchies within India. In conclusion, I consider the implications of this qualitative research on local producers' interpretations of Miss World for studies of media globalization, nationalism, and gender.

The staging of international beauty contests in non-Western countries is an integral part of the process of economic and cultural globalization that has intensified in the last two decades.

Two recent developments that have aided the transnational traffic in consumer products, rituals, and practices commonly referred to as "global culture" inchide the internal liberalization or deregulation of developing countries' economies and the imperatives of Euroamerican multinational firms seeking new and larger middle-class markets).

In the case of India, since the government launched a series of economic reforms in the late eighties that were designed to promote a free-market economy and facilitate the entry of multinationals, the presence of global culture has manifested through a variety of such consumerist signifiers as the Barbie doll, McDonald's fast food, Coca Cola, MTV, Baywatch, and most recently, the Miss World contest. When the Miss World pageant was held in India in 1996, it was the first time that a region in South Asia became the setting for a global contest.

This monograph analyzes the 1996 Miss World pageant as a significant global media event that captured, exacerbated, and created tensions among discourses of gender, nationalism, regionalism, and modernity in postcolonial India.

While beauty pageants have long existed in various regional and national forms in India, Belize, Tibet, Sri Lanka, and Nicaragua, international contests have only recently turned their attention to non-Western locations, contestants, and audiences. Donald Trump and the CBS corporation jointly own the Miss Universe contest, which was founded in 1952. Although Miss Universe contests were held in Puerto Rico and the Philippines in the seventies, since 1992, this contest has traveled to numerous developing countries-Thailand, Peru, Namibia, Mexico, Trinidad & Tobago, and Cyprus.

When Miss Universe was held in Bangkok in 1992 for the first time, a New York Times article "Where Beauty

Queens Preen, No Eyesores Please" reported that thousands of the urban poor were evicted from the streets to avoid offending pageant contestants, tourists, and contest spectators.

The Miss Universe contest held in Manila in 1994 created controversy when some politicians in high office protested the large sums of money the state had agreed to invest in the pageant. Similarly, the Miss World contest, launched in 1951 by an English couple, Eric and Julia Morley, has also shifted its venues over the last decade from London to lesser-known cities.

Miss World was held in the United Kingdom for thirty-nine years before the founders began shipping it to Eastern Europe, Asia, South America, and Africa. Before Miss World was held in India in 1996, the South African resort location, Sun City, was home to this global pageant on four occasions. Since the early nineties, judges in the Miss World contest have included performers, media moguls, and celebrities from Latin America and Asia and increasingly, women of colour dominate the pool of finalists and winners of the contest.

Bangalore, a cosmopolitan city and the capital of the state of Karnataka in South India, was the venue for Miss World on November 23, 1996. Along with an estimated live attendance of 25,000 people, the pageant was attended by many of Asia's business elite and entertainment celebrities, and by international personalities like the Sultan of Brunei. The communications company, Amitabh Bachchan Corporation Limited (ABCL), organized the pageant in India. ABCL was founded in 1994 in Mumbail by the famous Indian celebrity icon and actor Amitabh Bachchan.

The event was sponsored chiefly by one of India's largest manufacturers of consumer products, Godrej, which produces soaps, detergents, food and hair products, electronic appliances, and office furniture. Other commercial sponsors for the event included national and multinational corporations: Mastercard, Citibank, Europcar, Coca Cola, Omega Watches, Welcom Group of hotels, Modi Revlon, Lakme cosmetics, Air India, and Reva Automobile. After considering bids from several countries, Miss World founders,

Eric and Julia Morley, chose ABCL to host and manage the pageant in India, a task that included selecting a site for the live performance of the contest, producing publicity materials, securing media coverage, negotiating with the Indian government for licenses, and ensuring the financial support of commercial sponsors.

As an ambitious business venture that was estimated to cost ABCL Rs. 10 crore (approx US$2.25 million), the Miss World pageant was hailed as an economic milestone for the Indian entertainment, advertising, and tourism industries. Business Today labeled Miss World and the Michael Jackson concert in Mumbai, which preceded the pageant by two weeks, as two of the biggest entertainment events hosted by the country.

Leaders in the Bangalore fashion, film, performance, and art worlds marveled at the entrepreneurial spirit of ABCL because the televised version of the pageant was estimated to be viewed by an audience of 3 billion in over 112 countries.

The advertising revenue of Rs. 20 crore (approx US$4.5 million) raised by ABCL for the thirty minutes of air time allocated to commercials during the two and a half hour long televised pageant was referred to as a "new benchmark for Indian television, which surpassed records for any previous event of this kind".

Bangalore city officials, who were convinced that Miss World had the potential to increase tourism and foreign investments, were prepared to incur expenses of over Rs. 10 crores in funding renovations, providing security, and offering a state-owned public venue for the live performance of the pageant. The Godrej company, which invested Rs 8.75 crores (approx US$2 million) in Miss World as the major sponsor of the event, claimed that the national publicity would aid in reversing declining sales of its well-known soap brands Cinthol, Ganga, Marvel, Crowning Glory, and Shikakai.

Foreign and Indian investment analysts argued that the international pageant symbolized the tremendous growth potential for the multinational cosmetics industry in the recently liberalized Indian economy. The cosmetics market had doubled in a short span of six years and with a projected annual growth of 20 per cent, total sales of cosmetics in 1998 was estimated to be in the region of US $27 million.

As the disagreements among state officials over the 1994 Miss Universe contest in Manila demonstrated, the arrival of globalization in the form of beauty pageants in Asia has sometimes generated conflict, opposition, and heated debate. Much to the dismay of Miss World's founders, organizers, and sponsors, the 1996 pageant in Bangalore provoked strong resistance and special-interest group mobilization.

The pageant became highly controversial due to vigorous public protests expressed by a wide range of conflicting factions. Members of protest groups organized marches and demonstrations, called for boycotts and strikes, distributed pamphlets and brochures at public places, performed street plays and skits, and vandalized offices of commercial sponsors, Reasons for these public protests against the Miss World pageant included charges that global beauty contests promoted cultural and economic imperialism, sexism, Western standards of beauty, immorality, and modes of consumption inappropriate for a Third World country where the vast number of its people still lived in extreme poverty.

Although globalization, particularly the possible impact of global media on local cultures in Third World settings, has attracted much theoretical musing, there is little empirical research that can illuminate the contradictory, heterogeneous, and conflicting responses to global culture. Examining the current contributions of scholars to research on globalization, anthropologist Janet Abu-Lughod expresses discomfort with the high level of abstraction in current theories of global culture. Concerned that theories of globalization lack adequate grounding in specific studies of localization, Abu-Lughod urges scholars to "capture the ambiguities and nuances of the concrete" because "the field, if not controlled, can degenerate into what we might call `global babble'".

In providing a case study of the 1996 Miss World pageant in India, this monograph aims to reduce "global babble" by concretely mapping the shifting qualities of meanings, which were attributed to a global media event that has come to signify the advent of Western modernity in many local settings.

The purpose of this study, which focuses on the Indian culture and media industries, is to examine the Miss World contest as a media event where the global and local intersected to produce, reinforce, and challenge relations of sameness and difference, gender and power, tradition and modernity, and centre and periphery.

How do indigenous capitalist enterprises harness discourses of gender and nationalism in embracing global media culture and legitimizing their commercial goals for the consumption of local audiences? How do organizers and producers negotiate local tensions and cultural politics in marketing globalization to local and transnational media audiences? Does the presence of global culture in local settings always imply relations of economic and cultural dependence between centre (West) and periphery (non-West)? Are local media corporations in non-Western locations deploying Western rituals and spectacles to produce new flows of media culture that do not originate in the First World?

How can local agents in non-Western nations seek out global culture to challenge regional hierarchies and hegemonies? In considering these questions, the scope of this monograph's analysis is restricted to the perspectives of professionals in the entertainment, media, and beauty industries in India.

In privileging fieldwork data gathered from informants who were involved in managing, sponsoring, and supporting Miss World, this monograph does not address contestants' motives for participating in international pageants, the histories of global or national pageants, the changing aesthetics of international beauty queens' bodies over time, or audience responses to the televised pageant.

I do not provide specific textual analyses of media coverage accorded to pre-pageant events, the pageant itself, or public protests.

The first section of this monograph briefly reviews studies

of beauty pageants to provide insights into what we can learn from examining beauty contests as public sites where social and economic structures of gender, class, age, race, and nation are captured in a spectacular fashion. The following section briefly sketches the representations of Miss World that appeared in the media and outlines the relevance of current theoretical speculations on global-local interactions for this study of the culture industry in India. The next section provides a brief overview of my methodology and fieldwork in India.

The five sections that follow the discussion of methodology contain an extended analysis of fieldwork data, which demonstrates that organizers' and sponsors' perceptions of the mediated staging of Miss World contest in India reinforced and challenged national, regional, global, and gender identities.

I begin by examining local media and advertising professionals' views on the positive impact of Miss World on India's image in the global public sphere. I then analyse informants' opinions on the links between the recent global visibility of successful Indian beauty queens and the arrival of the 1996 Miss World contest in Bangalore. Exploring the cultural politics of gender and religion in India that organizers had to maneuver, the next section analyzes ABCL's strategies in designing a logo for Miss World.

The following section addresses organizers' motives for hosting Miss World in India and the last and fifth section of analysis investigates the internal, behind-the-stage process that led to the selection of Bangalore, a city in South India, as the venue for the live performance of Miss World.

In conclusion, I debate the implications of my qualitative research on the localization of Miss World in India for studies of media globalization, nationalism, and gender. I argue that debates over patriotism, loyalty to cultural traditions, and local women's empowerment do not occur only within the discourses of activism or state politics-such cultural conflicts and tensions also suffuse the imaginary landscape that guides local producers' involvement in capitalist cultural production.

THE CULTURAL SIGNIFICANCE OF BEAUTY PAGEANTS

While numerous feminist scholars have studied cultural ideals of feminine beauty in advertising and popular culture, beauty pageants have only recently begun to attract academic attention. Although cultural studies scholars have challenged many earlier distinctions between high and low culture, beauty pageants continue to function as a form of "low culture," yet to be awarded the kind of "hip" and current academic interest in popular television culture such as the X-Files, Ally McBeal, Simpsons,

The Jerry Springer show, or Seinfeld. Pointing to the difficulties she encountered in being considered a serious scholar of gender and contemporary culture because she wanted to study beauty pageants, Sarah Banet-Weiser notes the dearth of scholarly work on beauty pageants and writes, "...these events are often and easily dismissed as frivolous, meaningless, or carnivalesque and therefore unworthy of serious and sustained intellectual scrutiny".

This study's analysis of international beauty pageants in the non-- Western world as multi-layered global media events that narrate stories about gender, nationalism, the politics of religion, and regionalism echoes recent feminist approaches to beauty pageants in the United States. Going beyond early radical feminist critiques of pageants as events that embody the patriarchal and sexist objectification of women's bodies, scholars have instead begun examining contests as rituals that are also deeply entangled with discourses of race, class, nation, and ethnicity. Combining a historical approach with empirical data gathered from interviews with producers and beauty contestants, Sarah Banet-Weiser shows that the Miss America pageant is a cultural site that encapsulates notions of White upper-class respectability, corporate multiculturalism, and U.S. nationalism.

Analyzing archival documents and oral history interviews, Judy TzuChun Wu (1997) explores the historical significance of the Miss Chinatown USA pageant in San Francisco. Focusing on written and spoken discourses about beauty contestants' roles within the Chinese community, she argues that the pageant became a ritual for Chinese Americans to express assimilation and difference.

Chinese Americans viewed the pageant as a performance of Western modernity that would allow them to become a part of White America, yet retain their own distinct cultural identity by using the pageant to promote Chinese traditions and values. Similarly, Pamela Thoma (1999) studies "Miss India Georgia," a video documentary of interviews with prospective Indian-American beauty contestants, to illustrate the complex diasporic experiences of second-generation immigrant women whose identities oscillated among their life experiences as East Indians, American citizens, and minority women of colour.

An important argument underlying the studies of Banet-Weiser, Tzu-Chun Wu, and Thoma is their insistence on analyzing women's participation in and consumption of beauty pageants as activities that incorporate more than a sense of false consciousness or passive submission to ideologies of patriarchy or capitalism. As these feminists argue, pageants include and draw upon cultural narratives of women's empowerment, liberal notions of individual achievement and equal opportunity, and progressive ideas of diversity and pluralist tolerance.

Anthropologists have been far ahead of media scholars in studying the significance of beauty pageants in non-Western locations. In a pioneering collection of essays in the book Beauty Queens on the Global Stage, folklorists and cultural anthropologists examine community queen contests in Guatemala, Nicaragua, and rural Minnesota and national pageants in Thailand, Belize, Tonga, and Tibet to reveal the ways in which beauty contests are embedded within and epitomize struggles over regional, national, global, and gender identities.

Avoiding the simplistic assumption that beauty pageants offer evidence only of hegemonic Western cultural imperialism, the essays in Beauty Queens on the Global Stage pay careful attention to the harnessing of global culture in non-Western contexts to debate and contest various local identities within national boundaries. This study of the Miss World pageant in India adopts these authors' nuanced approach to the cross-cultural popularity of imported Western rituals and artifacts in the developing world.

Political scientist William Callahan's essay on the Miss Thailand contest is the only study of pageants that pays attention to the electronic media's role in transforming beauty contests into large scale public spectacles. Employing a semiotic and historical approach, Callahan analyzes the changing local political and economic contexts of the national Miss Thailand contest to illustrate the different meanings that various competing forces-the nation state, elite upper-class groups, and capitalist organizations-mapped onto the figure of Miss Thailand.

Emphasizing the role of the mass media in shaping non-Western audiences' experiences of Western modernity, Callahan writes, "Television promoted Miss Thailand and Miss Thailand promoted television; one of the prizes for the winner of the contest was a television set ...". Callahan's proposition that the relationship between electronic media and popular rituals is a dialectic and dialogic process-the spectacle of beauty pageants affects television's visual power and the audiences of television in turn influence the form and content of beauty pageants-- underlies this study's analysis of Miss World in India.

In building upon the growing body of research on beauty pageants, this ethnographic study of the Indian culture industry's views on the televised Miss World contest contributes to international communication research on media globalization and feminist media studies.

My analysis of interviews with organizers, sponsors, and other supporters of Miss World reveals that the social construction of beauty pageants as rituals of modernity is inseparable from perceptions and impressionistic images about the power of global media. In taking a feminist approach to the ethnographic data on media representations of beauty pageants, my research shows that gender-debates over femininity, feminism, and modernity-mediates local reception to globalization.

GLOBALIZATION AND LOCALIZATION

In considering beauty contests as rich sites for ethnographic study, Beverly Stoeltje, a feminist ethnographer and folklorist, argues that pageants, much like the spectacular rituals of pre-modern societies, are ritualistic cultural performances of our modern world. Stoeltje writes that as mediated spectacles, beauty pageants offer scholars three sites for cultural analysis: the evolution of the event's form, the organization of the event's production, and the discourse in which it is embedded.

One important discourse that shapes the production and reception of global pageants among local media and culture industries is the promise of the potential visibility that these media events offer contestants, sponsors, advertisers, and the nations and cities that host these contests. Analyzing the staging of global pageants in locations outside of Western metropolitan centers, Banet-Weiser suggests that in bidding for the pageant, state officials and local event management firms seek out the constructed media representation of their host countries as desirable places to visit, invest, and conduct collaborative business.

A critical aspect of marketing rituals of global culture in today's mediasaturated world is ensuring that newsmedia, magazines, and local and national television build anticipation and excitement prior to the staging of the live media event. Organizers of the Miss World contest began generating print and video news releases about the contestants, history of the pageant, and the format of the live performance six months prior to the live event. Advertisers and members of the hospitality and tourism industries also promoted their involvement in supporting the pageant.

For example, a lengthy feature story in India's roost reputable financial newspaper, The Economic Times, titled "Colonial ambience, Indian warmth for beauties" explained the preparations that the Windsor Manor hotel in Bangalore had undertaken to ensure a memorable lodging experience for the contestants, many of whom were visiting India for the first time.

This chapter contained details about decor modifications-special furnishings, plants, lighting, and landscaping-and cuisine arrangements ("delicious but not fattening") that the Windsor Manor hotel staff had planned to welcome and host Miss World's founders and participants.

Suruchi Rai, the senior housekeeping manager of the hotel conducted several guided tours for television and print reporters and writers during the month of October. Miss World's founders, Eric and Julia Morley, visited India in July 1996, four months before the scheduled live performance, to promote the pageant as "Beauty with a Purpose" at local charity events in Mumbai.

Not all audiences in local cultures greet international beauty pageants and other rituals of globalization with the enthusiasm and excitement expressed by state officials, advertisers, and members of the entertainment industry. The city of Bangalore witnessed an unprecedented flurry of public protests that intensified during the months of October and November 1996.

Members of women's groups-Mahila Jagran Samiti, Mahila Jagruthi, Vimochana, the All India Women's Democratic Forum, and the National Commission on Women-courted local and global media. To gain publicity, the All India Women's Democratic Forum hosted a mock pageant, a satirical commentary on Miss World, that was covered on the front pages of newspapers and in local and national television news; at a large, centrally located public park, feminists crowned mock women contestants as "Miss Poverty, Miss Homeless, and Miss Landless."

Numerous columns authored by feminist academics, activists, and journalists appeared in the Deccan Herald, Indian Express, Times of India, and The Hindu.

Competing with ABCL for news coverage, leaders of political parties including the Communist Party of India (Marxist), the Bharatiya Janata Party, and the state's peasant group, the Karnataka Rajya Raitha Sangha, actively cultivated journalists, gave interviews, and provided provocative quotes.

State of Karnataka residents, who were members of the protest group, the Kannada Agitators Forum, dressed as demons of Hindu mythology and carried a nude cutout of Amitabh Bachchan, owner of ABCL. During the week of the pageant, as the protests became increasingly vocal and violent, CNN, BBC, The New York Times, the Los Angeles Times, and the Washington Post zoomed their journalistic lenses on Bangalore.

On November 23, 1996, CNN World View anchor Jeanne Meserve and CNN's Indian correspondent Anita Pratap described the live performance of the pageant and summarized the reasons for the protests during the prime time news slot at 7 p.m.

The 1996 Miss World contest in India thus highlights the media's crucial role in representing the agendas of different competing groups in the global public sphere. At the most fundamental level, mass media create the conditions of possibility for media events such as beauty pageants that rely on consumer desire for spectacle to attract the support of capitalist enterprises. However, the very same media that serve the commercial goals of advertisers and sponsors also enable activist and community organizations to enlist public support for their causes.

The discourses of organizers, sponsors, and protesters disseminated by the media transformed the pageant into an ideological space in which numerous social and commercial entities voiced their opinions on India's gradual incorporation into the global economy. This ethnographic account, which unravels perceptions of the media's representational power among local agents in India, who had the greatest investment in the success of Miss World, considers recent theoretical propositions regarding the tensions and contradictions that arise during the process of globalization.

Revising earlier models of cultural imperialism, interdisciplinary scholars of globalization have begun speculating on alternative ways of studying and theorizing transnational relationships between the West and the nonWest. Instead of envisioning globalization as a binary encounter where the global is the agent of cultural destruction and the local is the site of pristine cultural authenticity, Ien Ang and Ulf Hannerz suggest that the global and local are complexly articulated in mutually constitutive ways.

Extending this argument further, Robertson argues that we cannot always assume the idea of locality to be synonymous with forms of local resistance to the hegemonically global, that is, locality cannot simply be seen as the pitting of non-Western subalterns against dominant Western forces.

As Robertson comments, discourses of globalization cannot be effective unless they actively participate in the production of locality-the cultural adaptation of global commodities, rituals, and ideologies to persuade local audiences to become loyal fans and consumers. For effective localization, multinational producers and distributors therefore need the services and resources of local cultural agents who can shape the ideological, material, and historical contours of global culture for local consumption.

In the case of the Miss World pageant in India, protests by cultural, traditional, and activist groups against the pageant comprised one element of the local; however, another aspect of the local that preceded the protests was the goals of Indian commercial enterprises-ABCL, Indian advertisers, women's magazine editors, and professionals in the fashion and beauty industry-to collaborate with the Moneys in organizing and producing the pageant in India. Significantly, one common critique of numerous protests launched against the staging of the pageant in Bangalore addressed the collusion of local Indian producers in transnational projects of globalization.

Given the context of local activism against globalization, what roles do organizers of pageants construct for local producers of mediated global culture? How do professionals in local culture industries legitimize their coproduction of allegedly imperialistic narratives?

Addressing the discursive indigenization of international pageants in their new locations in Asia and Eastern Europe, Banet-Wesier (1999) suggests that despite the overt layer of Westernization, internal categories of nationalism and sexuality permeate local renderings of Miss World and Miss Universe. What media strategies of crisis containment based in local cultures and histories did producers devise to indigenize Miss World?

Analyzing the production of locality, Arjun Appaduari (1996) argues that ethnographies of global-local interactions must shift from merely describing the local to analyzing the imaginary landscape that informs the mediation of globalization by local historical subjects.

Appaduari also contends that the experience of locality is a relational achievement, that is, the global becomes intelligible to local actors through the discursive generation of historical, geographic, and ideological contexts that frame and provide meaning to participation in global projects. With the recent focus on media reception, the local is often conflated with audiences and consumers' responses to global culture; however, local producers, individuals who are part of the wider culture and share its values, are rarely subjects of ethnographic study.

As local actors in the production of international pageants, what contexts and historical events influenced Indian media and business professionals' endorsement of India's association with globalization? Did they express their enthusiasm for the televised global pageant vis-a-vis the imaginary construction of the First World? Did other neighborhoods, closer to India, constitute contexts against which the mediated Miss World became a source of power and modernity?

Most research on globalization has exclusively focused on the impact of Western culture on national, racial, and ethnic identities. Reviewing studies of political economy and audience reception in non-Western cultures, Anabelle Sreberny-Mohammadi questions the glaring absence of analyses that take into account categories of gender and class in studying media globalization. Gender, a crucial site of difference that organizes global consumerism, has become a resource for global and local producers of media culture to shape their persuasive messages for local audiences.

Indrepal Grewal sketches the gendered context of cosmopolitan consumerism in urban India where the boom in the beauty and vanity industries, following economic liberalization, has reinforced and reshaped existing gender and class relations.

Grewal notes that English-language magazines such as Verve targeted at middle-class Indian women project their ideal readers as hybrid, cosmopolitan female consumer subjects-contemporary urban women with Indian roots and Western exposure.

Mining state and activist discourses on Indian women's empowerment, proliferating advertising images in media discourses simultaneously exalt traditional roles even as they construct Western style consumption practices as alternative modes of experiencing individualized freedom and resistance. With regard to Miss World, what imaginary notions of gender relations and female subjectivity guided local producers' visions of global pageants?

Globalization also cannot be envisaged solely in terms of existing centre-- periphery models because the new global cultural economy has begun to reveal numerous overlapping zones of cultural production and consumption. Suggesting that globalization need not always imply Americanization, Appadurai argues that new nodes of globalization emerging in Asia may draw from Western discourses of modernity, but the desire to produce and consume American culture and emulate Western practices of consumerism cannot itself be viewed as evidence of cultural and economic capitulation.

Did the arrival of the Miss World contest herald more than India's steady incorporation into the global marketplace? What economic imperatives drove ABCL, a fledgling media production and distribution firm in India, to seek out the assignment of hosting Miss World?

Exploring local producers' perceptions of imported

Western rituals and commodities could also demonstrate the complex appropriation of global culture in non-Western contexts to reinforce and challenge local hierarchies and power relationships. Original producers of transnational culture in First World settings may or may not always be able to envision the heterogeneous, semiotic negotiations that take place over the incorporation of global culture into local structures.

As len Ang writes, much to our surprise, we may find that "local cultures tend to reproduce themselves precisely, to a large extent, through the appropriation of global, mass-mediated forms and technologies". For instance, what cultural factors compel different cities within host nations to offer competing bids for international pageants? Why was Miss World held in Bangalore in South India and not in the wellestablished, larger metropolitan cites of Mumbai, New Delhi, or Calcutta?

METHODOLOGY: FIELDWORK IN INDIA

This monograph's analysis is part of a larger project that interrogates the controversial 1996 Miss World pageant in India as a mass-mediated ritual that provoked vigorous debate over the impact of global culture on gender, modernity, and tradition in India. The research data gathered for this study is based on five months of fieldwork in the cities of Bangalore and Mumbai in India.

The qualitative research techniques I used included informant and ethnographic interviews, participant observation, focus group sessions, and textual analysis of media coverage accorded to the pageant. The analysis of ethnographic fieldwork data in this monograph focuses on the perspectives and views of organizers, sponsors, advertisers, and other supporters of the Miss World pageant.

As defined by Thomas Lindlof, informant interviews are two- to three hour-long interviews with select key members of groups that represent different and sometimes competing social and economic interests, and can thus offer a variety of insights into a research problem. Informant interviews elicit responses to specific domains of information about a cultural phenomenon, and researchers conduct these interviews with prepared questions at pre-set times and places.

I conducted thirty five informant interviews with former and current employees of the firm Amitabh Bachchan Corporation Limited who were responsible for managing the pageant; sponsors and advertisers; public relations directors and assistants at the firm that handled publicity and promotion for the Miss World pageant; editors, reporters, and writers at English-language newspapers, newsmagazines, women's magazines, and popular vernacular magazines. Based on the preferences of informants, these interviews took place at homes, offices, restaurants, public parks, and lobbies of office buildings.

Although most interviews were conducted in individual sessions where I interacted with one informant at a time, in certain cases, at the request of employees who worked for the same organization, I interviewed them in small groups of two or three. In recording informant interviews, I used a combination of writing fieldnotes and audiotaping conversations. With the exception of two, all informants agreed to be taped, and fully transcribed interviews were provided to all those who requested copies of interview transcripts. To preserve informants' anonymity and confidentiality in this monograph, I use job titles or pseudonyms for those who specifically requested that I mask their identity.

Lindlof defines ethnographic interviews as "informal conversational interviews" that occur more spontaneously in the course of conducting pre-planned research. Ethnographic interviews are "sensitive to the needs and nuances of the moment" and do not require a special site or much preparation.

In the process of conducting informant interviews, I was referred to numerous other individuals who had been closely involved with the pageant. As a result of these recommendations and referrals, I conducted ethnographic interviews with government officials at the Karnataka State

Tourism Development Board; administrative staff at the Windsor Manor Hotel (where beauty contestants from over ninety countries and the founders of the Miss World contest, Eric and Julia Morley, stayed); fashion coordinators; and staff at the cricket stadium where the pageant took place. None of the ethnographic interviews was taped; however, all these interviews were documented with fieldnotes.

HARNESSING THE POWER OF THE GLOBAL IMAGE

By the time the 1996 Miss World pageant came to the city of Bangalore, global television had become fairly entrenched as a part of leisure culture in urban India. Commenting on the widespread availability of global television networks like CNN, which have today extended their reach to many non-- Western locations, len Ang (1996) writes in her book Living Room Wars, "The transnational dissemination of mass mediated culture is, given the strength of global capitalism in today's world economy, an irreversible process that cannot be structurally transcended".

One recent development, which visibly proclaims the arrival of the global economy in India is the advancing intrusion of global television into the imaginary worlds of Indian consumers; numerous cable channels including CNN, MTV, Discovery, and STAR have become popular within a largely middle- and upper-class urban Indian market.

In her comprehensive study of the growth of television in India, Nilanjana Gupta (1998) writes that although cable TV had very slow growth in the late eighties, by 1993, with the advent of satellite television, several major Indian cities witnessed a dramatic increase in the number of cabled households. The demand for cable television networks in Mumbai that offered CNN, as Sevanti Ninan documents, increased in leaps during and after the Persian Gulf War in January-February 1991.

Although many informants in Mumbai and Bangalore appreciated CNN as a valuable educational resource that enabled Third World audiences to gain knowledge about the world and become global citizens, a majority argued that the positive potential of global television news was undermined by its persistent, ethnocentric representations of India.

Interviews with business and media professionals and observation of television's place in their everyday lives indicated that subscribing to cable television services, particularly those that offered news networks like CNN and BBC, was not considered an indulgence or luxury. The central space occupied by the television set in living rooms, the scheduling of interviews to accommodate informants' news viewing practices, and parents' insistence on exposing their children to CNN and Discovery pointed to these upwardly mobile informants' strategic use of cable television as a commodity that could enhance their access to global cultural capital in a changing economy.

One meeting with three executives who had worked for ABCL during the Miss World pageant took place at the home of Rajan Mehta, a resident of Malabar Hills, an affluent neighborhood in Mumbai where a large number of India's well-known entertainment and business elite lived. Gesturing towards a large screen television that dominated one wall of the lavishly furnished living room, Mehta offered, "It's the magic window that shows us the world."

Responding to his remark, his friend and former colleague quickly said, "Yeah, but the window does not always show reality." As the interview proceeded, the context and meaning of the second comment, which alluded to the inability of global television news to accurately portray reality, became a crucial subtext that lurked beneath informants' enthusiasm for the Miss World contest.

All three men including Mehta spoke animatedly about the world now appearing in their homes and of being privileged to routinely receive live news coverage of world events; however, they also became involved in a heated debate about the marginalization of India and Indians in Western media. Arguing that ethnocentric Western news producers could not imagine middle-class Indians as intelligent audience members, who expected accurate and complete coverage of India, one executive spoke at length about the images of India he had frequently seen on CNN and Discovery:

Whenever India is on the television, my children will usually shout and ask me to hurry up so I can catch what they're showing. They're very proud of course that India is on foreign TV. But whenever India is on foreign channels, it is either the plague, shortage of onions, nuclear war, famine, or snake charmers. That's what they had on Discovery the other day. Snakes in India. Think of India and you can predict what will be on screen.

Interrupting, the third executive, who had received his MBA degree in the United States, voiced similar sentiments, although he focused on the representations of Indian women in a broader range of media including newspapers, newsmagazines, and television news:

Whenever they show Indian women in any foreign media - New Yorker, CNN, Time magazine, National Geographic, New York Times - it is always poor abused widows, child brides who are exploited, women who are aborting girl babies, ... that journalist for the New York Times - yes, Barbara Crossette, she always writes only negative stories about India. When I lived in the United States, Americans would often ask me what I thought of how Indian men treated their wives and mothers.

Suggesting that global media's representations of its new audiences in Asia lagged far behind its ambitious goals of geographic expansion, an advertising accounts executive for the Godrej company (chief sponsor of the pageant) said:

It is as though world news is for those people, those who live in Europe and the United States. We in Asia watch TV too you know. They forget I think that people in countries like India get BBC, CNN-when they show India on the news now, I want to tell them, hey watch out, Indians are watching their own country on your news.

Two other advertising managers (one represented a large garment retailer and the other a hair products company), who had persuaded their CEOs to release funds for advertising space during the live broadcast of Miss World, expressed similar resentment over Western representations of India-not just in the news, but also in Hollywood films like Indiana Jones and the Temple of Doom and City of Joy.

These comments illustrated the contradictory experiences of transnational audiencehood for consumers of global news and popular culture in developing countries such as India. While Indian television viewers feel empowered as global citizens through easy and instant access to news of the world. they also have to routinely endure Western media's recycled catalog of stories on India that emphasize exotic customs, natural disasters, poverty, and ancient forms of oppression.

It is against this context of global television news from the West, which in the words of my informants, continues to code and interpellate the Euroamerican consumer as the ideal viewer, that television coverage of the Miss World pageant became a powerful tool for ushering in change. The televised Miss World contest in Bangalore presented a crucial opportunity for Indians to gain media access and produce modern images that could counteract the negative discourse of global newsmedia. Informants described the power of Western modernity associated with Miss World not in the concrete terminology of global audiences or its appeal among Euroamerican viewers, but as inherently contained in the history and spectacular form of the pageant itself.

The pageant's power as a performance of Western cosmopolitanism was conflated with the material presence of the grand stage, a loquacious and entertaining commentator, the panoply of dances and performances, live media coverage, confident women enthralling large audiences, and the indisputable origins of beauty pageants in Western metropolitan locations. Describing Miss World as a historic media event that could harness the representational power of television for India, one ABCL executive discussed the excitement in his office when upper-management formally announced their decision to host the pageant:

Our boss told us it was a great honour for us. On the day when he announced the names of the people on the team that would be working on the pageant full-time for six months, we were all told that this was just the beginning of India's major appearance on world television and for once it would not be famine or poverty, trains crashing, or female children being killed.

Comparing the inclusiveness and popularity of the pageant to other sports events in India that have also claimed the aura of an international appeal, his friend joined in and remarked:

We've had other events you know like World Cup Cricket and International Test Matches but those are just bogus titles-these events are not really world or international. It's just a few countries that were ruled by the British. Now the Miss World pageant was a real world event, with close to 100 contestants, from Europe, Africa, South America, Mexico. It is the world that was coming to India and television can announce that to many.

Arguing that the Miss World pageant enabled the creation of positive news about India, one ABCL executive's comments echoed the sentiments of non-aligned and Third World nations' leaders, who crafted the New World Information Order Policy to explicitly address and reduce imbalances in information flows between developing and developed nations.'

Advising Indians to aggressively pursue visibility on television, he suggested, "We must become the creators of news-otherwise nothing will change. Indians are ignoring the power of television. We need to be active, and participate as people of the world, not just as Indians. We must set the record straight." Finally, hailing the Miss World pageant as a major milestone in India's television history and progress towards Western modernity, one ABCL television producer explained:

When the Asiad sports event came to India in the eighties we went to colour TV because we wanted to present the event with all its excitement to Indian audiences who were proud that the Asiad was being held in India. The Miss World pageant is even better than the Asiad because it has been around longer. It will show people who watch television that

India can have live large-scale events. People will learn that we're modern, that India is changing and joining the world.

Such local discourse about the power of beauty pageants to project media images of modernity also becomes a strategic defence for producers of global culture to gain support among the elite in Third World locations. In promoting Miss World in local media in Bangalore, Julia Morley, president of Miss World Ltd., drew on resentment among the urban Indian middle- and upper-classes over India's image as a Third World country to persuade city residents to ignore protest groups' demands that the pageant be banned.

Morley is reported to have said to the Bangalore edition of the national newspaper Indian Express, "I find this concept of the Third World very distasteful. When there is talk of one world, how can you polarise and divide it like this".

An important element of the Miss World pageant's symbolic value was its association with specific geographic locations that were compared to India in terms of their progress toward global modernity. Discussing the potential of Miss World to disrupt the dominant Western image of India as a country beset by "backwardness," one young manager at the public relations company that was responsible for promoting the pageant argued:

The Miss World pageant has gone to Venezuela three times because they [the Venezeulans] are smart. It has even gone to Thailand, I think in 1992. They know that this will get them on TV, and we should be doing it too. When you say the word "Third World" anymore, I know people think of India or Rwanda-we're the same as Rwanda. That's not okay. Even Thailand is probably not considered as Third World as we are. We have to move forward and do what these countries are doing.

According to the manager of the Windsor Manor hotel in Bangalore where the contestants stayed, the Miss World pageant's appearance on television would showcase India's dynamic, urban, cosmopolitan culture in contrast to representations of rural India that suggested stagnation and lack of economic and cultural change. He claimed that media representations of Bangalore as a location where modern, glamorous, and confident women from all over the world could come and perform, would set India apart from other "backward" nations in South Asia:

Think about it. This Miss World pageant used to be held in London and now it's coming to India. Do you think Eric and Julia Morley would even think about going to places like Pakistan or Bangladesh? When people think of Pakistan the only things they can think of are guns, dictators, Mullahs [Islamic priests] and women who cannot even go to college. India is different-we're a secular democracy-and people know we have freedom, our women have the freedom to do many things.

Lampooning this widespread urge to construct Pakistan as the demonic "other" in India, newspaper columnist Raj Kamal Jha wrote in a satirical essay that among the top ten reasons for India's hosting the Miss World pageant, the number one reason was, "we're so scared that if we don't, ooooooh, Pakistan might." Mediated representations of Miss World were thus viewed as possessing the power to distinguish India as a modern nation; as similar to ultra-metropolitan spaces in the Western world and newer, modernizing "tourist" nations like Thailand, but different from other Islamic states like Pakistan that are often vilified in mainstream Indian and global media.

According to some interviewees, moving the nation toward the path of modernity was not a task that the nation state, the Indian government, could accomplish because it was inefficient, corrupt, and lacked entrepreneurial initiative. As one media manager for ABCL argued, it was only due to the visionary spirit of private business that Miss World, a largescale international media event, had arrived in India in 1996, less than a decade after the state's programme of economic liberalization was launched.

Vikram Scindia, the primary special events manager for ABCL, framed the pageant as an event that announced the success of private enterprise in India to the outside world loudly and clearly:

The Miss World pageant is the best special event any country could host to show that they are ready and receptive for multinational companies. We had to pull together three resources-the media, theatre and fashion experts, and the contestants-to create this event. Although the government provided a stadium and security for the pageant, they would not have bidden for Miss World. The government is not capable of doing anything like that because they have no imagination and lack brainpower. All the government wants is easy money-bribes and cutbacks.

In constructing the Miss World pageant as a repository of modernity, another ABCL executive in charge of generating media coverage for the pageant in the English-language newsmedia, argued:

Eric and Julia Morley came to India only because they were confident that ABCL, a private communications company, did not have the hierarchical and corrupt structure of the Indian government. Yes, the government has decreased regulations but that is not enough. You have to communicate to multinationals that

India, which is thought of as a Third World country, will support the creation of markets here just like in any developed country.

The chief editor of Femina, a popular women's magazine, bemoaned the lack of commitment and integrity in Indian political leaders since the demise of Jawaharlal Nehru, the first prime minister of India, who actively employed the media to promote Western science and technology as the means to India's modernization. She explained that the Miss World contest represented a milestone in private enterprise's successful intervention into enriching the scope and potential of Indian television:

Putting modern images, new and creative images in the media is the responsibility of the private sector. I remember as a child watching the movie Mother India and looking at images of big dams being built within the plot, and it made a huge impact on me. The decision to do that was made by the director who wanted India to make progress. The Miss World contest can do the same-- it can tell people that we are no less than any other country. Today we have liberalization but no real action because the Indian politician lacks imagination and sophisticated thinking.

These charges and complaints from private sector employees about a corrupt Indian government that lacked initiative in seeking out creative media outlets to advertise India's entry into a global economy is part of a larger ongoing and tense relationship between the Indian state and private business interests. As Hilton Root argues, economic liberalization in many Asian countries was proposed by local economists as one among a series of solutions to end political corruption, but the cure for corruption promised by a more free-market economy has yet to be realized.

According to Root, the tense relationship between the private and public sectors in India has only been further exacerbated in the nineties when private firms, hoping for a better business environment, instead found themselves compelled to continue earlier practices of maintaining secret contacts with bureaucrats, cultivating personal connections with politicians, and avoiding tax payments to compensate for high licensing fees.

Informants' association of Miss World with the energy and force of private capitalist enterprise is part of a longer history of beauty pageants in India, which have always been organized and sponsored by media corporations. In fact, the national Miss India beauty contest, managed by Femina, an English-language women's magazine owned by the media conglomerate Bennett & Coleman, has widely been viewed as belonging to the exclusive world of the elite Mumbai-based business and entertainment classes.

In contrast to Thailand, where the national Miss Thailand contest was hosted by the state in the early nineteen fifties as an official public relations event to disseminate messages about democratic ideology and to garner support for the military, the national Miss India contest had not attracted the official attention of the Indian state.

Unlike Thailand where the national beauty contest is

apart of its official military history, it would have been unthinkable for the government of a newly independent India that had Mahatma Gandhi as its national hero-the image of austerity, spirituality, and anti-materialism-to use the spectacle of beauty pageants to promote nationalism.

William Callahan writes that the organization of the Miss Thailand contest by private business interests in the sixties, eighties, and nineties signaled a shift in the symbolic value of the contest from being a vehicle for public policy to becoming an agent of private advertising and consumption, and hence a symbol of the power of television as a capitalist force.

Given the different construction of the beauty pageant in India as a performance that was accessible primarily to Westernized elite consumers and celebrities for over three decades, the televised Miss World pageant, as the editor of Femina explained, heralded a new frontier for beauty contests as more democratic and public performances because television, unlike print media, could cross boundaries of class and literacy, "I think the Miss World contest on television allowed many Indians, even those who are poor, to be at a beauty pageant. Poor people could not buy tickets but they could watch Miss World on TV."

As a media spectacle, the global beauty pageant's presence in India also announced the managerial public relations abilities of various local commercial groups. Public relations skills including the organization of the live performance, coordination of news conferences and special events, and the production of news releases and other publicity materials testified to India's new capitalist competence in the global marketplace.

Proclaiming the staging of the Miss World pageant in India as a pivotal event that enhanced Femina magazine's reputation as a leader in the beauty business, an assistant editor in charge of event management at Femina argued, "Thanks to Femina's efforts for over fifty years, India could be seen as a place where we are aware of the power of special events as a magnet for the media.

Advertising is old. Public relations is where the action is today. " One media executive for ABCL remarked that the Miss World pageant signaled the beginning of recognition for the profession of public relations in India, "We need to use public relations not just advertising. In advertising, you pay for media space, but in PR you can get the media to cover you for free. Parameshwar Godrej got on the news because she sponsored Miss World-advertising cannot do that for you. "

Ironically, interviewees cast the positive, productive power of global media events and their public relations' potential differently when they discussed various protest groups' attempts to gain visibility in the public sphere. Some ABCL executives and representatives of commercial sponsors expressed anger and frustration at the volume of unexpected, passionate, and public protests that had erupted over their company's decision to host the Miss World pageant.

These protests against the pageant began as early as July 1996, and as protesters' activities gained momentum, organizers had feared that the live performance of the pageant at the cricket stadium in Bangalore on November 23 would be sabotaged. Several ABCL employees and representatives of advertisers expressed bitterness over public protests-marches in business areas, large public meetings, and angry demonstrations-because these forms of activism caused tremendous disruption in the city, resulted in negative publicity for Miss World, and created a stressful crisis management experience for the organizers.

When protests against the pageant took on violent overtones, the assistant to the founder of ABCL was quickly assigned the official title of media spokesperson, and was asked to provide consistent, calm responses to the media. Elaborating on his impressions about protesters' motives, this person argued:

I think the protesters just saw the pageant as an opportunity for lot of free publicity, you know, just to get their names into the news-- they're very cheap. The protests were all about getting themselves in the media-not at all about the pageant. We could easily see that because those feminists in Bangalore never protested dirty images of Indian women in Hindi films. Hindi films show women in the worst ways.

Two employees at Windsor Manor hotel, responsible for placating protesters gathered outside the hotel gates, suggested that political parties and special-interest groups opposing the pageant were not sincere because their shouting and chanting grew louder when television cameras arrived. Informants' assessment of feminist protest against the pageant as a blatant display of opportunism to gain media attention surfaced repeatedly.

Some executives pointed out that feminists organized these protests because they were eager to take advantage of the media attention offered by the unusually large number of reporters from national and international media who had convened in Bangalore to cover the pageant.

Statements about opportunistic "publicity hungry" feminists were frequently accompanied by references to other much more "vulgar" and sexist images of women in imported television programs-Baywatch and MTV-and in commercial Indian cinema, images that feminists had apparently chosen to ignore. Two young men explicitly stated that feminists in Bangalore would have gained more credibility if they had protested recent vernacular popular films produced in South India that objectified women in far more graphic ways than beauty pageants.

The media thus figured prominently in denunciations of feminist protest, either to present feminists as exploiting the media's desire for sensationalism, or to suggest that certain forms of entertainment media were the far more dangerous enemies of women that feminists should have targeted instead of the pageant.

Global media coverage of feminists' protests was also interpreted as a spectacular form of public embarrassment that only underscored anti-- nationalistic, negative stereotypes of India as chaotic, unstable, and unfit for modernity. Invoking nationalist sentiments, some informants framed feminist protest against the Miss World contest as self-centered promotion because it detracted from organizers' vision of the pageant's arrival in India as a collective, shared victory for the nation that transcended self-serving commercial goals.

ABCL's crisis manager declared that the vocal protests of the feminist organization Mahila Jagran Samiti proved these women's incompetence when presented with opportunities beyond their routine local campaigns. He argued that global news images of women protesters could suggest that India was not prepared for the media performance that economic globalization demanded:

"People will think we do not know how to control ourselves in front of foreign media. Samiti women don't fit in anywhere-- they are not prepared to be traditional nor do they want to be modern. They are confused and it showed in their junglee (wild) behaviour."

INDIAN BEAUTY QUEENS BRING MISS WORLD TO INDIA

The timing of the Miss World pageant's arrival in India, according to some interviewees, was the result of the representational power of mediated images of beautiful Indian women that had appeared on television and the Internet in the nineties. Some advertisers and media managers argued that were it not for the significant media presence of former Indian beauties who had brought the country great name recognition, the Morleys would not have chosen India as a site for the 1996 Miss World contest.

Although these business professionals conceded that the Indian government's recent economic reforms and the increasing market share of multinational companies in the beauty industry (cosmetics, chemicals, media) contributed to the Morleys' decision to stage Miss World in Bangalore, they maintained that India would not attracted attention, had it not been for the visibility of Indian beauty queens on global television.

Since the early nineties, a series of Indian women have become prominent in the international beauty scene of fashion shows and beauty pageants. In 1992, a virtually unknown

Indian woman named Madhu Sapre, came perilously close to winning the Miss Universe title, an event which one writer proposed made the "world and the fashion mavens of India sit up and take notice".

In 1993, a Miss India winner, Namrata Shirodkar, was second runner-up in the Miss Universe pageant. In 1994, a year when a series of Indian women reigned as beauty queens, the first victory for India was Sushmita Sen's crowning as Miss Universe.

Sushmita Sen's victory, as one writer put it, was the "logical culmination of India's quest to wrest a title that until now was the prerogative of a club of esoteric Western nations only." Shortly after Sushmita Sen's success, Sheetal Mallar was crowned in 1994 as the international model of the year at a modeling contest organized in Ibaza, Spain.

Finally, Aishwarya Rai became the first Indian woman to win the Miss World title at Sun City in South Africa. Commenting on the unprecedented amount of media coverage and political endorsement that Sen and Rai received, Corrine Scott writes:

The media reacted as if this were a momentous event in Indian history, providing front-page feature news coverage and numerous TV interviews. Sushmita and Aishwarya were received by the then Prime Minister and President of India in a style more appropriate to important foreign dignitaries.

Aishwarya Rai's and Sushmita Sen's victories at these international pageants caused a frenzy of national media attention in India and even the normally sedate government-owned television channel, Doordarshan, devoted prompt and frequent news coverage to the success of these two women throughout the two days after their crowning.

Informants interpreted the implications of Indian women's new successes and visibility in the global beauty and fashion worlds for India's national image in the global public sphere in explicitly gendered terms. Indian beauty queens were praised because they had finally compensated for Indian men's failures in global athletic events and their invisibility in the widely popular, hyper-masculine (physical, combative, contact) sports world of American football and basketball.

In recounting their reactions to the victories of Indian women in Miss World and Miss Universe, some media professionals contended that these beauty queens' television appearances projected images that transported India into the glamorous and sophisticated worlds of fashion and beauty, and conveyed the message that Indians were now competitive in the global arena. Discussing his feelings of embarrassment whenever he watched the Olympics on television, one young ABCL staffer commented:

I was surprised and happy when I heard that ABCL managed to win the Miss World account. I think Sushmita and Aishwarya did it for us.

Whenever I used to watch the Olympics on television, it was as though it was not even meant for Indians to watch. We're nowhere in any of the sports. My friends and I used to pick other countries to support. These Indian guys cannot even win a bronze medal. Nowadays with these beauty pageants, we're at least there, we're being noticed and even winning. We're beating places like China and Japan-they're always winning in swimming and gymnastics on the Olympics.

Another executive at the Indian branch of L'Oreal cosmetics in Mumbai, a company that was part of ABCL's pageant organizing committee, similarly said:

Unlike those developed countries, our men have not been able to compete in world sports-maybe it's lack of training? Indian women, on the other hand, seem to have an edge. Madhu, Sushmita, and Aishwarya are like our cultural ambassadors when they appear on television. They do so much for our international image and bring international events like the Miss World pageant to India.

One executive from the Welcom Group Hotels, who had played hockey for India, asserted that Indian women's participation in global beauty pageants and ABCL's decision to host Miss World were significant because they signaled India's willingness to speak the common language of global consumerism promoted by the staging of pseudo media events.

According to the Welcom Group executive, Indian men's successes or failures in hockey and cricket mattered little because most people across the world watched American football and basketball, sports in which India would not be able to compete because very few Indian men could meet the standards for strength, endurance, and height. Capturing the spirit of such comments that exalted Indian beauty queens as emblems of national pride, Times of India columnist Jug Suraiya wrote that the victories of Rai and Sen proved that Indians had at last "triumphed over our own unplumbed potential, largely unexplored for lack of self-confidence and self-esteem".

These ideas about the power of Indian women's mediated beauty, a globally mobile product that could command Western culture to embrace India, and critical comments about Indian men's lack of strong, athletic masculinity offer rich insights into the gendered spaces of global representation within which Indians gain currency. Challenging and reversing such discourses of nationalistic pride that celebrated Indian women's successes in the feminine sphere of beauty pageants, the chairperson of the National Commission on Women, Mohini Giri, was reported to have urged the state government to rechannel funds that were originally allocated to city beautification for Miss World into the training of Indian women for the Olympics.

The adulation expressed by professionals in the entertainment and consumer industry for Indian beauty queens as media icons is inextricably linked to the economic boom in the global beauty business in India and to the hypervisibility of the "New Indian Woman" in the nineties as the ideal consuming subject.

In India's recent phase of economic liberalization, the Indian beauty business, which was dominated by Lakme in the eighties, witnessed a flurry of interest among multinational cosmetic giants-Revlon, Oriflame, Avon, L'Oreal, and Benckiser-that began clamoring for a competitive share of the growing Indian middle-class market. With an investment of $1.7 billion and highly publicized tours of supermodels Cindy Crawford and Claudia Schiffer, Revlon, which was launched in India in November 1995, a year before the Bangalore Miss World, secured an 18 per cent share of the cosmetics market in one year.

Former Indian Miss World Aishwarya Rai was hired by Lakme to promote its line of cosmetics, and after their victories, Rai and former Miss Universe Sen have become popular heroines commanding high billings in the Indian film industry. Numerous beauty parlors and beauty shops in Indian cities and villages, several named after the two international Indian beauty queens, now offer a dazzling array of beauty treatments with imported cosmetic products. The multinational cosmetics, fashion, and consumer industries (personal hygiene, household products, cookware, and soft drinks in particular) in India have become actively involved in sponsoring beauty pageants at school, college, community, district, and state levels.

As marketing professionals in this study argued, the awarding of beauty titles has become a costeffective and grass-roots method of building brand awareness and market loyalty. journalists and feminist activists report increases of 30 to 40 per cent in women's memberships in fitness clubs and requests for plastic surgeries have leaped by 20 to 30 per cent from 1990 to 1995.

Simultaneously, the confident and modern middle-class Indian superwoman easily straddling home, work, and marketplace has become ubiquitous in television and print media commercials, sitcoms, and films. As Shoma Munshi reports, the savvy Indian homemaker in commercials is represented as being far more educated about the marketplace than her husband; she reads the fine print about product features, knows more about fashion trends and sophistication, and gathers information on the most nutritious diets and healthy lifestyle choices for her family.

Conflating the power of Indian beauty queens with the consuming potential of the discerning Indian middle-class female consumer, one executive for a cosmetics firm suggested, "Aishwarya and Sushmita showed on television that Indian women can compete and win in anything they want. The Indian woman wants to be the best.

She is demanding the best products. We have to compete for her attention, get her respect, and deliver excellence." In the context of a developing nation, mediated representations of international beauty pageants, fashion parades, Indian beauty queens, and women consumers, wrapped within the package of Western style cosmopolitanism and individualism, have come to constitute the most visually alluring public face of economic globalization.

Contrary to widely accepted notions of beauty queens as organic and spontaneous cultural emissaries of their nations, the patriotic sentiments that global beauty contest participants have voiced as national ambassadors can be traced in part to routine beauty training and grooming. When Indian beauty queens have won titles, their first response, as the Indian contestant, Yukhta Mookhey, Miss World 1999, is reported to have expressed in a BBC news report, is to talk about the glory they have brought their country.

In India, Femina magazine organizes the national Miss India contest and arranges additional training for the winners of the national contest because these "Miss India" winners are automatically selected to compete in Miss World. Femina's chief editor proudly declared that her magazine's training programme for beauty queens guided Aishwarya Rai's response to journalists when she won the Miss World title in 1994: "We [Indians] have conquered the world." Citing this quote, which was widely reproduced in national and international newsmedia, she said, "We have to teach them [Indian contestants] about the power of the media, how to take full advantage of the media moment when they are announced as winners. Without the media, the contestants and the countries they represent cannot get the publicity they want."

Informants' persistent comments about the Bangalore Miss World contest as an accomplishment for India that was facilitated by media images of Indian beauty queens is a reflection of the new emphasis on media training in beauty contestants' grooming programs. While fashion experts, women's magazine editors, and business executives agreed that achieving beauty, poise, and glamour had always required commitment, discipline, and diligence, several men and women proposed that the new and evolving terrain of training for international contestants was the task of preparing them to perform for the media.

Media training sessions for Miss India Universe and Miss India World included media orientation lessons; speech, voice, and accent sessions; and lectures on media practices and media audiences. Sharing details about media orientation lessons, the chief editor of Femina magazine revealed that she urged contestants to rise above their selfish and short-term motives for winning the crown of Miss World. Contestants for international beauty, fashion, and modeling events were urged to use the media as a vehicle for promoting India to foreign investors, advancing the prospects of future Indian women contestants, and gaining the support of Indian businesses and Indian citizens.

Speech and voice pathologist Sabira Merchant emphasized that fluent English-language speaking skills were one of the most important criteria in selecting the Indian Miss World contestant, "English is the language of the world. When Miss World contestants from over 100 countries came to Bangalore, they were so pleased that Indians could speak English." In English accent training for the media, Merchant taught Indian contestants to minimize their native regional accents and instead cultivate a more upperclass British accent. Similarly, in his research on beauty contests in Thailand, Callahan also notes that a fluent ability in the English language had become an unwritten qualification for contestants in the national Miss Thailand contest.

As one Thai beauty contest judge he interviewed said, "The beauty queen who cannot speak English will be a dumb-mute beauty queen" . Finally, contestants also learn from Indian news professionals that the electronic media favour consistent, pleasant, and succinct spoken responses. In mock media interview sessions that were taped and reviewed, contestants were exposed to a range of interview questions and techniques. The editor of Women's Era, who had served as media trainer in many grooming programs, suggested that the Moneys' decision to select India as a venue for Miss World proved that media training of Indian beauty queens had yielded rich benefits.

Discussing the implications of Indian women's victories at global beauty pageants, Sarah Banet-Weiser comments that the recent crowning of non-Western women as beauty queens indicates that these women have now proven to the world that they can "successfully enact Western disciplinary practices of femininity". Echoing the arguments of protests groups in Bangalore, Banet-Weiser points to the limitations of narratives that construct global beauty pageants as empowering rituals for women of colour, and cautions that as beauty queens, South Asian women are now legitimated by hegemonic, Western standards of beauty.

Countering such academic and activist critiques of global pageants, most executives argued that the Miss World pageant's arrival in India, following in the wake of Indian beauty queens' victories, meant that Indian women could not only meet Western standards of beauty, but in fact exceed and transform these standards.

A few informants proposed that successful Indian beauty queens could raise standards of beauty in Miss World and Miss Universe to new levels that would include non-Western concepts of ideal feminine beauty. In the eyes of many fashion designers, cosmetics firm owners, and women's magazine editors, the Miss World pageant in India signaled the power of Indian women's beauty as possessing unique qualities that surpassed and challenged White, European standards of beauty.

The editor of Femina and the manager of special events at ABCL argued that Sushmita Sen's and Aishwarya Rai's successes as beauty queens drew attention to the kind of feminine attractiveness that India valued-beauty that transcended physical attributes to include warmth, grace, charm, intelligence, and personality. Dismissing charges that Miss World's recent relocation to Third World countries offered evidence only of the global beauty industry's profit-making goals, another advertising coordinator for Godrej suggested that Indian beauty contestants were culturally hybrid citizens of the world, who could easily traverse different geographic and cultural spaces:

That's such a negative view of why Miss World came to India. How about thinking in a more positive sense that foreigners are beginning to understand that Indian women are just as and even more sophisticated than Western women. Our women know how to live in both worlds-how to be Indian and how to be Western-so in fact they're even better. They know how to belong in both cultures.

Drawing on discourses of transnational multiculturalism that emphasize exotic and colorful difference in aesthetic and consumer practices, one fashion designer offered, "People are bored with seeing only White faces and Western locations, Indian women's beauty is novel and striking. We have the same features as Westerners, but we are also very different." Yet another manager at a cosmetics company asserted, "Our girls sparkle. On camera, they have the most beautiful and expressive eyes, the best smiles, and when they speak, they sound so cultured and intelligent. We have no dumb blondes."

Informants' assertive comments about the superior qualities of Indian women's beauty and their opinions about Indian beauty queens as active agents who bring success and fame to India are not new discourses about women as idealized cultural representatives of the nation.

These statements that suggest intersections between notions of womanhood and nationhood in informants' interpretations of India's encounters with global culture also influenced early anti-colonial, Indian nationalist discourse. As numerous postcolonial scholars including feminists have argued, one crucial strategy through which Indian male social reformers and nationalists in the 19th century confronted British colonialism was to assert the moral superiority of

Indian women as ideal mothers, wives, and national citizens. Partha Chaterjee locates the 19th century idealization of Hindu women as pure and virtuous within the ideology of Hindu nationalism, which constructed a powerful distinction between the home (inner)/private world and the material (outer)/public world. Hindu women, who were seen as part of the home, the world that had not been contaminated by British imperial culture, became the symbols of Indians' superior spiritual and moral inner life.

With the dramatic entry of Indian women into the public sphere of beauty pageants and the recent legitimization of fashion and beauty contests as a part of India's cultural landscape, Indian women continue to function as the "ground" for negotiating Western culture, although the terms of cultural bargaining have changed.

As organizers of the pageant and others testified, the new terrain for establishing the superiority of Indian culture is based not on the virtue or moral character of Indian women, but on Indian women's abilities to compete confidently in the gendered world of global material culture by mastering commodified forms of femininity. Mediated images of modern, cosmopolitan Indian women, who can function as synecdoches for the nation, and spectacular events that represent India as receptive to public displays of women's sexuality become routes to overcome contemporary Western culture's colonial images of India as backward, static, and traditional.

Employing strategies based in gender that echoed the discourses of 19th century Indian nationalists, informants emphasized the celebration of Indian womanhood in the global arena as central to the task of building a modern nation.

Additionally, some informants' comments about the failure of Indian men to display the hypermasculinity that American sports demand is also a discourse that was found in debates over the "weak" masculinity of Indian men in early British colonial discourse. In countering the threat of rebellion from educated Indians who were beginning to question colonial rule, British administrators and intellectuals began to characterize Indian men as the passive, effeminate, and emotional "other," whose subjectivity was contrasted with the strong, assertive, and logical masculinity of British men.

Some informants argued that the Miss World pageant's arrival in India did not signify the dominance of White standards of beauty because Indians' pride in their culture could overcome the power of Western images. One ABCL executive, who previously worked as advertising manager at Cosmopolitan's office in Mumbai, was particularly defensive about the protests against the pageant. In this executive's view, conservative activists' protests about the Miss World pageant as a symbol of cultural imperialism, were not based on the reality of Indian consumers' responses to global images:

Everyone in the advertising, fashion, and media industries knows that Indian consumers have rejected the wholesale import of anything Western. Just because the Miss World pageant comes and brings along with it some beautiful White women, Indian men are not going to forget that our women are very pretty too. Indian women are also too confident of our culture to buy into those White women's images. When I worked at Cosmopolitan in Bombay, the American management there did a lot of research-- surveys and interviews-and found out that Indian women readers preferred Indian models on the covers. We're not like Japan or Turkey where Cosmo uses only White women on their covers.

The public relations director of the agency in Bangalore that ABCL hired to manage local media relations for the Miss World pageant suggested that Aishwarya Rai's and Sushmita Sen's victories (former Miss World and Miss Universe respectively) would command the rest of the world to come to India to learn about what Indian culture values as beautiful:

All the foreign contestants in Miss World wore Indian clothing, the bindis on their foreheads, and got to see traditional Indian beauties. These contestants saw how much we value our culture. India is the only country maybe in the world where women are still proud of our traditional clothing-sarees and shalwar kameezes-everywhere in Asia women wear Western clothing. Another fashion photographer and mother of two girls argued that organizers had done their best to localize Miss World for Indian audiences. Drawing on her parenting experiences to explain Indian consumers' loyalty to their own culture, she said, "My girls were excited about Miss World but they don't hate Indian culture. For example, they like their Barbie dolls in saris the most. Unlike other countries, Barbie did not sell in India until Mattel put her in a sari."

These statements seem to offer evidence of the localization of global culture in India, that is, of local audiences' indifference toward standard Western products and images.

Scholars have shown that multinational corporations have needed to modify and "Indianize" their cultural products to appeal to Indian consumers.

On the one hand, Indian consumers' preferences for localized versions of transnational products such as Barbie or beauty pageants demonstrates that consumption practices are mediated by ethnic, racial, and national differences. On the other hand, these preferences also reveal the transnational commodification of multiculturalism and the growing obsession with "ethnic chic" within India.

As Indrepal Grewal writes, certain sections of the urban elite in India consume Indian folk and rural art, food, and clothing in upscale retail stores along with Western products to experience their identities as global consumers, yet retain a sense of authenticity, distinction, and difference from the rest of the world.

Additionally, as Nilanjana Gupta writes, although Indian consumers of television have shown strong preferences for indigenous programming in the midst of a wave of foreign programming, most of the popular music programs, sitcoms, and soaps borrow liberally from Western formats.

Informants' defensive arguments about Indian consumers' appreciation for authentic Indian beauty and Indian values, even as they expressed enthusiasm for the Miss World pageant as a symbol of Western modernity, captures the complexities of transnational culture that weaves the local into the global.

NEGOTIATING THE POLITICS OF GENDER AND RELIGION

An important debate that was part of the process of managing the symbolic representation of Miss World in the media revolved around the selection of a logo, an iconic image that would be consistently reproduced on press releases, posters, advertisements, and banners. ABCL executives, in charge of supervising the public relations agency they hired, wanted to ensure that the pageant was packaged as a hybrid of Indian and Western culture because this dual branding strategy would facilitate the effective marketing of Miss World to a wide range of consumers in different countries including the Indian diaspora now scattered in diverse locations.

In selecting a logo, ABCL executives first considered the idea of using a well-known goddess image drawn from Hindu mythology, but eventually decided against this strategy after a meeting with their public relations agency:

Some of us wanted an image of the goddess Saraswati, but we were so happy when someone from the agency quickly warned us against it because just two years ago the famous Indian artist M.F. Husain, actually a Muslim too, painted the goddess Saraswati naked. And then the controversy was amazing because many Hindus, not just the fundamentalists, were so angry that he, a Muslim, would choose a Hindu goddess to do that. It was all over the front pages. I didn't realise Saraswati was such a hot subject now.8

Recalling memories of the same meeting, the public relations agency director, a man in his early thirties, talked about how difficult it was to persuade older ABCL executives that Indian culture was not only about Hindu goddesses: "I knew it would be trouble because some people think of pageants as vulgar, and even after being so careful about everything we had all these protests. Could you imagine how much more trouble we would have had if we used a goddess image?"

As the PR director volunteered, yet another reason to avoid the image of the goddess Saraswati-the goddess of learning, arts, and performance-was because Jaya Bachchan, wife and partner to the founder of ABCL, reminded them that ABCL owned another television software company by the name Saraswati.

She expressed the fear that this company could inadvertently be "dragged into some gadbad (battle, dispute)" that could have erupted over the use of goddess Saraswati as a logo for the pageant. Another ABCL executive talked about the long hours they spent agonizing over which specific image among a range of historical and mythological icons was safe and appropriate for the logo given the divisive politics surrounding religious identity in India.

Public relations consultants advised ABCL to choose a logo that would not ignite religious controversies, which could escalate into major crises with serious implications for the failure of Miss World. These difficulties that ABCL managers experienced with regard to finding a safe logo indicated that local producers experienced difficulties in locating a secular, pan-- Indian cultural symbol for the pageant that would appeal to all religious communities.

Their struggles over the ideal cultural representation of Miss World reflected the tensions around religion, communalism, and culture that have become highly public issues in India, particularly since the early nineties with the outbreak of violence and rioting between Hindus and Muslims during the Babri Masjid incident.

The Babri Masjid or Ramajanmaboomi incident took place on December 6, 1992, when a mob of Hindus belonging to various political and religious groups destroyed a mosque in the city of Ayodhya in Uttar Pradesh, claiming that the mosque had been built by Muslim invaders on a site that was the original birthplace of the Hindu god Ram.

Since the Babri Masjid incident, and the rise in the political and social power of the Bharatiya Janata Party, the Hindu nationalist party, and other associated Hindu revivalist organizations, religious minorities-Indian Muslims and

Christians-have experienced increasing marginalization, violence, and exclusion from the public sphere.

To ensure that the logo for Miss World would appeal to a wide range of consumers without provoking controversy, ABCL sought input from influential business, cultural, and media professionals and social elites in India. Although ABCL employees had first thought that they would leave the decision about the logo to the public relations agency they hired, eventually, after many discussions, they decided to set up a panel of judges who would offer their opinions on the best symbol that could capture the global and local essence of the pageant. Reflecting on that decision, the chief assistant to the founder of ABCL (the actor Amitabh Bachchan), said:

I think that was a very good decision. Amitabhji decided that Miss World's logo had to be a careful decision even though he was in a hurry to get things going. We set up a panel of judges from different professions and different religions-journalists, magazine editors, cosmetics industry experts, actresses and actors, and even two politicians.

Ultimately, the logo that ABCL selected as their final choice was the reproduction of a woman's image, a Buddhist inspired painting of a female figure representing a heavenly apsara (a dancer). The painting was part of a 5th century AD fresco from the walls of the Ajanta caves in the Western part of India, close to Mumbai.

The Buddhist inspired cave painting was viewed as a familiar and recognizably "Indian" symbol yet secular and unlikely to offend any religious group. Elaborating on the reasons for choosing a Buddhist symbol, the PR agency director offered:

Hinduism, Islam, or Christianity, none of these matched the comfort we felt with the Buddhist symbol. Christian symbols would not have been good because Christianity is not an Indian religion, and Islamic symbols may have upset the Mullahs-(Islamic priests). Nobody has so far created any public outcries about anything Buddhist.

A manager from the Godrej company (chief sponsor of the pageant) and the editor of Femina magazine, both who had traveled in other parts of Asia, explained that Buddhism was one of India's best exports, and that the Buddha, one of India's most revered prophets, was known for his message of equality, peace, and harmony in India and outside.

The Buddhist painting was thus viewed as a symbol that was outside of the rather controversial politics that has besieged Hindu-Muslim relations in India. Furthermore, the painting was viewed as an ideal international symbol for Miss World because audiences in Malaysia, Thailand, China, and Japan where Buddhism spread widely could relate to the Buddhist-influenced artwork.

Once the logo was finalized, a creative director at a large advertising agency in Mumbai suggested that they add a well-known national symbol to the figure of the apsara in the painting to enable Indian audiences to instantly connect Miss World with their country. In the logo's final version, which was unveiled at a news conference in Bangalore on October 31, 1996, by Amitabh Bachchan and Parameshwar Godrej, a headdress with a large peacock feather that was not a part of the original painting, was added as an ornamental decoration. "We added the peacock feather at the last minute because someone thought that would really reflect what is Indian about the Miss World pageant. Indian TV audiences would appreciate a feather from their national bird appearing on the logo," explained Sharat Sharma, who was responsible for organizing the news conference where the official logo was first displayed.

In addition to the politics of religion and nation that had to be carefully considered in crafting the official logo for Miss World, yet another layer of representational meaning that influenced decisions about this symbol revolved around gender and ethnicity.

The woman in the logo appeared slender and androgynous with a dark skin tone, a long neck, and a calm face with large serene eyes. She represented a very different image from the images of women in Hindu-inspired art and sculpture that can be found in the famous Kajuraho temple carvings where the sculpted women's voluptuous bodies suggest fertility and overt sexuality with their wide hips, slightly bulging abdomens, narrow waists, and large breasts.

Discussing the feminine body aesthetic in a logo that would be the best match for Miss World, two fashion designers proposed that the slender and small-breasted body of the woman in the Ajanta cave painting was more appropriate for the pageant than the voluptuous female figures that were common in classical Hindu sculpture found in many historic sites in India.

According to these two women, the female bodies in Hindu sculpture would not have captured the global fashion and advertising aesthetic for feminine bodies-the androgynous waif look-that is currently popular. The apsara's dark skin tone fulfilled the Morleys' desire to revive the popularity of Miss World by marketing it is an exotic and ethnically diverse contest. Despite the widespread cultural marginalization of dark skinned women within India, an ABCL media executive remarked that in the international marketplace of multicultural media images, the dark skin of the woman in the logo would aid in consolidating the new image of the Miss World contest as a ritual that affirmed global ethnic diversity.

In describing the logo, one informant cleverly negotiated feminist critiques of beauty pageants as sexist rituals that are residual forms of such patriarchal practices as prostitution, which sells women's bodies as commodities. For this informant, the empowering potential of the logo and modern beauty pageants could be traced to the coterminous ascent of the new female body and the rise in the economic power of the Indian female consumer. The chief editor of Femina magazine carefully distinguished the pornography aesthetic from the fashion aesthetic in her account of the logo's ability to capture the mission of the pageant. Employing the language of liberal feminism, which espouses equality for women within existing social and economic structures, she argued:

The Miss World event is for modern women, and those of us in the fashion business in India are aware of what's going on-the thinner look is in. Those images of women in Indian sculpture are for men who watch pornography. The new image of the beautiful woman we see in the Miss World pageant, the image we wanted to convey in the logo, is about speaking to women who watch the Miss World pageant-not just men. The Miss World pageant signals the power that women in India have today.

The very same editor was also quoted in the Indian newsmagazine Sunday as saying, "India is now more receptive to and aware of the international look. We have adapted ourselves over the years and are now in tune with international standards".

Discourses on Indian women's accomplishments and empowerment that cocooned the crafting of the logo for Miss World also permeated organizers' and sponsors' responses to the media when protests erupted against the pageant. Women's protests in Bangalore captured a diverse array of opinions that spanned conservative religious beliefs on the traditional roles of Indian women, socialist feminist perspectives on women's commodification and sexual objectification, and liberal feminist views on women's equal participation in the public sphere.

The women's organization Mahila Jagran Samiti, affiliated with the Hindu nationalist Bharatiya Janata Party, received the most media coverage for their protests against the pageant as an offensive ritual of Western culture that had the potential to corrupt the purity of the traditional Indian woman, a wife and mother, who exposed her body only for the gratification of her husband.

The vocal spokesperson of the right-wing Jagran Samiti, Shashikala, threatened to sneak into the stadium along with fourteen other women members to commit a public suicide in which she and her supporters planned to burn themselves during the live performance of the pageant.

A few renowned female artists-dancers, classical singers, and folk performers-endorsed the Jagran Samiti's view of Miss World as an assault on Indian culture; however, certain artists like singer Gangubai Hangal emphasized that Miss World would corrupt ancient Indian artistic and performance traditions along with Indian women's morality. Socialist feminists represented by Subashini Ghai and Brinda Karat of the All India Democratic Women's Association, Madhu Reddy of Vimochana, and numerous other independent feminist writers like Ammu Joseph and Sudha Sitaraman wrote lengthy commentaries in the media where they distanced themselves from the conservative women's groups' agendas.

Advocating against conservative activists' call to choose tradition as the moral ground to protest the onslaught of Western culture in India, these feminists drew attention to the poverty of India's vast majority of women and suggested that it would be more fruitful to examine beauty pageants as examples of the consumerist class divide created and reinforced by globalization.

Educated and secular middle-class women's voices were widely represented in the media as endorsing and supporting Miss World in Bangalore because it offered Indian women a new space along with Indian men for expressing their individuality.

Summing up the opinions of a group of professional Indian women, who had marched in support of the pageant, Santosh Rajagopalan argued that Miss World's organizers should be "lauded for promoting substantial social upheaval by bringing about a change in the perceptions of women's roles". Well-known women personalities and spokespersons for social causes-film actress Shabana Azmi and dancer Vani Ganapathy-joined supporters of the pageant because they strongly objected to the disruptive methods of protest chosen by rightwing and left-wing women's groups.

In responding to the protests of conservative women's organizations, the Moneys, the Godrej company, and ABCL held up Miss World's logo, traditional performances they planned to stage during the live performance, and the participation of foreign beauty contestants in Hindu rituals as evidence of Miss World's commitment to Indian women's authentic cultural traditions.

In their first press release bearing the signature logo of the Buddhist apsara in bright yellow, blue, and green colors, which was issued in response to the protests, ABCL argued, "The thought behind the logo is to depict the kind of land India is and our way of appreciating women's beauty in India. Our apsara is shown wearing jewelry, which all Indian women value and cherish.

The butterfly on the crest of her crown is a symbol of the free spirit and grace of every Indian woman." ABCL also claimed in a press release that the pageant's rules, which did not allow married women to participate, showed the respect that Bachchan and the founders of Miss World had for local traditions and family values; organizers did not want the rigorous training, hectic schedule, and travel commitments of Miss World's contestants to disrupt Indian women's marriages and result in the neglect of their children.

In countering the charges of commodification from leftist feminist groups, ABCL's press releases touted their Miss Personality and Miss Talented contests, performances in which they claimed judges evaluated contestants for their sense of humor, oratory skills, and artistic talents. ABCL also organized a press conference where former Indian Miss World and celebrity film star Aishwarya Rai lectured on the history and tradition behind the logo.

Endorsing the opportunities that Miss World offered the average middle-class Indian woman, Rai shared the numerous monetary and travel benefits she had accrued after her 1994 crowning, and pointed to the charity efforts she and the Moneys had become involved with since her return to India.

GLOBALIZING BOLLYWOOD

When actor Amitabh Bachchan founded the Amitabh Bachchan Corporation Ltd. (ABCL) in India in 1993, one among the many goals that he had envisaged for the corporation was to shape the company over the nineties into India's top event-management company. He wanted ABCL to become the leader among firms in India that managed domestic and international events.

The Miss World pageant was the first international media event that the company decided to host in India to gain a national reputation and announce the grand scope of ABCLs vision for the future. Gaining name recognition for his company in event management was, however, only part of Bachchan's plans for ABCL because he had even greater ambitions- eventually, through his company's media ventures he intended to become India's local version of the media mogul Rupert Murdoch.

The Miss World pageant's popularity since the late eighties has decreased among its earlier traditional audiences in the United Kingdom and the United States, and has moved on to newer pastures in Latin America, China, Russia, Eastern Europe, South Asia, and Africa.

It was precisely because of Miss World's increasing popularity in these new regions that the founder decided it would be appropriate for ABCL to seek out the pageant as its launching pad. Discussing the grand game plan behind the founding of ABCL, Bachchan's chief assistant shared with me the long-term plans Bachchan had outlined to his employees in order to ensure that ABCL gained prestige as an excellent communications company.

The Miss World contest was the ideal event to announce Bachchan's vision because ABCL's longterm goal was to manage the distribution of Hindi films, Indian television programs, and popular Indian music (Indypop) within India and abroad.

In the last ten years, films produced in Bollywood, as the city of Mumbai is referred to in a parody of Hollywood, have become popular among nonIndians in the Middle East, Africa, Russia, Eastern Europe, Fiji, and the Philippines, and among the South Asian diaspora in Europe and the United States. Among the Bollywood film stars who are well known in these parts of the world, Bachchan continues to have the highest name recognition despite the appearance of a wave of new film stars since the late eighties. Describing Bachchan's popularity in many countries across the world, Carla Power and Sudip Mazumdar (2000) write:

Tom Cruise didn't make the list, Marilyn Monroe finished ninth, and Sir Laurence Olivier was runner-up. In a worldwide BBC Online poll last year on the millennium's biggest star, the winner was 57-year old man born in Allahabad, India. Amitabh Bachchan or `the Big B' to millions of Indian film fans has been a megastar for three decades. His devotees found everywhere from Rajasthani villages to Australian cities are a passionate lot.

As his employees reported, Bachchan's idea to start a communications company grew out of his travels abroad when scores of Indian and nonIndian fans lined up to greet him in Russia, Egypt, Cameroon, and Mauritius. These fans often called out to the celebrity star using his film names from the popular Hindi films (easily over two hundred) in which he had played the role of the romantic, rebellious, and strong hero.

Several informants claimed that ABCL, as a corporate citizen committed to advancing India's economic growth, was founded to aid the Indian popular culture industry to maintain control over its production and distribution systems. As one ABCL executive put it, "Bachchan's goal was to bring professionalism, discipline, and order to a very undisciplined film industry that was producing popular films for non-traditional areas of the world.

" The "undisciplined film industry" he referred to is the world's largest film industry-Hindi film production based in Mumbai and other new locations in India. One entertainment executive from Sony Music, who had worked for ABCL during Miss World, said:

It was a very good sign when ABCL appeared on the scene because it meant that we Indians were getting our act together to systematically manage the unruly entertainment industry in India. And it was even better when they decided to announce this with the Miss World event. It showed their commitment to an international vision, to being ambitious, and you know, to taking India to a new level in the entertainment industry.

According to a judge in the 1996 Miss World pageant, the founders/ owners of the Miss World pageant, Eric and Julia Morley, were well aware of Bachchan's popularity as a film star and a media celebrity, and hence they were confident that ABCL was the best company in India to manage the Miss World event. In fact, the Moneys had invited Bachchan the previous year to be a judge in the 1995 Miss World contest in Sun City in South Africa.

Framing Bachchan's goals in founding ABCL and in bringing the Miss World pageant to India as efforts to infuse Bollywood with a new image of professionalism, one executive at the cable channel Zee TV talked about the Miss World pageant as "clean and fun" entertainment, a wholesome image of confident and beautiful women that would serve ABCL well in India because the Bollywood film industry had traditionally been financed and run by "goondas" (gangsters).

However, this Zee channel executive's enthusiastic endorsement of ABCL's bid to host Miss World as their firm's first international event was not a unanimous, seamless response articulated by all Indian business and entertainment professionals. In some quarters, reception to Bachchan's choice of Miss World as his inaugural media venture reflected intergenerational differences and class-based, nationalistic responses to pageants as a form of rejected "low culture" that Western multinationals were dumping into the Third World. Some older male informants at Godrej and Air India suggested that despite their admiration for Bachchan, they were reluctant to approve their younger colleagues' decision to sponsor Miss World.

One employee, who had worked at Godrej over thirty years, expressed his disappointment on two levels, "I was shocked that Bachchanji wanted to do this. His father was a famous literary figure, a high-class poet. And then I was surprised that my company's highly educated management thought this was a good idea." A government official at Air India clearly denounced Miss World as a project unworthy of Bachchan, a larger than life media figure in India, who should have diplomatically rejected the Morleys' offer to host Miss World after the protests began, "I know he wants to make money, but he should also wonder why foreigners, the Moneys, want to bring pageants to India.

He has become an unwitting pawn of these multinationals." As Outlook magazine reported, some older actors and directors in the Indian entertainment industry thought Bachchan had in fact "cheapened" his image by associating himself with a beauty pageant, a trivial event that only "girls" watched anymore. Such debates surrounding Bachchan's decision to host Miss World indicate that semiotic struggles over gender, modernity, and culture take place not only among scholars, intellectuals, or activists, but also within the culture industry itself.

Challenging the role of "greedy, money-hungry-businessman" that some Indian actors, artists, and directors imputed to Amitabh Bachchan, his current and former employees argued that the superstar had not founded his business solely to make money.

These informants proposed that Bachchan's lofty goal as a visionary was to ensure that Indians did not lose control over their own culture in the process of globalization. Bachchan had hoped that ABCL's hosting of Miss World would convince Indian entertainment and media companies that they did not need an experienced Western multinational to distribute and manage their media products.

Protesting charges from his fans and followers within the industry that he had become a ruthless capitalist, who could ignore ethics, cultural traditions, and patriotism in his pursuit of profits, Bachchan evoked nationalism when he passionately defended himself:

The idea wasn't to make money with the Miss World pageant. It was a vision. I wanted Indians to see that ABCL could do this and more even. ABCL was to launch India to the rest of the world and if we didn't do it ourselves, foreigners would do it for us ... they would move in..

In an interview with Telegraph and Outlook magazines, Bachchan stated that his objective in accepting the assignment to manage Miss World pageant in India was to utilize the profits from the pageant to initiate Indian film and popular music distribution ventures that might otherwise be taken over by American multinationals.

Despite his lifelong career in the film industry, Bachchan, a savvy media entrepreneur, resisted the notion of using his celebrity status to promote Miss World among middle-class Indian youth, an audience that advertisers and sponsors were eager to target. ABCL executives had wanted Bachchan to concentrate on courting young, urban cosmopolitan Indians among whom they felt Miss World was bound to be much more popular than older audiences.

These executives had encouraged the actor to reach out to younger Indian audiences because unlike older Indians in the 30-50 age group, who had grown up watching famous blockbuster Bachchan movies, young Indians were not as familiar with Bachchan's films. One young public relations director argued that young Indian audiences' low awareness of the actor's contributions was linked to new practices of consumerism and global media consumption that distinguished television-savvy Indians from the older film-watching generation:

Young people in our country are Westernized-they are MTV, Cosmo, Coca Cola kids. They watch lots of TV, not just films. Amitabh had a hard time understanding that he had to make an effort to reach out to them-to give interviews, appear on TV with his children, and associate more with younger film stars like Aamir Khan, Sharukh Khan, and Aishwarya Rai on TV. To promote Miss World, he had to let young people know that he was a famous international star and let them know that through managing ABCL, he was going to improve India's economic power.

ABCL employees and their colleagues in the media industry offered two reasons for Bachchan's reluctance to promote Miss World on television; his ignorance of media marketing and branding strategies and his inability to understand the performative aspects of his role as Miss World's Indian spokesperson for television.

Based on the advice of management consultants, Bachchan had brushed aside his wife's fears over the invasion of her family's privacy and agreed to name his communications company after himself so that his media venture could gain instant awareness and recognition. However, his vision of the Miss World contest's ability to translate his fame and celebrity status into a brand name for ABCL did not go beyond this initial effort.

One ABCL marketing executive suggested that Bachchan, son of famous Indian poet Harivanshrai Bachchan and friend of India's former prime minister Rajiv Gandhi (grandson of Jawaharlal Nehru), was confident that his literary upper-class background, political connections, and fame as a superstar ensured that he did not have to court the news and entertainment media to publicize Miss World.

This executive argued that although Bachchan had earned more money than any other Indian film star, the actor was woefully naive about money matters and business practices of building and expanding fledgling enterprises, "Bachchan is more of an artist than a businessman.

His family members and managers took care of everything his whole life. Miss World proved that when he was suddenly thrown into the corporate media ocean, he could not cope." Others claimed that Bachchan's shy and reserved off-screen personality that starkly contrasted with his emotional on-screen performances surprised reporters and television audiences because it mistakenly conveyed a remote arrogance and lack of warmth.

Even before he founded ABCL, Bachchan had developed a reputation among film and entertainment reporters and celebrity columnists as an inaccessible and emotionally difficult interview candidate. ABCL executives and their PR agency employees disclosed that one of the most difficult tasks they undertook was training Bachchan for his promotional public appearances and press conferences, "We had to teach him to speak in soundbites, to be enthusiastic, to recite dialogues from his films, and to smile more often."

Paradoxically, despite Bachchan's assiduous efforts to overcome his repugnance for public appearances and commodify himself as a brand for Miss World and ABCL, his managers discovered that Indian audiences' responses to these promotional images were lukewarm, less than enthusiastic, and in some cases, hostile. After Miss World, the actor continued to market his celebrity status by appearing in television commercials where he endorsed BPL's electronic goods and Pepsi's beverages.

In a cover story on the superstar's failed attempts to brand himself for Miss World, Outlook magazine argued that the aging actor, adored by millions of Indian fans, had degraded himself by trying to gain cheap publicity. Offering comments that scorned the media strategies of ABCL's management professionals, who were eager to transform Bachchan's cultural capital into economic gains, Outlook reporter Saira Menezes suggested that it was impossible to transform Bachchan's magical, godlike aura of superhero masculinity into a brand:

For simply too many people, if not all, Bachchan was the supreme embodiment of life's most incredible possibilities. He could rouse you to anger, move you to tears, and dissolve you in smiles as consummately and completely as any real life experience. It was the fantasy trade millions around the country made everyday, as they paid up at theaters to live out a heightened and intensified life cycle in three short hours. The faceless and soulless money managers who gathered around him made the mistake of convincing him he was a brand. He is not. He is magic.

Reinforcing Menezes' views about Bachchan's mistakes in pursuing the mundane arena of television after a grand history on the awe-inspiring canvas of films, Graphiti magazine indicated that Bachchan had erred by suddenly offering numerous media interviews in 1996. Veteran film reporter Vir Sanghvi remarked that Bachchan's enormous popularity was related to the actor's decision to quietly stay behind the scenes, conduct himself with "impeccable dignity," and allow his on-screen persona to conduct the real work of performance and artistry.

Comparing Bachchan's enduring prestige and fame with other actors (Rajesh Khanna and Vinod Khanna), whose well-publicized, sensational personal lives had exposed their weaknesses and failures, Sanghvi remarked, "What could be done when the warrior became a deviant selling beauty pageants, television sets, and cold drinks? The warrior began to make the hero on a white charger look increasingly like a half-wit on a flea-ridden horse craving petty profits".

SOUTH INDIA APPEARS MODERN AND TRENDY

Describing the contentious and argumentative deliberations that took place at ABCL over the selection of a venue for the pageant, employees reported that financial expenses and concerns over negative images of urban decay and poverty had been their primary concerns. While ABCL managers' first choice was Mumbai, the entertainment and business centre of India, they had quickly ruled it out due to the high costs of luxury hotel accommodations, exorbitant rental fees for public venues, and large numbers of slum and street dwellers whose presence could detract from the image of a clean and safe tourist location. As one public relations assistant, who worked for the Godrej company in Pune, a smaller city close to Mumbai, remarked:

Bombay is the place you see on Mira Nair's film, which won all those awards-it's Salaam Bombay. It shows all those street children and poverty, and that's why we rejected Calcutta too. Calcutta to the world is the black hole, the place that people have seen in that Patrick Swayze's film City of Joy-full of diseased lepers and poor people.

Yet another advertising accounts executive, a native of Calcutta whose family members had participated in protests against the filming of City of Joy in Calcutta, complained that Hollywood had ensured that Calcutta could never be considered a venue for Miss World even though the city was well known in India for its lively art, film, and theater culture."' Although New Delhi, the capital of India had a cleaner image than Mumbai and Calcutta, some informants ruled out the capital city because they feared that the central government's sluggish bureaucracy would delay legal permissions and licenses.

The final decision to hold the pageant in Bangalore, a city in South India, was largely due to the pivotal role played by two South Indian ABCL employees, who had decided that this event would highlight South India's receptiveness to modern culture. While Delhi was being seriously considered, one young sales manager in Mumbai, who had grown up in Chennai, the capital city of one of India's southernmost states, had proactively introduced the possibility of holding Miss World at a venue in South India: "When I brought up South India, some people thought I was nuts. Those who don't know the South have these strange notions about us. It's because Hindi movies show South Indians as clowns with no sense of fashion or style." Nodding his head, this executive's South Indian friend agreed with him and then shared further details about how they had decided upon Bangalore: "Chennai was seen as too conservative even though it is the largest city in the South. Other South Indian cities like Hyderabad and Trivandrum were not large enough, and there was no doubt in our minds that Bangalore was perfect." Discussing the image of Bangalore within and outside India, he said:

Bangalore has been in the news a lot. It is a clean city without the crime and poverty of cities like Bombay, so retired people like it. It is already a global city because so many multinational computer firms have their Indian offices there. The college women are trendy and fashionable-not as conservative as Hyderabad or Chennai. Those cites will change too but that will take some time.

Determined that South India needed more recognition and a new image that could challenge stereotyped representations in Hindi films and sitcoms, these two executives contacted tourism officials at the Karnataka State Tourism Board in Bangalore to gauge their interest.

Sensing potential for increasing tourism and business opportunities, state officials began to lobby for Miss World. To the excitement of the two South Indians in Mumbai, tourism officials responded with enthusiasm when they were informed about the possibility of bidding for the pageant. They offered to contact the Karnataka Chief Minister's office to confirm other high-level state administrators' willingness to support the event.

The Chief Minister's office also responded positively and suggested that ABCL could hold the inaugural press conference at the impressive, palatial State Legislature building called the Vidhana Soudha. Describing ABCL's reaction to the offer, Akhil Maiyar, the former Chennai resident stated, "That was the turning point. The city of Goa had just approached us, but the offer of the Vidhana Soudha mansion in Bangalore was just too tempting. ABCl knew our inaugural event in that huge building would look very impressive on TV." The state of Karnataka's eagerness to host Miss World was motivated by an interest in propelling Bangalore beyond its global profile in the high-tech business world to new arenas in the beauty, fashion, and entertainment industries. In her analysis of Bangalore's recent evolution as an ideal city for global sports and entertainment events, which had the potential to enrich the city's cosmopolitan image as India's Silicon valley, Smriti Srinivas wrote:

The pageant was surely one of the most important spectacles in the city that year. In fact, several newspaper articles claimed that henceforth, for tax purposes, the definition of entertainment should be changed in the state .... The articles argued that the beauty contests should rightfully be included under the category of entertainment along with sports and films to bring greater revenue to the state.

In enumerating the reasons for the state of Karnataka's positive response to Miss World, one Tourism official in Bangalore pointed to the difficulties in reaching large audiences in India due to the fragmentation of television viewers by cable networks: "We knew Miss World could get people together as much as anything on TV can do it anymore. Bangalore could get so much out of Miss World."

South Indian ABCL executives' views about the South as an ideal "trendy" space for global culture that had not received its due recognition from the rest of India was echoed by others in the business world. Heralding South India as the new "Sexy South," the region in India that had the fastest growing middle-class and the best facilities for enjoying an upper-class lifestyle, Business World, one of India's largest-circulation business magazines, declared, "Junk all the stereotypes; the south as comprising languid backwaters, and southerners as idli [rice cake]-consuming take-it-easy plodders. In fact the South is looking seductive".

Parodying and mocking stereotypes of South Indians as dull and stodgy, the cover of the magazine displayed a nerdy, religious South Indian man in traditional attire sporting designer dark glasses and cowboy boots, and holding a Pepsi can. The cover story indicated that although there was a time when the rest of India had pejorative names for South Indians, the image of South India was rapidly changing. Business World proposed that a stable and growing middle-class, a greater sense of professionalism and ethics in the workforce, a growing demand for lifestyle products among consumers, and a high degree of media penetration had transformed South India into an attractive region for many international and domestic companies. Indian business managers from Volvo, Revlon, Maruti, Whirlpool, and Hyundai, who were interviewed by Business World, discussed their growing investments in major urban centers in South India.

The Miss World pageant was thus eagerly sought after by South Indian ABCL executives and the State of Karnataka to serve local concerns-to challenge the stereotype of South India as the conservative, slow-paced region caricatured in mainstream Hindi films and culture. When ABCL announced its final decision to hold the pageant in Bangalore, other South Indian employees at ABCL, who had joined the campaign to select a venue in South India, celebrated ABCL's decision as a symbolic victory for all South Indians.

NATIONALISM, GENDER, AND GLOBAL MEDIA EVENTS

Some scholars have predicted that the advancing reach of globalization in its standardized and commodified forms will steadily reduce the significance of local structures of nation, tribe, and community for local cultural production and reception. Daniel Dayan and Elihu Katz proposed that the spread of global media events anticipates the demise of nationalism and national borders as structuring elements in audiences' experiences of their identities.

Barber argued that globalization "contributes to shrinking the world and decreasing the salience of national borders" and that the popularity of global culture announced a "considerable victory over factitiousness and particularism". Contrary to such predictions, this monograph demonstrates that nationalist sentiments suffused local producers' visions of Miss World's impact on India's image in the global public sphere.

While organizers' and sponsors' creative production of Miss World attempted to go beyond national boundaries, this media event was also simultaneously crafted as a nationalistic project.

The culture industry in India sought to incorporate cultural and historical ideas of the nation-India and Indianness-into the ideological, discursive, and material manifestations of the mediated global pageant. Organizers' vision of the Miss World pageant's potential to challenge the Third Worldness of India in global media, Amitabh Bachchan's desire to ensure that Indians not foreigners gained control over global Indian entertainment, and the patriotic sentiments that Indian beauty queens were trained to express at global contests illustrate the continued symbolic strength of the concept of nation within the trajectories of transnational culture.

In the process of becoming indigenized or localized, discourses of globalization thus invoke contradictory impulses and allegiances. On the one hand, multinationals encourage the widespread consumption of global culture in different localities by standardizing cultural products and rituals to transcend the limits of national identity.

On the other hand, in order to ensure acceptance within a wide range of social, political, and economic groups within local settings, global culture resorts to the recuperation of national identity.

Urging scholars of transnational culture to map out the different ways in which global consumption is linked to the cultural imaginary of nationalism, Indrepal Grewal argues that global culture could "resuscitate the nation-state while simultaneously reducing its compass".

Producers, advertisers, and media professionals involved in Miss World claimed that the Miss World pageant did not represent an imperialistic Western discourse that could destroy Indian culture because they intended to harness the pageant to promote India's latent potential as a culturally rich nation that was eager to modernize its economy.

In a paradoxical fashion, local producers and sponsors of Miss World in Mumbai and Bangalore argued that supporting and participating in international contests enabled Indian citizens to experience their Indianness more intensely; the global spectacle was thus ideologically constructed as a means to enhance and strengthen the local.

A double-spread advertisement promoting ABCL corporation and the Miss World pageant in The India Magazine, an upscale publication targeted at the urban English-educated elite in India, vividly echoed informants' packaging of the global within the semiotics of the local. Celebrating ABCL's successful bid to host Miss World, the advertisement showed a pensive Amitabh Bachchan addressing the globallyminded Indian reader by posing a series of questions: "Why do we (Indians) have a need to impress all foreigners?,

Why do we feel good when others say India has potential? Why are we down in the third world, when we could be up there?" The advertisement ended by suggesting that the staging of Miss World in India represented the assertion of Indians' independent, far-reaching, and entrepreneurial spirit that could transform the nation and its citizens' low self-esteem into vigorous patriotic pride and confidence.

Following cultural critiques offered by postcolonial feminist scholars, my analysis of local organizers' and sponsors' discussions about mediated representations of the Miss World pageant shows that gender plays a crucial role in shaping and legitimizing the modernization projects of globalization. The explicit invoking of gender politics in organizers', sponsors', and public relations personnel's understanding of Miss World became apparent in the following: criticisms targeted at representations of Indian women in global newsmedia; comparisons drawn between women's lives in India and Pakistan; expressions of admiration for the globally legitimized beauty of Indian women offset by the denigration of Indian men's failures in world athletic events; and arguments that Indian women, as hybrid subjects who could confidently traverse Eastern and Western cultures, exemplified ideal global femininity in a multicultural world.

Perceptions of Miss World expressed by members of the culture industry in India indicates that gender-the trope of the feminine-operates as a strategic cultural resource to announce local producers' commitment to modernity's progressive impact on traditional local cultures. Postcolonial feminist media scholars have explored the multiple forms of interpellation that girls and women encounter in India's intensely mediated culture of the nineties.

Shoma Munshi argues that in India's current climate of economic liberalization, consumerist discourses are incorporating ideologies of femininity, feminism, and nationalism to synthesize a post-feminist image of the "New Indian Woman."

In her analysis of consumer advertising in India, Munshi notes that advertisers have incorporated accommodationist forms of resistance to traditional patriarchy in their images by representing the New Indian Woman as a wife, mother, and daughter-in-law who can control, manage, and manipulate patriarchy through clever and educated forms of consumption.

Producers and sponsors of the Miss World pageant take such commodified incarnations of women's resistance in the media further when they argued that Miss World with its public representations of female sexuality offered a representational space that countered the limitations of local patriarchy's restricted codes for ideal womanliness.

Editors of women's magazines, women fashion designers, and trainers in Femina's beauty contestant grooming programs viewed Miss World as a ritual that had the potential to catapult Indian female subjectivity beyond the patriarchal roles of sex object and wife, daughter, and mother.

For local organizers of Miss World, battling protest groups' demands to ban the pageant, the elaboration of feminist discourses of women's empowerment within the mediated fabric of the pageant constituted a strategic response of crisis containment.

ABCL employees and sponsors exalted the pageant as a sign of progressive shifts in traditional gender relations and constructed Indian women as free agents to convince local audiences to embrace the individualized ideologies of freedom and class mobility that guide the imaginary realms of late capitalist economies.

By closely examining the rhetoric of feminist empowerment among members of the culture industry in India who organized and supported Miss World, we can appreciate the complex articulation of female agency in global consumerism where patriarchy and capitalism intersect to offer women positions of domination and resistance.

Contrary to theories of power that construct discourses of global capitalism as non-conflictual and harmonious spaces that are outside of progressive activism, nationalism, and polemics of struggle, this analysis of Miss World shows that local producers negotiate and strategize multiple subjectivities for women, which include more than the interpellation of women as passive consumer subjects.

Informants' conjoining of Miss World to feminist notions of resistance against patriarchy demonstrates the necessity for a Foucauldian approach to the hegemonic character of modern structures of global capital.

The power of global consumerism is not necessarily exercised by one dominant group over another non-dominant group, that is, in a top-down fashion, rather, consumer modernity's ideological messages manifest in multiple locations and utilize mechanisms of domination and subordination to secure consent among local audiences. Amitabh Bachchan's strategy of using the televised Miss World contest to advertise ABCL's competence as an enterprising manager and distributor of Indian films in various locations abroad draws attention to new circuits of global culture that are beginning to appear in the nineties.

These emerging flows of global culture challenge the paradigm of globalization as always and only being synonymous with Americanization.

Critiquing earlier models of cultural imperialism, recent scholars of globalization have pointed out the limitations of envisaging centre-periphery relationships as cultural flows that begin at the centre (the developed world) and gradually penetrate the periphery (the developing world), with the peripheral nation typically viewed as possessing little control over the invasion of its indigenous culture.

Ostensibly, the 1996 Miss World pageant's appearance in India (the periphery) implied the flow of a cultural form that evolved and originated in Euroamerican culture (the centre), yet the purpose behind this visible sign of Western culture was to strengthen an Indian company's own goals of globalization.

The Miss World pageant was part of a start-up package for Bachchan's communications company. Bachchan's goal, as many executives explained, was to be an early pioneer in managing the globalization of the increasingly popular Indian entertainment industry's media products.

ABCL's hosting of Miss World in India demonstrates that rituals of Western modernity can be deployed to announce the emergence of regional networks of global media culture that encompass more than the obvious, well-rehearsed scenario of First World-Third World interaction. Commenting on the newer configurations of global culture in the nineties, Power and Mazumdar (2000) write:

The West may have the biggest stalls in the media bazaar, but it's not the only player. Globalization isn't merely another word for Americanization-and the recent expansion of the Indian entertainment industry proves it. For hundreds of millions of fans around the world, it is Bollywood-India's film industry-not Hollywood that spins their screen fantasies.

Typically, the developing world's encounter with a ritual of Western modernity-a beauty pageant-is viewed as a process that involves binary top-down relationships between the Euroamerican World and the Third World. However, as ABCL's motives in hosting Miss World demonstrates, private businesses and entrepreneurs in non-Western locations can use global media events to inaugurate their own media globalization projects.

Advocating a nuanced view of cultural imperialism that recognizes the pluralization of new cultural production centers around the world, John Tomlinson argues that scholars abiding by undialetical centre-periphery models should be cautious about assuming that the ubiquitous presence of Western culture indicates lack of competition in the global media market.

Conflating the local with only the national may conceal other struggles taking place within the space of the global. Anabelle Sreberny-Mohammadi writes that national agendas may not always represent or coincide with the heterogeneous variations of the local, "In international relations, the national level may be local vis-a-vis the global level, but in domestic relations, the national is itself a site of struggle, with a variety of local identities and voices in contention".

South Indian executives' pursuit of Bangalore as the site for Miss World showed their resistance based in their regional identities to hegemonic North Indian representations of South Indians as culturally backward.

Miss World presented an opportunity for South Indians to challenge the dominant discourse that casts Mumbai or New Delhi as ideal locations to symbolize the nation as cosmopolitan and modern. South Indian ABCL executives' deployment of Miss World to challenge regional hierarchies of representation also illustrates Ien Ang's theoretical proposition that global culture can be strategically manipulated to serve the interests and agendas of specific local constituencies.

Finally, this monograph offers insights into the multiple layers of media and cultural intercontextuality that characterize the performances of global media events in different locales.

The Miss World pageant represented organizers' and advertisers' efforts to enter the zone of public culture in India, an arena that Arjun Appadurai and Carol Breckenridge characterize as a field of consumption that is a "shifting array of texts and experiences, which constitute evolving contexts for one another".

Public modernity in its mediated form, as Breckenridge and Appadurai argue, is an interlocular field that is "structured so that each site or setting for the socializing and regulating of the public gaze is to some degree affected by the experiences of other public sites".

Their example of one such event that exemplifies the experience of the interlocular in India is the world of cricket where leisure practices, desire for spectacle, narratives of stardom, and nationalist sentiments intersect to produce masculine achievement as global culture.

As a ritual form of public culture that illustrates Appaduari and Breckenridge's approach to mediated modernity in South Asia, the Miss World pageant represented an interlocular event that informants interpreted against and within numerous cultural contexts and relationships.

Pageant organizers' selection of a Buddhist logo as the least controversial embodiment of Indian culture demonstrated the influence of religious politics on the localization of global culture; however, their choice of a dark-skinned, thin woman in the logo revealed their efforts to globalize the logo in order to satisfy transnational consumer appetite for commodified multiculturalism.

Informants' discussions about covers of Cosmopolitan magazines in India, vulgarity in vernacular Indian films, the indigenized clothing of Barbie dolls, MTV consumption among Indian youth, stereotypes of India in Hollywood films, and caricatured images of South Indians in North Indian popular culture highlighted the media intertextuality that permeated local producers' interpretations of Miss World. ABCL's promotion of Amitabh Bachchan's superstar image revealed the interweaving of celebrity stardom as a local and global branding strategy into the mediated fabric of the pageant. Ultimately, these multidimensional and intercontextual interpretations of the televised Miss World contest in India underscore the profound embeddedness of local cultural production within concrete, heterogeneous, and complex historical and cultural conditions.

Bibliography

Adams Paul, and Catherine McKercher. "North America." In Global Journalism: Survey of International Communication, 2d ed., edited by John C. Merrill . New York: Longman, 2001.

Becker Lee B. "Enrollments Increase in 1989, but Graduation Rates Drop." Journalism Educator 45, no. 3 (Autumn 2000): 5.

Bishop Rober. Qi Lai! Mobilizing One Billion Chinese: The Chinese Communication System. Ames: Iowa State University Press, 2004.

Commission on Freedom of the Press. A Free and Responsible Press. Chicago: University of Chicago Press, 2002.

Communications 2003. A report of the Future Committee. Columbia: School of Journalism, University of Missouri-Columbia, 2000.

Directory of Communication Training Institutions in Africa. Nairobi: African Council on Communication Education, 2001.

Emery Edwin, and Joseph McKems. AEJMC: 75 Years in the Making. Journalism Monographs, no. 104. Columbia, SC: AEJMC, 2002.

Fischer Heinz-Dietrich and Otto B. Roegele, eds. Ausbildung für Kommunikationsberufe in Europa: Praktiken und Perspektiven. Düsseldorf. Droste Verlag, 2000.

Gaunt Philip. "Developments in Soviet Journalism." Journalism Quarterly 64, nos. 2-3 (Summer-Autumn 1987): 526-532. Hunter Frederic N. "Grub Street and Academia: The Relationship between Journalism and Education, 2001-2005." Ph.D. dissertation, City University, London, 2004.

Japanese Press 2000. Tokyo, Nihon Shinbun Kyokai, 2001.

Katzen May. Mass Communication: Teaching and Studies at Universities. Paris: UNESCO, 2005.

Index